Woman Suffrage and Women's Rights

Woman Suffrage and Women's Rights

Ellen Carol DuBois

NEW YORK UNIVERSITY PRESS
New York and London

NEW YORK UNIVERSITY PRESS
New York and London

Library of Congress Cataloging-in-Publication Data
Woman suffrage and women's rights / [edited by] Ellen Carol DuBois.
p. cm.
Includes index.
ISBN 0-8147-1900-7 (clothbound : acid-free paper)
ISBN 0-8147-1901-5 (pbk. : acid-free paper)
1. Women's rights—United States—History. 2. Women—Suffrage—
United States—History. 3. Women—United States—Social conditions.
I. DuBois, Ellen Carol, 1947–
HQ1236.5.U6 W63 1998
305.42'0973—ddc21   98-19698
                                        CIP

New York University Press books are printed on acid-free paper,
and their binding materials are chosen for strength and durability.

Manufactured in the United States of America

10 9 8 7 6 5 4 3 2 1

Contents

    All illustrations appear as a group after page 120.

Acknowledgments

Each one of these essays had appended to it names of colleagues and friends whom I thanked. Put together as a composite list, these acknowledgments constitute the intellectual and political colleagueship of twenty years. Thanks for many years of help and support to Amy Bridges, Mari Jo Buhle, Phillida Bunkle, Nancy F. Cott, Barbara Epstein, Ann Ferguson, Ann D. Gordon, Linda Gordon, Vivian Gornick, Amber Hollibaugh, Cora Kaplan, Elizabeth Lapovsky Kennedy, Carolyn Korsmeyer, Jill Lewis, Esther Newton, Gayle Rubin, Rochelle Ruthchild, Mary Ryan, Anne Firor Scott, Ann Snitow, Judith Stacey, David Thelen, Carol Vance, Judith R. Walkowitz, Marilyn B. Young, and Eli Zaretsky. For help with the previously unpublished essays in the current volume, I owe special thanks to Joyce Appleby, Lois Banner, Alice Echols, Eric Foner, Dan Horowitz, Jan Reiff, Molly Shanley, Kay Trimberger, and Jon Wiener. And a hardworking cadre of graduate students helped me to prepare this volume: Mike Bottoms, Anastasia Christman, Lisa Materson, Rebecca Mead, Gail Ostregren, Allison Sneider and Rumi Yasutake. Robert Cooney, of Point Reyes, California, and proprietor of the greatest suffrage photography archives anywhere, collaborated with me on the illustrations; effusive thanks to him. Despina Papazoglou Gimbel and Andrew Katz guided the manuscript through production with style and enthusiasm. Finally, Niko Pfund was wonderfully responsive when I came to him about New York University Press's publishing this collection, and doing so within the sesquicentennial anniversary of the Seneca Falls Convention; and Cecelia Cancellaro was wonderfully prophetic in encouraging me to contact Niko.

1

The Last Suffragist

An Intellectual and Political Autobiography

From the beginning, my decision to focus my scholarship on woman suffrage ran against the grain of the developing field of women's history. In 1969, the year I selected my dissertation topic, women's history was only an aspiration, albeit a widespread one. *Feminism* was still a word that even those of us who would go on to revive it were uncomfortable using. In graduate history programs all over the country, young women like myself were realizing that the history of women in the United States was an enormous unexplored territory, rich with compelling analytical questions. Our interest in women's history was more a product of our political activism than our career aspirations. In buildings other than the ones where we took our graduate seminars, on evenings when we were not reading in preparation for our qualifying exams, we were writing feminist manifestos, attending meetings, calling demonstrations, and forming women's liberation organizations.

I was a graduate student at Northwestern, at the same time helping form the Chicago Women's Liberation Union. Determined to unify our political and scholarly selves (and protected by a robust economy from too-great anxieties about our future careers), my generation wanted to contribute to a historical practice that would be useful, that would not only document social change but help realize it. Meanwhile, a few miles down the road, the signal 1960s organization Students for a Democratic Society was so committed to stopping the war in Vietnam by any means necessary that it was in the process of destroying its own existence. I have often wondered about the preoccupation of men of my generation with fighting either in or against the war and what role this played in the new prominence of women in traditionally male environments such as the university.

For the most part, women's historians of the late 1960s and early 1970s were directing their scholarly energies toward women's private lives—family, childrearing, sexuality.[1] This was a perspective that was shaped by many factors. First, the entire practice of history was in the midst of a tremendous paradigm shift that would eventually go by the term *social history*.[2] Itself an intellectual response to the larger politics and culture of "the sixties," social history directed historians' attention away from the designated rulers to the masses of common folk, with whom we believed the real fate of society lay. My teacher at the time, Jesse Lemisch, had called this new historical practice "history from the bottom up," and those of us who adopted it did so with a crusading fervor.[3] We were dedicated to a democratic approach to the power to make history, as much in our role of historian as in that of citizen. Although social history would eventually—two decades later—provide the basis for an invigorated approach to political history, for the time being, politics, at least in the formal sense of elections, officeholding, and government, was outside its purview.

In addition, there was the strong sense that politics was not the place to find women's overlooked and suppressed historical importance—their *agency*, to use the word that was coming to symbolize social historians' intent to subvert old-fashioned notions of historical significance. The relation between "public" and "private" life would soon surface as one of the fundamental problematics of modern feminist thought, but initially, women's historians observed the distinction even as they began to challenge it. Public life, where women had been the objects of sustained and multifaceted discrimination, did not seem the arena in which women were going to be restored to history at the level to which we aspired. Indeed, that approach had been tried by an earlier generation of women's historians and had manifestly failed to bring women into history.[4] Given the frameworks of social history, to identify women's *agency*, historians would have to focus on the things that most women did most of the time, on the very private and family concerns that had been considered too trivial and personal for historical investigation.

A major factor in the lack of interest in political history was the larger disillusionment and contempt that surrounded formal politics in these years. The rise and fall of hopes for modern liberalism during the Kennedy-Johnson years, the inexorable growth of the war in Vietnam, the electoral corruption and executive criminality of Watergate left many convinced of the uselessness of choosing between parties and of the impossibility of controlling the arrogance of power at the ballot box. I voted in November 1968, shortly after my twenty-first birthday, but cannot remember which minor candidate I preferred to Hubert Humphrey and the Democrats. In 1980, I reluctantly voted for Jimmy Carter over Ronald Reagan, but most of my friends refused this lesser-evil ploy. The twelve years of reactionary Republicanism ushered in at that point eventually forced renegades from Democratic liberalism back into electoral politics, but not until unbelievable damage was wrought on the social fabric and feminists and progressives of all sorts learned the painful lesson that who voted for what had significance.

From the very beginning of my work on suffrage, therefore, I felt compelled to defend my decision—to explain why the long struggle to win the vote was worth studying, what it could contribute to the field of women's history. I made my first effort at answering this question even before completing my dissertation, in an article in 1975 in *Feminist Studies*, a new journal that declared by its name that it intended not only to cultivate women's studies but to keep it vitally connected to the feminist movement. (See Chapter 2.) The question, as I posed it then, still seems to me to be a valid and crucial one: Why was woman suffrage the demand around which women's boldest aspirations for emancipation coalesced in the nineteenth century? Why was political equality at the core of radical feminism in this period?

My answer, structured in response to the focus on private life that so characterized both women's history and women's liberation in the mid-1970s, was that precisely by bypassing the private sphere and focusing on the male monopoly of the public sphere, pioneering suffragists sent shock waves through the whole set of structures that relegated women to the family. Because political participation was not based on family life, women's demands for inclusion represented an aspiration for power and place independent of the structures of the family and women's subordination in it. If I had had access to the terms developed twenty years later, I would have written that women's demands for suffrage uniquely threatened to disrupt and reorganize the relations of gender. Later, I could make this point by suggesting an analogy between the central role that suffrage played in first-wave feminism and that abortion played in the second wave: simultaneously a concrete reform and a symbol of women's freedom, widely appreciated as such by supporters and opponents alike.

This first attempt to express, as I called it at the time, "the radicalism of woman suffrage" left certain crucial questions unanswered that would shape my work over the next twenty years. Why was politics, more than other aspects of public life, such as wage labor, the focus of women's rights battles against male privilege? If woman suffrage began as a radical feminist movement, why did the eventual enfranchisement of women not do more to emancipate women? And perhaps most obvious, what did I mean by "radical feminism"?

We called ourselves "radical feminists" then. The first time I spoke at an academic conference (at the 1970 meetings of the American Psychological Association!), I proudly claimed this mantle, only to be usurped at the edge of the political spectrum by copresenter Robin Morgan, who declared herself a "revolutionary feminist." Radical feminism signified a movement that aimed to challenge the social order as profoundly as did the labor and civil rights movements. This was a complex claim that both assumed the link between feminism and other radical movements and insisted on feminism's distinctiveness. The determination in these years to establish what we called the "autonomy" of women's historic struggle for liberation is difficult to recall, inasmuch as feminism is infinitely more legitimate now than it was then, far stronger than the politics of class and race toward which we felt, in the 1970s, so much like junior partners. To insist on the autonomy of our questions about women's subordination, our judgment about crucial issues, our methods of social change, was the political expression of women's newly stubborn claims for independence on a personal level. Over the years, as feminism grew while the larger enthusiasm for radical change withered, I became less concerned with insisting on autonomy and more with drawing attention to the connection between feminism and other battles for social justice.

The constant factor through all this, I hope, has been my attempt to encompass both the bond and the tension between the general aspiration for justice and democracy and the particular claims of feminism. Still trying to express this two decades later, I characterized the dynamic I was seeking to convey in terms of "the hyphen," as that which connects even as it separates the two terms of the relationship. I borrowed the metaphor of the hyphen from Mary Bailey, who had used it in connection with the development of modern American "Marxist-Feminism":[5]

> As Marxist-Feminists we straddle an uneasy horse. We have not worked out what this means, this hyphen. . . . All too often, all this has meant is that we are Marxists to our feminist sisters and feminists to our Marxist brothers. The gravest danger facing us right now is that we will settle for this hyphen . . . as a self-explanation . . . a counter, a cipher, instead of a project. . . . What intervenes in this relationship of two terms is desire, on every level. Hyphen as wish. We have heard its whisperings.

A hyphen seems such a formal, grammatical device; and yet Bailey turned it into poetry, by using it to invoke something quite different— the "desire" to bring together the two elements it separated. Full theoretical reconciliation became less important than long-range vision and political aspiration.

My second major attempt to make my case for the role of the political in the history of women was the centerpiece of a symposium on "Politics and Culture in Women's History," first delivered at the 1978 annual meeting of the Organization of American Historians, under the title "Feminism and Women's History" and published, also in *Feminist Studies*, in 1980. (See Chapter 3.) My concern was that not just suffragism but the whole political dimension of women's history was getting short shrift, and with it, attention to the character of women's subordination.[6] The women's liberation movement had opened up the meaning of the word *political* through its claim that "the personal is the political," that is, that power relationships characterized even the most seemingly private of encounters between men and women, from lovemaking to housekeeping. I embraced this expanded definition but also wanted to restore something of the more organized, collective, and public dimension to politics and to indicate that, ultimately, feminist goals had to be won at this level.

Much more polemical than "The Radicalism of the Woman Suffrage Movement," "Politics and Culture" needs to be set in the particular context of that moment. After less than a decade, the field of women's history was on the verge of achieving academic legitimacy, as a whole series of strong first monographs appeared, drawing professional attention and students.[7] The idea of a historical practice influenced by a political movement outside the university was by no means seen as professionally acceptable. "Women's history" smacked too much of a constituency, a clientele, a partisan perspective. I was concerned that, just as women's history was beginning to find acceptance in the academy, the intellectual legitimacy of bringing openly feminist questions to the field was coming under attack, and my argument was meant to alert women's historians to this threat.[8]

Despite this sense of an external threat to my young field, the article I wrote was a challenge to developments within the feminist community of women's historians. One could say I was looking for aspects of women's history practice that conceded too much to, or coincided too closely with, the apolitical spirit of academic history. I argued that women's history was taking shape around an interpretive framework associated with the term *women's culture*, which left little room for the place of feminist politics. Women's culture, I contended, was an interpretation that focused on women's ability to relocate themselves away from the pressures and limitations of male dominance in an environment defined more by their own repressed needs and perspectives; I preferred a more frontal attack on male privilege. As Alice Echols has argued, feminism in the 1970s was making its own move in this direction, but with a self-consciously ideological case for the necessity of establishing separate institutions for and by women.[9]

As several of the other symposium participants pointed out at the time, my definition of the historical phenomenon of women's culture was not as precise as my criticisms of it were pointed.[10] Did I mean antebellum women's arguments in defense of separate spheres; forms of social activism, such as moral reform and temperance, that rested on notions of women's distinctive (and superior) morality; ideologies resting on notions of the difference of the sexes rather than on their common humanity; women's intimacies with one another; or all of the above? With respect to the actual period in question, I was trying to locate women's rights ideas in opposition to antebellum notions about the special virtues and distinct integrity of "woman's sphere," especially as these ideas were embraced and expressed by women. At a more general level, my argument was that some of the resources necessary to envision and forge truly different power relations between the sexes needed to be taken from the hands of men themselves. Again to rely on an expression that came later, I was disagreeing with Audre Lorde's famous slogan that "the master's tools" could never "dismantle the master's house."[11] In this I was influenced by the venerable Caribbean historian C. L. R. James, who had briefly been my teacher at Northwestern in 1969. James's assumption was the opposite of Lorde's: the tools the oppressed most needed were precisely those of the master, turned to their own purposes.[12]

Rereading "Politics and Culture" now, I find it one of my more dated articles, precisely because it was so keyed to the developments of the moment. I was motivated by the continuing disregard for the subject of suffragism (even a favorable critic of my work pointed to the "pallid nature" of suffrage as a demand);[13] also by the idealization of the mutuality and harmony that allegedly characterized women's relations with one another. Sometimes it seemed to me that the assumption of women's natural sisterhood was an antidote to the frequency of—and pain attendant on—conflict among women. My objections were especially directed to the work of Carroll Smith-Rosenberg, who had just published her pathbreaking article on "the female world of love and ritual."[14] She concentrated on the intense affection so common among nineteenth-century women, while my own concerns lay in identifying and studying conflict, especially political, including among women. I did not appreciate at the time how Smith-Rosenberg's work was initiating one of the most innovative dimensions of women's history: the study of women's intimate relations with one another. Nonetheless, I still think that the controversy was productive, generating one of women's history's first theoretical debates.[15] By giving name to this framework, the symposium sharpened awareness of the issues involved, which reemerged later in controversies around themes of "equality" versus "difference" in women's history.

But where to begin my own study of woman suffrage? My generation's feminism had been forged in the era of civil rights, the "mother movement" of the 1960s.[16] Hence locating the origins of the women's rights perspective in the 1830s, at the point at which abolitionism led "nominally free" women (to use Angelina Grimké's words) to recognize and protest their own kind of enslavement, was so obvious as to be virtually automatic.[17] The impact of abolitionism on the history of American feminism is a theme to which I have returned repeatedly, finding in it clues to everything from the ability of women's rights pioneers to critique the ideology of woman's separate sphere, to their insights into the sexual dimensions of women's subordination, to the enduring, if contradictory, link between race and gender in the American feminist tradition. In the 1970s, I emphasized the dissenting perspective on sexual difference that emerged among abolitionist women, the insistence that male and female, like black and white, faded in the face of human and moral oneness before God. (See Chapter 4.)

However, the narrative line on which I was concentrating at this point, like the political process I was living through, was that of "the emergence of an independent women's movement."[18] In retrospect, my understanding exhibited a tendentious character, as if feminism, struggling through the soil of women's subordination, *had to* surface in history. While committed to the dialectic of radicalism and feminism, my account was decidedly tilted toward separation rather than attachment. To me, abolitionist-feminists, like women's liberationists 130 years later, appeared as junior partners in an extraordinary radical enterprise, profiting from the conviction that fundamental social relationships could be revolutionized yet held back by their not being first and foremost members of a women's movement.

Impatient for nineteenth-century suffragism to appear in all its initial boldness, I hurried forward, moving too quickly through the women's rights battles of the 1850s that would catch my eye two decades later. These battles, which focused on the impact of marriage on women's status, struck me (quite incorrectly) as more limited than the goal of political equality, which spoke to all women regardless of marital status. The women's rights framework of the 1850s did help me see why and how the demand for political equality so elegantly captured women's claims for individuality, for personhood, and for equality with men. But I was eager to get to the years after the Civil War, when the franchise became the focus of the feminist struggle and "women's rights" folded into "woman suffrage." Indeed, in my finished dissertation and subsequent book, as a member of a determinedly antiwar generation I virtually ignored the Civil War to concentrate my attention on Radical Reconstruction.[19]

An article published in an early collection of feminist writings, which was graced with the very 1970s title of *Capitalist Patriarchy and the Case for Socialist Feminism*, recounted the insights and insurgencies that came so quickly to feminists once they embarked on the creation of a women's movement in the early Reconstruction years. (See Chapter 5.) Although my goal was to emphasize the primacy of the suffrage demand, I also wanted to confront the fundamental mischaracterization that has always dogged it: that political equality was a "single issue" that ignored all the other dimensions—sexual, economic—of women's emancipation. As evidence to the contrary, I demonstrated the dramatic expansion of interest in wage-earning women and in the sexual dimension of women's subordination that accompanied the rise of attention to woman suffrage in the late 1860s. When I wrote this article, I had begun my first teaching job, at the State University of New York at Buffalo, home to one of the first women's studies programs in the country, and feminist students only a few years younger than myself were bringing some very challenging political questions to the history I was teaching them.

Much more difficult than tracing either the abolitionist inheritance or the full feminist flower of nineteenth-century suffragism was understanding the moment of transition between the two, when the priorities of blacks' and women's emancipation came into conflict and choices between them had to be made; this became the focus of my dissertation and of the book that resulted from it. The 1867–1869 crisis that occurred when woman suffragists realized their inability to win inclusion in the Fourteenth and Fifteenth amendments not only led to animosity between suffragists and defenders of freedmen's rights; it also split suffragists into competing camps just at the moment that they launched a serious drive for political equality. This episode is one of those turning points in history that requires, indeed deserves, continually revised interpretation, so fundamental were the issues involved, so irresolvable the conflicts facing the participants, so painful the choices they faced.

I have since revisited the Reconstruction crisis in suffragism and have changed my own understandings of it considerably. When I first confronted the conflict within the suffrage movement over the Fourteenth and Fifteenth amendments, my judgment was that this was a necessary, productive, and, though painful, positive development in the history of American feminism. I reacted strongly to the condemnation that was heaped on the renegade wing of woman suffragists and concentrated on defending Elizabeth Cady Stanton and Susan B. Anthony as its leaders. At this point, my emphasis was on what was gained in terms of freedom to express openly feminist themes and goals. My willingness to entertain conflict as a productive and progressive process was surely at work here, as I argued that the split within the suffrage movement in the late 1860s worked to advanced its visibility and broaden its base.

I returned to these questions a decade later, in connection with the bicentennial of the federal Constitution and the new attention it was directing to the history of citizenship.[20] I now had much more to say about the Reconstruction shifts in the woman suffrage movement in terms of their impact on the historical link between black freedom and women's emancipation. Far from being an abstract and lawyerly formulation, the post-Civil War call for "universal suffrage," devised by feminists to link the demands for political rights for ex-slaves and for women, had a substantial, militant following among American women and a major impact on suffrage strategy. This formulation had the effect of joining the claims of race and sex and emphasizing the position of African American women, who asserted both. (See Chapter 6.) In 1874, the U. S. Supreme Court finally rejected the case for universal suffrage in *Minor v. Happersett*, and only then did suffragists turn from arguing that citizenship brought with it political rights for all to winning the more limited goal of enfranchisement just for women. (See Chapter 7.) The shift from universal suffrage to woman suffrage, which I had once regarded as the moment that independent feminism had "emerged," now appeared more a political defeat, with reactionary consequences for both the suffrage movement and the American constitutional tradition.

By the mid-1980s, the feminist movement was no longer a junior partner and was being called on to look seriously into its own racial politics.[21] My original argument about woman suffrage had always been vulnerable to charges that it underplayed the racism unleashed among feminists by their break with abolitionists, and now these criticisms hit their mark.[22] By the 1980s, black feminism had reached a sort of critical mass in terms of visibility and distinctiveness of political message.[23] Now I saw how the shift away from universal suffrage and toward an exclusive focus on (to use Stanton's words) "an aristocracy of sex" worked in reactionary ways to constrict the movement's reach. In the place of the movement's original high-minded universality, suffrage arguments focused exclusively on the need for the vote among white, middle-class, educated women, which was inevitably counterposed with what they regarded as the unwarranted political power of men who were their natural inferiors. My commitment to "the hyphen," to achieving a balance between independent feminism and multifaceted radicalism, now led me to see things in a new light. Political conditions around me were now alerting me to the importance no longer merely of legitimating feminism but of ensuring that its reach was broad and its impact democratic.

My rereading of Reconstruction suffragism was also a reaction to an all-encompassing, paradigm-rattling debate about whether "equality" was an adequate theoretical basis for challenging women's subordination or whether it just led to minor integrations of women into a still male-defined world. A wing of feminism had begun to develop around the celebration and elaboration of women's "difference" from men as a means to deeper sorts of change. More has been written about this than about any other theoretical shift in modern feminism.[24] Here I endeavor only to situate this debate historically. While clearly a development out of the earlier claims for "women's culture," elaborations of "difference feminism" went much further, both in time and in theoretical reach, calling into question basic elements of progressive political theory such as individualism, the desirability of expanded rights, and liberal thought itself.

The first hints of this theoretical offensive came from France in the 1970s, but in the United States the popularity of difference feminism can be dated from the publication of social psychologist Carol Gilligan's book *In a Different Voice* in 1982.[25] Not since Kate Millett had declared war on "sexual politics" had a feminist theoretical development been so certified outside the movement as a significant intellectual "event."[26] As a result of these debates, I took my place squarely in the camp of "equality."

The debate over equality and feminism was crucially shaped by the larger atmosphere of Reagan-era politics, notably the collapse of progressive politics and the demonization of liberal ideas. Some might think that to credit the disrepute into which the equal rights tradition of feminism came in these years to a larger right-wing turn in American politics is reductionist, inasmuch as most of the claims of difference feminists were not intentionally conservative or antifeminist. I do not argue that everything discovered or argued by feminist scholarship in these years was so colored by the larger political reaction as to be wrong or useless. But the further we get from these years, the more obvious it seems to me that feminists and progressives of all sorts were under a terrible cloud of political impossibility during them. Insurgent conservativism rode all too easily over what little there was of an openly left-wing opposition and went on to drive liberalism itself into full-fledged retreat. Feminists had only two alternatives: to pull back our forces and defend liberal premises we had once sought to transcend or to change direction and question our liberal roots altogether. Both had their dangers, but no one, not even a professional historian, is insulated from the limited choices history itself presents us with, and I elected the former.

A crucial event that illuminates the political context of the feminist questioning of equality was the "Sears case," an episode of great significance for feminist scholarship in the early 1980s.[27] My first knowledge of the case came from another women's historian, who confided that I had been "right" to warn that women's culture arguments would eventually be turned to antifeminist uses. The Equal Employment Opportunity Commission had charged the Sears Company with sexual discrimination. The case had been filed in the final months of the Carter administration, but it was heard in 1982, before a judge appointed by

President Ronald Reagan, and Sears shaped its defense accordingly. Sears reasoned that arguments about the historical "difference" in women's values, choices, and lifestyles could be used to attribute women's current absence from high-paying sales positions to women's own choices rather than to the corporation's discriminatory employment policies. The defense located—after several tries—a reputable women's historian willing to so testify.[28]

This was a painful irony for the field of women's history. The notion of women's agency was here being marshaled against the commitment to social change with which it had originally been paired. What had once been called "inequality" was now being labeled "difference." It was gratifying that most women's historians went on record as objecting to the testimony of Sears's expert, but the sorry truth was that the defense's use of history in its case was consistent with the emphasis women's historians had placed on nineteenth-century women's role in creating their own, distinct "sphere" and the satisfaction it had provided them.[29]

Nowhere was the intersection of the right-wing insurgencies of the 1980s and the path of women's history more important than with respect to the family and sexuality, the history and political significance of which modern feminists had been the first to explore. A "new" right, like the "new" left and the "new" feminism, had learned to focus on the frustrations and yearnings fostered in private life and the political possibilities these offered. In this rapidly changing atmosphere, where simply to speak of family concerns or to claim to speak in a woman's voice was no longer the distinguishing mark of feminism, positions on the relation of home and work in modern women's lives and on the possibilities of sexual freedom became clouded and confused. The badge of feminism was now claimed by those who argued that women's interests were *not* served by liberalized divorce laws, an all-out drive for equality in the labor force, increased sexual choices, or even the easy availability of legal abortion.[30]

In the early years of the Republican insurgency, the most explosive of these crossover feminist issues was pornography. In the late 1970s, a feminist attack on pornography began to grow in influence.[31] Ten years earlier, women's liberation had done important work in opening up and politicizing the issue of rape, which so many women had suffered in shame and isolation. The antirape movement metamorphosed into the antipornography movement, a development that was very much encouraged by the growing power of the right wing, which found it more useful and malleable than the campaign to eliminate rape. Antipornography ordinances drawn up by feminists Catharine MacKinnon and Andrea Dworkin were enacted in several midwestern cities. In 1985, President Reagan appointed a high-level commission, chaired by his attorney general Edwin Meese, to study the issue and come up with recommendations. So promising was distaste for pornography as a concern that could draw women into politics that feminists had a difficult time maintaining control over it.

I was educated in the way that these sexuality and family issues played out over the political spectrum while I was in San Francisco and New York, where I was on leave, off and on, from 1978 through 1982. In the company of a small study group of feminists in San Francisco, I observed other feminists raging against the American Civil Liberties Union for defending "the rights of pornographers" and new-right women claiming the legacy of Martin Luther King, Jr., to defend the civil rights of "our unborn brothers and sisters."[32] Later, in New York, I became a full-fledged participant in what eventually was nicknamed "the feminist sex wars," the *götterdämmerung* of which took place in April 1982 at Barnard College.[33] There, feminists who were determined to challenge the conservative drift of contemporary sexual politics, and especially the antipornography movement, presented their case. In recent years it has become fashionable to condemn the partisan excesses and unnecessary polarizations of the sex wars, but my own judgment is that this was an important, useful, and even exemplary intervention of feminist scholars in feminist politics.[34] The attention generated by the Barnard conference helped halt, perhaps even reverse, the right-wing direction in the feminist approach to sexuality.

For the Barnard "sex conference," Linda Gordon and I coauthored a historical examination of the range and impact of sexual politics in American feminism. (See Chapter 8.) Like others at the time, we were coming to understand that feminism was a complex political tradition with multiple tendencies that we needed to distinguish and, at times like this, choose among.[35] This was my first experience with coauthorship, and despite the fact that I regarded myself as a good feminist and democrat, I was surprised that our joint product was indeed something that neither of us could have produced alone but that represented what we both had to say.[36] Our argument was that women's sense of sexual endangerment had to be understood in terms of both the changing historical conditions they faced and the ideological formulations available to mobilize their fears. In particular, we contrasted the symbolic use nineteenth-century feminists made of prostitution and twentieth-century feminists made of rape as representative notions of sexual threat. We offered a complex portrait of the past in order to show that feminism in the present had more than one tradition of sexual politics on which to draw and that, as the conditions of women's lives have changed, a sexual politics that pursues pleasure as well as guards against danger is now much more feasible. Several years before discursive analysis became all the rage, we were exploring how women's widespread but inchoate feelings of danger and oppression were organized around a historically shifting series of demands, in order to give them meaning and political significance.

I incorporated several of these themes as I continued to work my way forward in the history of suffragism. The impact of both the feminist sex wars and the Reagan-era political atmosphere is obvious in a paper on late-nineteenth-century feminist conflicts over religion and sexuality that I gave at the Fifth Berkshire Conference on the History of Women in 1982. (See Chapter 9.) I had always shied away from this period because I found its politics less personally congenial than the democratic radicalism of the Reconstruction years, but now I felt obligated to try to grasp Gilded Age suffragism's conservative turn. Aileen Kraditor's very influential 1967 *Ideas of the Woman Suffrage Movement*, identified and named this late-nineteenth-century shift as a move from "justice" to "expediency" arguments, but Kraditor did not actually explain the shift.[37] Influenced by the rise of the Moral Majority and other fundamentalist-based conservative politics in the 1980s, I linked sexual conservatism and the Protestant Christian revival in the Gilded Age, especially as manifested in the success of the Woman's Christian Temperance Union in joining suffragism and a deeply domestic understanding of womanhood. And as always, I worked my way through this period by means of the writings of Elizabeth Cady Stanton, whose own religious and sexual dissent helped me expand my sense of feminist possibilities.

Here is the place to acknowledge the degree to which Elizabeth Cady Stanton has consistently been at the forefront of my writings on nineteenth-century suffragism. A reasonable critique of my work is that often, when writing of "suffragism" or "women's rights," I am really referring to Stanton and the women who shared her ideas. And yet I have always found Stanton's insights into women's subordination so extraordinarily rich, the meanings of her words so multiple, that returning to them time after time seems no more limited to me than concentrating on the study of any other timeless thinker. But it is the thought that is timeless; the thinker died in 1902, well before woman suffrage finally found its place in the U. S. Constitution. If I was to follow the woman suffrage movement through to its conclusion, as it seemed to me I was obliged to do given my claims about its radicalism at inception, I would have to find another figure to trace. This is how I first settled on a study of Harriot Stanton Blatch, as a surrogate for her mother.

Ultimately, my study of Blatch took me sixteen years, so I have much more to say about my relationship to her than that she was a stand-in for her mother. Feminist biographers have written a great deal by about the intensity of identification between themselves and their subjects, but it was precisely because of my reverence for Elizabeth Cady Stanton that I did not want to write her biography.[38] I did not want to write a filiapietistic account of her life and did not think I had enough critical distance from her ideas to write a book with an "edge" to it, which is the kind of history I do best. By writing a life of the daughter instead of the mother I found a much better vehicle, one that both more accurately represented my own position as fictive daughter and allowed me the emotional and historical distance necessary to put my subject's contributions in their proper place. From Harriot's perspective, even Elizabeth became clearer. So, for instance, I finally understood the mother's 1897 advocacy of educated suffrage on the basis of her daughter's public accusation that this position was "at odds with the principles of a lifetime."[39]

As it turned out, Harriot Stanton Blatch had her own historical riches to offer me, as she led me through the revival of suffrage militancy and feminist vision that reappeared in the last decade of women's drive for the vote. (See Chapter 10.) Blatch's approach to women's emancipation was sufficiently connected to and yet separate from her mother's to serve as a perfect vehicle for following the American suffrage movement into its final decades. Her leadership helped the movement shift from a nineteenth-century women's rights ideology, born of natural-rights ideas and focused on political notions of independence and power, to a twentieth-century feminist version, reflecting social democratic ideas and concentrating on economics. The category of "class" and the importance of wage labor stood at the center of her contributions to Progressive Era suffragism. The image of woman as worker was coming to replace that of woman as mother as the emblem of modernizing womanhood, and Blatch helped author this shift.[40]

The historiography of women's culture reentered my scholarly sights at this point. By the late 1980s, the notion of women's culture had been brought forward in time and, therefore, to an accommodation with the vigorous reform activity so characteristic of middle- and upper-class women in the Progressive Era. The resulting notion of a "women's *political* culture" retained a commitment to following a separate and distinct female path through history, even as this path clearly went straight through the political territory that was once the center of "men's sphere." Paula Baker's 1985 article "The Domestication of American Politics" was often identified as the foundation of this analysis, although my own reading, quite different from others', is that Baker traces not only the evolution of "separate spheres" ideology into politics but its demise precisely at the moment of women's enfranchisement.[41] In my perspective, Harriot Stanton Blatch serves as a crucial figure for (some) women's eagerness to jettison the legacy of women's political differentness, their claims to be above partisanship, ambition, and the struggle for power.

Unlike most other students of suffragism, I have not paid particular attention to the movement's dramatic final years. One reason is that my historical guide, Harriot Blatch, was absorbed in other issues—world war and then the growing debate over labor legislation for women only—after 1916. Nor was she alone; from the perspective of many of the other innovators of twentieth-century suffragism, who also were not at the final barricades, the battle seems to have been over before it was over, the vote won before it was won.[42] Also, it seemed to me that too-close attention to the drama of suffragism's last years, both between activists and the Wilson administration and between dissenting camps of suffragists, leads to an exclusive focus on tactics, to questions that I did not think were fundamental, and to a narrative line climaxing with the Nineteenth Amendment and concluding in 1920.

History does not end as cleanly as novels do, and this classical periodization did not fit my sense of the continuing implications of the suffrage tradition after 1920. Historians have a habit of moving backward in their studies, looking for ever-deeper roots. I felt compelled to go forward, to find still-flowering branches. My work on Harriot Blatch led me from the winning of the Nineteenth Amendment directly into the process by which the woman suffrage movement was incorporated into the historical record. (See Chapter 11.) In the 1930s, the last decade of her life, Blatch was dedicated to establishing her mother's place in the history of the woman suffrage movement. Other suffrage veterans had their own cases to make and defend from history, and Blatch fought with them over what the vote had meant, how it had been won, and, above all, who was responsible for winning it. I came to see that even the question with which I had begun my own work—what made the suffrage demand so radical at its inception—was part of a historical debate that reached this far back. In the 1930s, Blatch disagreed energetically with the contention of her friend Mary Beard (another ex-suffragist) that oppression was overstressed in the history of women, at the expense of the "force" that women had exerted in shaping the past.[43] Offering the evidence of her mother's leadership, Blatch argued that there was much Beard did not know—that had been forgotten—about the richness of the women's rights tradition and the links between woman suffrage and the full range of social justice concerns. Force and oppression, agency and subordination, could and must be linked in understanding women's history, she contended.

My article on this subject, "Making Women's History" (Chapter 11), published in 1991, was shaped by its own contemporary context: "attacks of official, right-wing critics of 'history from the bottom up.'" By the late 1980s, Republican politicians and officials had come to appreciate how much the writing and teaching of U.S. history had changed under the influence of the social history paradigm of the late 1960s. Shielding their own political purposes behind a "just-the-facts" appeal to objectivity, conservative forces charged American historians with advancing a left-wing agenda that taught students to hate their country and distrust their government. This was a compliment of sorts: apparently, reinterpretations of American history had made enough of an impact to deserve such an all-out assault.[44] From this perspective, my account of the early stages of woman suffrage historiography was a rumination on the relationship of history making and political engagement. On the one hand, I criticized these amateur, politically motivated historians of suffrage for simplifying the historical narrative and suppressing debate over its meaning. Yet, on the other hand, I appreciated that it was precisely because of their open feminist commitment that they had begun the work of preserving the suffrage record, of turning the past into history; without them, there might not be a historical record over which to argue. Taken together, these observations suggested a standard for responsible history, one that was both politically engaged and committed to full disclosure and democratic debate.

Arguably, the first historian of suffrage to rise to this criterion had been Eleanor Flexner, author of the 1959 book *Century of Struggle*, with which every historian of suffragism begins her research. Flexner was the first to insert Blatch alongside the more familiar figures of Alice Paul and Carrie Chapman Catt in her account of the achievements of Progressive Era suffragism. Over the years, as the political environment in which I had become a feminist and women's historian receded, I realized how much my own work owed to Flexner's, and how much I had taken for granted her careful balance of political commitment and historical integrity. In 1988, aware that time was passing, I requested and received permission to talk with her and drove to Massachusetts to meet her. The interview provided the basis for an article that concentrated on what I called the "left feminism" at the core of Flexner's vision of suffrage history, her commitment to exploring both women's systematic oppression and its relation to the larger problem of inequality, her mastery of the art of the hyphen. (See Chapter 12.)

Having gone through the terrors of the McCarthyite 1950s, Flexner herself was at great pains to underplay her left-wing politics. But to me, bringing this element of her analysis into the open was the only way to make sense of her achievement. Where prior historians of suffrage looked backward to victories already won, Flexner looked forward to battles yet to be fought. In particular, *Century of Struggle* is shaped by an awareness of the emerging civil rights struggle. How else to explain Flexner's two most distinctive achievements: the very fact that she wrote on women's rights at all, surrounded as she was by the most vigorous antifeminist sentiment of the entire twentieth century, and her extraordinarily prescient insistence on bringing African American women into the mainstream of suffrage historiography?[45]

In 1988, I moved from the State University of New York at Buffalo to UCLA. Coming to the West shook up my understandings of women's history. Faced with groups of students who represented a different and new (to me) racial and ethnic mix, my sense of the context of women's history, both past and present, shifted. I could see the northeastern bias of the "master" narratives in women's history, learned the importance of "region," and became fascinated with the history of western suffrage. The rise of "multiculturalism," so influential on the heavily immigrant, multiracial campus of UCLA, reopened for me questions of the history and meanings of "race." The first product of this was my coediting, with Vicki L. Ruiz, of *Unequal Sisters: A Multicultural Reader in U.S. Women's History.*[46]

Poised on the American edge of the Pacific Rim, I also become aware of the importance of situating American history in a global environment. This was reflected in another elaboration of my suffrage interest: looking into the international dimension of the movement. My work on woman suffrage around the world was first presented to a male-dominated socialist colloquium. (See Chapter 13.)[47] In reviewing this piece, published in 1991 in the British Marxist journal *New Left Review,* it seems to me that it forms a fitting pair with "The Radicalism of the Woman Suffrage Movement," written sixteen years before. (See Chapter 2.) The earlier article was directed at a feminist audience and argued for the originality of the suffrage demand; the later one, written for a socialist audience, argued for the link between woman suffrage and the larger left tradition. Significantly, this was the article that provided me with the metaphor on which I have relied so much in this survey of my intellectual development. The notion of the hyphen, that which both separates and links "socialism" and "feminism," best expressed my historical observation that a thriving and independent women's movement and an environment friendly to socialism both were necessary to produce a progressive suffragism and a democratic sort of feminism.

For most of the time that I have been working on the history of woman suffrage, few have shared my interest. The word *suffrage* remained as antiquated (and regularly misspelled) as it had been when I wrote my first graduate paper on the subject. But in the 1990s, women and politics has become a popular issue. On the coattails of Bill Clinton's presidency, many women were elected to public office, constituting the famous "year of the woman" in 1992. Politics at the highest level turned increasingly on "women's issues," most notably abortion rights. A gender gap in voting, which had been a factor at least since 1980, now drew pundits' attention. Women's greater liberalism (pacifism, preference for Democrats, inclination to social spending) was taken for granted as fundamentally female, rather than as the widespread impact of twenty years of liberal feminism.

In the last half decade, the scholarship on suffrage has blossomed. By a very rough estimate, already in the 1990s more monographs and collections of articles on the woman suffrage movement in the United States have been published than in the entire period between 1960 and 1990.[48] Even more remarkable is the renascence of interest in the subject outside the academy. In 1995, the seventy-fifth anniversary of the Nineteenth Amendment was marked by widespread grassroots celebration; by contrast, the fiftieth anniversary, occurring during the infancy of the modern feminist revival, went virtually unobserved. The sesquicentennial of the Seneca Falls Convention will undoubtedly be marked even more widely, including by the publication of this collection.

In moving beyond the issue of votes for women, the last chapter in this collection, "A Vindication of Women's Rights," reflects this normalization of women in politics. On the surface, it appears to differ in emphasis from virtually everything else included here. (See Chapter 14.) It is a reconsideration of the history of the American women's movement that deliberately avoids a focus on woman suffrage, citizenship, and political participation. I argue instead for the emancipatory power of another strain in the American feminist tradition, which I label "women's rights" and characterize as a critique of the institution of marriage as it restrains both women's labor and their sexuality. However, emphasizing the way that marriage limits women's possibilities can be seen as the corollary of my original claim: that enfranchisement and citizenship, because they were roles that bypassed the family, offered a uniquely emancipating vista for women.

Even so, I ask myself, is what I understand by the term *feminism* changing yet again? Unlike many of my colleagues, I have never offered a definition of feminism that can link the present and the past to create a well-defined political tradition;[49] this despite the fact that my own scholarship has consistently been about the investigation and re-creation of that tradition. To be sure, I have consistently given emphasis to certain elements in the history of feminism, most notably to the achievement of greater individualism for more and more women. "Vindication of Women's Rights" elaborates this emphasis by juxtaposing the institution of marriage, as the source of women's subordination, with the call for greater personhood, played out over a two-hundred-year period.[50]

Still I resist a precise definition of feminism. Even a definition that turns on the battle against "oppression" or "patriarchy" shifts the indeterminacy of "feminism" to these other terms, the content of which comes only from a particular historical context. Instead, I confess to approaching historical feminism in a way that has everything to do with feminism in the present. If I were talking the talk of postmodernism, I might say that feminism is a discourse, that discourses are tools in the struggle for power, and that the meaning of feminism changes over time and in the hands of different groups.

And I would also say that, as a historian and as a feminist, I have been part and parcel of that discursive struggle for almost three decades. When I began, as part of a generation trying to face down modern contempt for feminism, my definition focused on the political independence of feminism from other movements. Later, as modern feminism grew more confident, I defined feminism so as to strengthen the left wing of it, in which I placed myself, by emphasizing the interplay between struggles for political power in the public sphere and association with other insurgent political movements. When the sexual politics of modern feminism began to take a turn that I thought conservative, I did my best to make history serve the case of a "pro-sex" feminism. Now, in the face of heated contests about family life, sexuality, and the scope and future of marriage, I am in the camp that seeks to push the limits of politically possible sexual and familial change, and I attempt to use the evidence of the past to do so. I hope that, through all this, I have met my own standards for historical responsibility as well as political engagement.

It has become a commonplace to say that how we approach the past has everything to do with where we are located in the present. The historian has to stand someplace to generate her questions of the past. But investigating the past is also connected to what we want from the future, for the historian is also trying to understand the trajectory of change of which she is a part. And if committed to intervening through political action to affect the contemporary trajectory—that is, to being an active citizen—the historian's perspective must be part of that effort, intended to effect or alter what the future brings. In virtually every one of my writings in this collection, I have insisted on the intimate relationship between the practice of women's history and the possibilities of modern feminist politics. Given how diffuse and compromised feminism has become, certainly as compared to the determined, focused movement of twenty years ago, the rhetorical character of some of these claims now causes me some embarrassment. And yet I am unwilling to give up my own personal "metanarrative," which is a sort of wishful progressivism seeking to recruit adherents; an insistence that things might get better, if only people refuse to be discouraged about making them so.

NOTES

1. Judith Zinsser, *History and Feminism: A Glass Half Full* (New York: Twayne, 1993).

2. James A. Henretta, "Social History as Lived and Written," *American Historical Review* 84, 5 (1979): 1293–1322.

3. Jesse Lemisch, "The American Revolution Seen from the Bottom Up," in

Barton Bernstein, ed., *Towards a New Past: Dissenting Essays in American History* (New York: Vintage Books, 1967).

4. Mari Jo Buhle, Ann D. Gordon, and Nancy E. Schrom, "Women in American Society: An Historical Contribution," *Radical America* 5, 4 (1971): 3–66.

5. See Chapter 12, note 5, below. As a member of the Marxist-Feminist groups that Bailey was describing, I was particularly fond of this quote.

6. Several years later, Judith M. Bennett made a similar plea in "Feminism and History," *Gender & History* 1, 3 (1989): 251–72.

7. I am thinking of Nancy F. Cott, *The Bonds of Womanhood: "Woman's Sphere" in New England, 1780–1835* (New Haven: Yale University Press, 1977); Linda Gordon, *Woman's Body, Woman's Right: A Social History of Birth Control in America* (New York: Grossman, 1976); Kathryn Kish Sklar, *Catharine Beecher: A Study in American Domesticity* (New Haven: Yale University Press, 1993). I would also include in this list my own book, *Feminism and Suffrage: The Emergence of an Independent Women's Movement in America, 1848–1869* (Ithaca: Cornell University Press, 1978). I am not including Aileen S. Kraditor, *Ideas of the Woman Suffrage Movement, 1890–1920* (New York: Columbia University Press, 1965), and William O'Neill, *Everyone Was Brave: The Rise and Fall of Feminism in America* (New York: Quadrangle Books, 1969), which were written almost a decade earlier.

8. The immediate stimulus for the piece was the hostile scholarly reception to one of the key books in the first wave of women's history, Linda Gordon's *Woman's Body, Woman's Right*. Despite the subtitle of the book (which was not Gordon's choice), *Woman's Body* was feminist political history, a brilliant rewriting of the history of the birth control movement from the perspective of women's liberation, and a prescient acknowledgment of the significance of the movement for reproductive rights to the future of contemporary feminism. Many reviewers criticized the book for its refusal to accept the birth control battle as won, its sometimes harsh evaluation of Margaret Sanger's political leadership, and its insistence that political rather than technological and scientific developments drove the history of birth control.

9. Alice Echols, *Daring to Be Bad* (Minneapolis: University of Minnesota Press, 1989), pp. 243–47. For an article that also reads contemporary feminist separatism back into history but argues for its contribution to feminist politics, see Estelle Freedman, "Separatism as Strategy: Female Institution Building and American Feminism, 1870–1930," *Feminist Studies* 5, 3 (1979): 512–29.

10. The other contributors were Mari Jo Buhle, Gerda Lerner, Carroll

Smith-Rosenberg, and Temma Kaplan. See *Feminist Studies* 6, 1 (spring 1980), 37–64.

11. Audre Lorde, "The Master's Tools," in *This Bridge Called My Back: Writings by Radical Women of Color*, ed. Cherríe Moraga and Gloria Anzaldúa (New York: Kitchen Table Women of Color Press, 1983).

12. C. L. R. James makes this argument both about cricket, the preeminent imperial sport that colonials eventually took over, and about the ideology of the French Revolution, which Touissant L'Ouverture made the basis for the first successful revolution of slaves in the Western world; see James's *Black Jacobins: Touissant L'Ouverture and the San Domingo Slave Revolution* (New York: Vintage Books, 1963) and *Beyond a Boundary* (New York: Pantheon, 1963).

13. Christine Stansell, review of *Feminism and Suffrage*, *Feminist Studies* 6, 1 (1980): 65–75.

14. Carroll Smith-Rosenberg, "The Female World of Love and Ritual," *Signs* 1, 1 (1975): 1–29.

15. Eventually, the most thorough overview of the women's culture paradigm came from Linda Kerber: "Separate Spheres, Female Worlds, Women's Place: The Rhetoric of Women's History," *Journal of American History* 75, 1 (1988): 9–39.

16. Sara Evans, *Personal Politics* (New York: Random House, 1979).

17. My first published article was "Struggling into Existence: The Feminism of Sarah and Angelina Grimké," *Women: A Journal of Liberation* 1, 3 (1970): 4–11.

18. This is the subtitle of the book that came from my dissertation, *Feminism and Suffrage* (Ithaca: Cornell University Press, 1978).

19. Two of the most recent books on women and the Civil War are Drew Gilpin Faust, *Mothers of Invention: Women of the Slaveholding South in the American Civil War* (Chapel Hill: University of North Carolina Press, 1996), and Elizabeth Leonard, *Yankee Women: Gender Battles in the Civil War* (New York: W. W. Norton, 1994).

20. "Outgrowing the Compact of the Fathers" (Chapter 6 in this book) was originally part of a special issue of the *Journal of American History*, "The Constitution and American Life" (1987, published in 1988 by Cornell University Press).

21. See, for instance, Nancy Hewitt, "Beyond the Search for Sisterhood," originally published in *Social History* 10 (1985): 299–321.

22. Bettina Aptheker, "Abolitionism, Women's Rights and the Battle over the Fifteenth Amendment," in *Women's Legacy: Essays on Race, Sex, and Class in American History* (Amherst: University of Massachusetts Press, 1982); Angela

Davis, *Women, Race and Class* (New York: Random House, 1981), pp. 70–86. Neither criticized my book directly, but rather responded by providing alternative interpretations of the conflicts over the Fourteenth and Fifteenth amendments that emphasized the racism of the Stanton/Anthony forces.

23. Paula Giddings, *When and Where I Enter: The Impact of Black Women on Race and Sex in America* (New York: William Morrow & Co., 1984); Michele Wallace, *Black Macho and the Myth of Superwoman* (New York: Dial Press, 1979); "Combahee River Collective Statement, 1974" in *Home Girls: A Black Feminist Anthology*, ed. Barbara Smith (New York: Kitchen Table Women of Color Press, 1983), pp. 272–82.

24. Joan W. Scott, "Deconstructing Equality-versus-Difference," *Feminist Studies* 14, 1 (1988): 33–50. The first historiographical overview to draw out this distinction was Hester Eisenstein, *Contemporary Feminist Thought* (Boston: G. K. Hall & Co., 1983).

25. Carol Gilligan, *In a Different Voice: Psychological Theory and Women's Development* (Cambridge: Harvard University Press, 1982).

26. Kate Millett, *Sexual Politics* (New York: Doubleday, 1970). Millett's face appeared on the cover of *Time* magazine.

27. Ruth Milkman, "Women's History and the Sears Case," *Feminist Studies* 12, 2 (1986): 375–400; Jon Wiener, "The Sears Case: Women's History on Trial," *The Nation* 241, 6 (1985): 161–69. Scott concludes her discussion in "Deconstructing Equality-versus-Difference" with a discussion of the Sears case.

28. Rosalind Rosenberg, "Offer of Proof," *Signs* 11, 4 (1986): 757–66.

29. I made this argument when I spoke on the Sears case, at the Socialist Scholars Conference, New York City, April 19, 1986.

30. Leonore Weitzman, *The Divorce Revolution: The Unexpected Social and Economic Consequences for Women and Children in America* (New York: Free Press, 1985); Felice Schwartz, "Executives and Organizations: Management Women and the New Facts of Life," *Harvard Business Review* 67, 1 (Jan.–Feb. 1989): 65–77; Catharine MacKinnon, *Feminism Unmodified: Discourses on Life and Law* (Cambridge: Harvard University Press, 1987), p. 99. MacKinnon offers a very complex discussion about abortion, but the essential point is that "so long as women do not control access to our sexuality, abortion facilitates women's heterosexual availability. In other words, under conditions of gender inequality, sexual liberation in this case does not free women; it frees male sexual aggression. The availability of abortion removes the one remaining legitimized reason that women have had for refusing sex besides the headache" (p. 9).

31. Lisa Duggan and Nan D. Hunter, *Sex Wars: Sexual Dissent and Political Culture* (New York: Routledge & Kegan Paul, 1995).

32. The group was coorganized by myself and anthropologist and pioneering feminist sex radical Gayle Rubin. Other members included Michelle Zimbalist Rosaldo, Mary Ryan, Barbara Epstein, Estelle Freedman, Kay Trimberger, Martha Vicinius, Judith Stacey, Barbara Haber, and Nancy Chodorow.

33. Carol S. Vance, ed., *Pleasure and Danger: Exploring Female Sexuality* (Boston: Routledge & Kegan Paul, 1984). See also Ann Snitow, Christine Stansell, and Sharon Thompson, eds., *Powers of Desire* (New York: Monthly Review Press, 1983).

34. See, for example, Ilene J. Philipson, "Beyond the Virgin and the Whore," in *Women, Class and the Feminist Imagination: A Socialist-Feminist Reader*, ed. Karen V. Hansen and Ilene J. Philipson (Philadelphia: Temple University Press, 1990), pp. 451–59.

35. Nancy Cott made this point in "What's in a Name: The Limits of 'Social Feminism,' or Expanding the Vocabulary of Women's History," *Journal of American History* 76, 3 (1989): 809–29.

36. I went on to collaborate on two books: with Gail Kelly, Elizabeth Kennedy, Caroline Korsmeyer, and Lillian Robinson on *Feminist Scholarship: Kindling in the Groves of Academe* (Urbana: University of Illinois Press, 1985), and with Vicki L. Ruiz in the editing of *Unequal Sisters: A Multicultural Reader in U.S. Women's History* (New York: Routledge & Kegan Paul, 1991). For a very good essay on feminist collaboration, see Elizabeth Lapovsky Kennedy, "In Pursuit of Connection: Reflections on Collaborative Work," *American Anthropologist* 97, 1 (1995): 26–34.

37. Kraditor, *Ideas of the Woman Suffrage Movement.*

38. See, most recently, Sara Alpern, Joyce Antler, Elisabeth Israels Perry, and Ingrid Winther Scobie, eds., *The Challenge of Feminist Biography: Writing the Lives of Modern American Women* (Urbana: University of Illinois Press, 1992).

39. Ellen Carol DuBois, *Harriot Stanton Blatch and the Winning of Woman Suffrage* (New Haven: Yale University Press, 1997), pp. 72–73.

40. Ellen Carol DuBois, "Harriot Stanton Blatch and the Transformation of Class Relations among Woman Suffragists," in *Gender, Class, Race, and Reform in the Progressive Era*, ed. Noralee Frankel and Nancy S. Dye (Lexington: University Press of Kentucky, 1991), pp. 162–79.

41. Paula Baker, "The Domestication of American Politics: Women and American Political Society, 1780–1920," *American Historical Review* 89 (1984): 620–49.

42. Crystal Eastman, Leonora O'Reilly, and even Mary Beard are other examples.

43. Among the many testimonies to Beard's influence on modern American

women's historians, see Nancy F. Cott, ed., *A Woman Making History: Mary Beard through Her Letters* (New Haven: Yale University Press, 1991); Bonnie G. Smith, "Seeing Mary Beard," *Feminist Studies* 10 (1984): 399–416; Suzanne Lebsock, "Reading Mary Beard," *Reviews in American History* 17, 2 (1989): 324–39; Ann Lane, ed., *Mary Ritter Beard: A Sourcebook* (Boston: Northeastern University Press, 1988); Berenice A. Carroll, "Mary Beard's *Woman as Force in History*: A Critique," *Massachusetts Review* 13, 1–2 (1972): 125–43.

44. Lawrence W. Levine, *Opening the American Mind: Canons, Culture, and History* (Boston: Beacon Press, 1996).

45. In 1994, Eleanor Flexner died. Since then, her papers, closed at her request during her lifetime, have become available at the Schlesinger Library, Radcliffe College, and her own history within the Left need not merely be inferred. Daniel Horowitz has begun this process, as a result of his efforts to make a very similar argument for the submerged left-wing politics of the feminist pioneer Betty Friedan ("Rethinking Betty Friedan and the *Feminine Mystique*: Labor Union Radicalism and Feminism in Cold War America," *American Quarterly* 48, 1 [1996]: 1–42). Note that the word *feminist* does not appear in the first edition of Flexner's *Century of Struggle* (Cambridge, Mass.: Belknap Press, 1959), because at that time, the word was claimed only by the National Woman's Party, in the 1950s a pro-Republican and avowedly anticommunist group. It was not until the 1972 revision (New York: Atheneum), after the women's liberation revival of feminism, that Flexner started to claim and use the word.

46. See note 36, above. On region and women's history, see Jacquelyn D. Hall, "Partial Truths," *Signs* 14, 4 (1989): 902–11. I addressed my understanding of the role of California in the woman suffrage movement in an exhibit on the history of woman suffrage from a western perspective, held at the Huntington Library from October 1995 through January 1996; the catalog for the exhibit is *Votes for Women: A Seventy-fifth Anniversary Album*, ed. Ellen DuBois and Karen Kearns (San Marino, Calif.: Huntington Library Press, 1995).

47. My interest in the subject was further stimulated by an invitation to speak at an international symposium on the history of woman suffrage sponsored by the government of New Zealand, the first country to enfranchise women (in 1893). The proceedings of the conference are published as *Suffrage and Beyond: International Feminist Perspectives*, ed. Caroline Daley and Melanie Nolan (Auckland: Auckland University Press, 1994).

48. These include Kristi Andersen, *After Suffrage: Women in Partisan and Electoral Politics before the New Deal* (Chicago: University of Chicago Press, 1996); Sara Hunter Graham, *Woman Suffrage and the New Democracy* (New Haven: Yale University Press, 1996); Suzanne Marilley, *Woman Suffrage and the*

Origins of Liberal Feminism the United States, 1820–1920 (Cambridge: Harvard University Press, 1996); Marjorie Spruill Wheeler, ed., *Votes for Women in Tennessee, the South and the Nation* (Knoxville: University of Tennessee Press, 1995); Marjorie Spruill Wheeler, ed., *One Woman, One Vote: Rediscovering the Woman Suffrage Movement* (Troutdale, Ore.: New Sage Press, 1995).

49. See, as one of many examples, Nancy Cott's definition in *The Grounding of Modern Feminism*: an opposition to sex hierarchy, a belief in the social construction of women's condition, a recognition of the collective character of womanhood ([New Haven: Yale University Press, 1987], p. 4).

50. Here I find myself in belated agreement with the distinction that Gerda Lerner made between "autonomy" and "legal equality" as more and less radical standards for feminist change ("Women's Rights and American Feminism" [1971], reprinted in *The Majority Finds its Past*, ed. Gerda Lerner [New York: Oxford University Press, 1979], p. 49). Ironically in light of my own usage, Lerner identifies autonomy with "feminism" and equality with "women's rights." My emphasis on individualism as the emancipatory core of feminism is stated most strongly in "Illusions without Feminism," a review of Elizabeth Fox-Genovese's *Feminism without Illusions, The Nation* 454, 2 (January 20, 1992): 57–60, and in "Comment on Karen Offen's 'Defining Feminism: A Comparative Historical Approach,'" *Signs* 15, 1 (1989): 195–97.

2

The Radicalism of the Woman Suffrage Movement

Notes toward the Reconstruction of Nineteenth-Century Feminism

The major theoretical contribution of contemporary feminism has been the identification of the family as a central institution of women's oppression.[1] On the basis of this understanding we are seeing the beginnings of a revisionist history of American feminism that challenges the significance that has traditionally been attributed to the woman suffrage movement. Aileen Kraditor and William O'Neill have suggested that the woman suffrage movement did not lead to female emancipation because it accepted women's traditional position within the home.[2] While attacking this "what-went-wrong" approach, Daniel Scott Smith has contended that suffragism should yield its claim to the central place in the history of nineteenth-century feminism to a phenomenon he calls "domestic feminism."[3] Similarly, in her study of the female moral reform movement of the 1830s, Carroll Smith-Rosenberg argues that "it can hardly be assumed that the demand for votes for women was more radical than" the moral reform movement's attack on the sexual double standard.[4]

These revisionist efforts are commendable in that they expand our sense of nineteenth-century feminism to include a much larger and more diverse group of women's activities than merely suffrage. On the other hand, I think they do a historical disservice to the woman suffrage

Originally published in *Feminist Studies* 3 (1975).

movement. Nineteenth-century feminists and antifeminists alike perceived the demand for the vote as the most radical element in women's
protest against their oppression and we are obliged to honor the percep-
tions of the historical actors in question. When considering nineteenth-
century feminism not as an intellectual tradition but as a social movement, as a politics that motivated people to action, twentieth-century
historians are in no position to redefine what was its most radical aspect.
What we can do is analyze the position of nineteenth-century women
and the nature of suffragism in order to understand why the demand for
the vote was the most radical program for women's emancipation possible in the nineteenth century.

I would like to suggest an interpretation of nineteenth-century suffragism that reconciles the perceived radicalism of the woman suffrage
movement with the historical centrality of the family to women's condition. My hypothesis is that the significance of the woman suffrage movement rested precisely on the fact that it bypassed woman's oppression
within the family, or private sphere, and demanded instead her admission to citizenship, and through it admission to the public arena. By focusing on the public sphere, and particularly on citizenship, suffragists
demanded for women a kind of power and a connection with the social
order not based on the institution of the family and their subordination
within it.

Recent scholarship has suggested that the sharp distinction between
public and private activities is a relatively modern historical phenomenon. In his work on the evolution of the idea of childhood in Western
Europe, Phillipe Aries demonstrates that there was considerable overlap
between family life and community life in the premodern period. He
traces a gradual separation of public and private life from the sixteenth
century to the nineteenth century, when "family" and "society" came finally to be viewed as distinct, even hostile, institutions.[5] This development seems to have been clear and compact in U.S. history. In seventeenth-century New England, all community functions—production,
socialization, civil government, religious life—presumed the family as
the basic unit of social organization.[6] The whole range of social roles
drew on familial roles. The adult male's position as producer, as citizen,
as member of the church, all flowed from his position as head of the fam-

ily. Similarly, women's exclusion from church and civil government and their secondary but necessary role in production coincided with their subordinate position within the family.[7] A few women enjoyed unusual economic or social privileges by virtue of their family connections, but, as Gerda Lerner has pointed out, this further demonstrated women's dependence on their domestic positions for the definition of their roles in community life.[8]

By the nineteenth century, this relationship between family and society had undergone considerable change. Although the family continued to perform many important social functions, it was no longer the sole unit around which the community was organized. The concept of the "individual" had emerged to rival it. In the nineteenth century, we can distinguish two forms of social organization—one based on this new creature, the individual, the other based on the family. These overlapping but distinct structures became identified, respectively, as the public sphere and the private sphere. The emergence of a form of social organization not based on the family meant the emergence of social roles not defined by familial roles. This was equally true for women and men. But because women and men had different positions *within* the family, the existence of nonfamilial roles had different implications for the sexes. For women, the emergence of a public sphere held out the revolutionary possibility of a new way to relate to society not defined by their subordinate position within the family.

However, only men emerged from their familial roles to enjoy participation in the public sphere. Women on the whole did not. Women were of course among the first industrial workers, but these were overwhelmingly unmarried women, for whom factory work was a brief episode before marriage. Adult women remained almost entirely within the private sphere, defined politically, economically, and socially by their familial roles. Thus, the public sphere became man's arena; the private, woman's. This gave the public/private distinction a clearly sexual character. This phenomenon, canonized as the nineteenth-century doctrine of sexual spheres, is somewhat difficult for us to grasp. We are fond of pointing out the historical durability of sexual roles into our own time and miss the enormous difference between the twentieth-century notion of sexual roles and the nineteenth-century idea of sexual spheres. The difference is a measure of the achievements of nineteenth-century feminism.

The contradiction between the alternative to familial roles that activity in the public sphere offered and the exclusion of women from such activity was particularly sharp with respect to civil government. In seventeenth-century New England, citizenship was justified on the basis of familial position; the freeholder was at once the head of the household and a citizen. By contrast, nineteenth-century citizenship was posed as a direct relationship between the individual and his government. In other words, patriarchy was no longer the *official* basis of civil government in modern industrial democracy. However, in reality, only men were permitted to become citizens. The exclusion of women from participation in political life in the early nineteenth century was so absolute and unchallenged that it did not require explicit prescription. It was simply assumed that political "persons" were male. The U.S. Constitution did not specify the sex of citizens until the Fourteenth Amendment was ratified in 1869, after women had begun actively to demand the vote. Prior to that, the equation between "male" and "person," the term used in the Constitution, was implicit. The same, by the way, was true of the founding charter of the American Anti-Slavery Society. Written in 1833, it defined the society's membership as "persons," but for six years admitted only men into that category.

The doctrine of separate sexual spheres was supreme in the nineteenth century and even suffragists were unable to challenge certain basic aspects of it. Most notably, they accepted the particular suitability of women to domestic activities, and therefore their special responsibility for the private sphere, and did not project a reorganization of the division of labor within the home. Antoinette Brown Blackwell, pioneer suffragist and minister, asserted that "the paramount social duties of women are household duties, avocations arising from their relations as wives and mothers. . . . The work nearest and dearest before the eyes of average womanhood is work within family boundaries—work within a sphere which men cannot enter."[9] No suffragist of whom I am aware, including the otherwise iconoclastic Elizabeth Cady Stanton, seriously suggested that men take equal responsibilities with women for domestic activities. "Sharing housework" may be a more uniquely twentieth-century feminist demand than "smashing monogamy." To nineteenth-century feminists, domestic activities seemed as "naturally" female as child-bearing, and as little subject to social manipulation.

Although suffragists accepted the peculiarly feminine character of the private sphere, their demand for the vote challenged the male monopoly of the public arena. This is what gave suffragism much of its feminist meaning. Suffragists accepted women's "special responsibility" for domestic activity but refused to concede that it prohibited them from participation in the public sphere. Moreover, unlike the demand that women be admitted to trades, professions, and education, the demand for citizenship applied to all women and it applied to them all of the time—to the housewife as much as to the single, self-supporting woman. By demanding a permanent, public role for all women, suffragists began to demolish the absolute, sexually defined barrier marking the public world of men off from the private world of women. Even though they did not develop a critical analysis of domestic life, the dialectical relationship between public and private spheres transformed their demand for admission to the public sphere into a basic challenge to the entire sexual structure. Thus, although she never criticized women's role in the family, Stanton was still able to write: "One may as well talk of separate spheres for the two ends of the magnet as for man and woman; they may have separate duties in the same sphere, but their true place is together everywhere."[10]

Suffragists' demand for a permanent, public role for all women allowed them to project a vision of female experience and action that went beyond the family and the subordination of women which the family upheld. Citizenship represented a relationship to the larger society that was entirely and explicitly outside the boundaries of women's familial relations. As citizens and voters, women would participate directly in society as individuals, not indirectly through their subordinate positions as wives and mothers. Mary Putnam Jacobi identified this as the revolutionary core of suffragism. The American state, she explained, is based on "individual cells," not households. She went on: "Confessedly, in embracing in this conception women, we do introduce a change which, though in itself purely ideal, underlies all the practical issues now in dispute. In this essentially modern conception, women also are brought into direct relations with the State, independent of their 'mates' or 'brood.'"[11] Without directly attacking women's position within the private sphere, suffragists touched the nerve of women's subordinate status by contending that women might be something other than wives and mothers. "Womanhood is the great fact in her life," Stanton was fond of saying; "wifehood and motherhood are but incidental relations."[12]

On one level, the logic behind the demand for woman suffrage in a country professing republican principles is obvious, and suffragists made liberal use of the tradition and rhetoric of the American Revolution. Yet this is not sufficient to explain why suffrage became the core of a *feminist* program, why enfranchisement was perceived as the key to female liberation. I hypothesize that because enfranchisement involved a way for women to relate to society independent of their familial relations, it was the key demand of nineteenth-century feminists. It was the cornerstone of a social movement that did not simply catalog and protest women's wrongs in the existing sexual order but also revealed the possibility of an alternate sexual order. Unlike the tradition of female protest, from the moral reformers of the 1830s to the temperance women of the 1880s, which was based in the private sphere and sought to reinterpret women's place within it, suffragism focused squarely on the public sphere.

In part, the feminist, liberating promise of enfranchisement rested on the concrete power that suffragists expected to obtain with the vote. Suffragists expected women to use the ballot to protect themselves and to impose their viewpoint on political issues. They anticipated that by strategic use of their political power women would break open new occupations, raise the level of their wage scales to that of men, win strikes, and force reforms in marriage and family law in order to protect themselves from sexual abuse, the loss of their children, and the unchecked tyranny of their husbands. The demand for suffrage drew together protest against all these abuses in a single demand for the right to shape the social order by way of the public sphere. No longer content either with maternal influence over the future voter's character or with an endless series of petitions from women to lawmakers, suffragists proposed that women participate directly in the political decisions that affected their lives. "Like all disfranchised classes, they began by asking to have certain wrongs redressed," Stanton wrote. But suffragism went beyond what she called "special grievances" to give women's protest "a larger scope."[13]

In evaluating suffragists' expectations of the power that the vote would bring women, it is important to keep in mind the structure of political power in the nineteenth century. Political decisions were less centralized in the federal government and more significant at the local level than they are now. Herbert Gutman's analysis of the assistance which local politicians gave labor activists in nineteenth-century Paterson, New Jersey, suggests that Susan B. Anthony's prediction that woman suffrage would win women's strikes had some basis in reality.[14]

Even granted the greater power of the individual voter over political decisions that would affect her or his life, suffragists did not understand the ballot as merely a weapon with which to protect their interests in the political process. They also expected enfranchisement to transform woman's consciousness, to reanchor her self-image, not in the subordination of her familial role but in the individuality and self-determination that they saw in citizenship. This was a particularly important aspect of the political thought of Elizabeth Cady Stanton, the chief ideologue of nineteenth-century suffragism. It is developed most fully in "Solitude of Self," the speech she thought her best. She wrote there: "Nothing strengthens the judgment and quickens the conscience like individual responsibility. Nothing adds such dignity to character as the recognition of one's self-sovereignty."[15] Elsewhere, she wrote that from the "higher stand-point" of enfranchisement, woman would become sensitive to the daily indignities which, without due appreciation for her own individuality, she ignored and accepted.[16] She developed the theme of the impact of enfranchisement on women's self-concept most fully in a speech simply titled "Self-Government the Best Means of Self-Development."[17]

Given the impact on consciousness that suffragists expected from the vote, they generally refused to redirect their efforts toward such partial enfranchisements as municipal or school suffrage. Although these limited suffrages would give women certain political powers, they were suffrages designed especially for women and justified on the basis of women's maternal responsibilities. Their achievement would not necessarily prove women's right to full and equal participation in the public sphere. Suffragists did not simply want political power; they wanted to be citizens, to stand in the same relation to civil government as men did. As a result, it was primarily clubwomen who worked for school and municipal suffrage, while those who identified themselves as suffragists continued to concentrate on the admission of women to full citizenship.[18]

An important index to the nature and degree of suffragism's challenge to the nineteenth-century sexual order was the kind and amount of opposition that it inspired. Antisuffragists focused on the family, its position vis-à-vis the state, and the revolutionary impact of female citizenship on that relation. In response to suffragists' demand that modern democracy include women, antisuffragists tried to reinstate a patriarchal theory of society and the state.[19] The family, they contended, was the virtual, if not the official, unit of civil government, and men represented and protected the women of their families in political affairs. Antisuffragists regularly charged that the enfranchisement of women would revolutionize the relations of the sexes and, in turn, the character and structure of the home and women's role within it. The 1867 New York Constitutional Convention expressed this fear for the future of the family when it rejected suffrage because it was an innovation "so revolutionary and sweeping, so openly at war with a distribution of duties and functions between the sexes as venerable and pervading as government itself, and involving transformations so radical in social and domestic life."[20]

Most suffragists were much more modest about the implications of enfranchisement for women's position within the family. They expected reform of family law, particularly of the marriage contract, and the abolition of such inequities as the husband's legal right to his wife's sexual services. They also anticipated that the transformation in woman's consciousness which enfranchisement would bring would improve the quality of family relations, particularly between wife and husband. Stanton argued that once women were enfranchised they would demand that democracy be the law of the family, as well as of the state.[21] Her comment suggests that, by introducing women into a form of social organization not based on patriarchal structures, she expected enfranchisement to permit women a much more critical perspective on the family itself. However, suffragists regularly denied the antisuffragists' charge that woman suffrage meant a revolution in the family. Most would have agreed with Jacobi that if antisuffragists wanted to argue that familial bonds were mere "political contrivances," requiring the disfranchisement of women to sustain them, suffragists had considerably more faith in the family as a "natural institution," able to survive women's entry into the public sphere.[22]

Suffragists worked hard to attract large numbers of women to the demand for the vote. They went beyond the methods of agitational propaganda, which they had learned as abolitionists, and beyond the skills of lobbying, which they had developed during Radical Reconstruction, to become organizers. As suffragists' efforts at outreach intensified, the family-bound realities of most women's lives forced more and more domestic imagery into their rhetoric and their arguments. Yet suffrage remained a distinctly minority movement in the nineteenth century. The very thing that made suffragism the most radical aspect of nineteenth-century feminism—its focus on the public sphere and on a nonfamilial role for women—was the cause of its failure to establish a mass base. It was not that nineteenth-century women were content, or had no grievances, but that they understood their grievances in the context of the private sphere. The lives of most nineteenth-century women were overwhelmingly limited to the private realities of wifehood and motherhood, and they experienced their discontent in the context of those relations. The enormous success of the Woman's Christian Temperance Union (WCTU), particularly as contrasted with the nineteenth-century suffrage movement, indicates the capacity for protest and activism among nineteenth-century women and the fact that this mass feminism was based in the private sphere. The WCTU commanded an army in the nineteenth century, while woman suffrage remained a guerrilla force.

Unlike the woman suffrage movement, the WCTU took as its starting point woman's position within the home; it cataloged the abuses she suffered there and it proposed reforms necessary to ameliorate her domestic situation. As the WCTU developed, its concerns went beyond the family to include the quality of community life, but its standard for nonfamilial relations remained the family and the moral values women had developed within it. The WCTU spoke to women in the language of their domestic realities, and they joined in the 1870s and 1880s in enormous numbers. Anchored in the private realm, the WCTU became the mass movement that nineteenth-century suffragism could not.

The WCTU's program reflected the same social reality that lay beyond suffragism—that the family was losing its central place in social organization to nondomestic institutions, from the saloon to the school to the legislature, and that woman's social power was accordingly weakened. Yet the WCTU, Luddite-like, defended the family and women's traditional but fast-fading authority within it. Its mottoes reflected this defensive goal: "For God and Home and Native Land"; "Home Protection." In 1883, the WCTU formally endorsed the demand for female enfranchisement but justified its action as necessary to protect the home and women within it, thus retaining its family-based analysis and its defensive character. The first resolutions introduced by Frances Willard in support of suffrage asked for the vote for women in their roles as wives and mothers, to enable them to protect their homes from the influence of the saloon.[23] This was the woman suffrage movement's approach to female oppression and the problem of spheres stood on its head— women entering the public arena to protect the primacy of the private sphere and women's position within it. Yet the very fact that the WCTU had to come to terms with suffrage and eventually supported it indicates that the woman suffrage movement had succeeded in becoming the defining focus of nineteenth-century feminism, with respect to which all organized female protest had to orient itself. Even though the WCTU organized and commanded the forces, the woman suffrage movement had defined the territory.

Suffrage became a mass movement in the twentieth century under quite different conditions, when women's position vis-à-vis the public and private spheres had shifted considerably. Despite, or perhaps because of, the home-based ideology with which they operated, the WCTU, women's clubs, and other branches of nineteenth-century feminism had introduced significant numbers of women to extradomestic concerns.[24] Charlotte Perkins Gilman noted the change among women in 1903: "The socialising of this hitherto subsocial, wholly domestic class, is a marked and marvelous event, now taking place with astonishing rapidity."[25] Similarly, Susan B. Anthony commented at the 1888 International Council of Women: "Forty years ago women had no place anywhere except in their homes, no pecuniary independence, no purpose in life save that which came through marriage. . . . In later years the way has been opened to every avenue of industry—to every profession. . . . What is true in the world of work is true in education, is true everywhere."[26] At the point that it could attract a mass base, suffragism no longer opened up such revolutionary vistas for women; they were already operating in the public world of work and politics. The scope and meaning of twentieth-century suffragism requires its own analysis, but the achievement of nineteenth-century suffragists was that they identified, however haltingly, a fundamental transformation of the family and the new possibilities for women's emancipation that this revealed.

NOTES

1. The clearest explanation of this is Juliet Mitchell, *Women's Estate* (Baltimore: Penguin Books, 1971).

2. Aileen Kraditor, ed., *Up from the Pedestal: Selected Writings in the History of American Feminism* (Chicago: Quadrangle Books, 1968), 21–24; William O'Neill, "Feminism as a Radical Ideology," in *Dissent: Explorations in the History of American Radicalism*, ed. Alfred F. Young (De Kalb: Northern Illinois University Press, 1968), 284.

3. Daniel Scott Smith, "Family Limitation, Sexual Control and Domestic Feminism in Victorian America," *Feminist Studies* 1, 3/4 (1973): 40–57; reprinted in *Clio's Consciousness Raised*, ed. Mary Hartman and Lois W. Banner (New York: Harper Torchbooks, 1974).

4. Carroll Smith-Rosenberg, "Beauty, the Beast, and the Militant Woman: Sex Roles and Social Stress in Jacksonian America," *American Quarterly* 23 (1971): 584.

5. Phillipe Aries, *Centuries of Childhood: A Social History of Family Life* (New York: Vintage Books, 1962), esp. 365–407.

6. Edmund Morgan, *The Puritan Family: Religion and Domestic Relations in Seventeenth-Century New England* (New York: Harper & Row, 1966), esp. chap. 6; John Demos, *A Little Commonwealth: Family Life in Plymouth Colony* (New York: Oxford University Press, 1970), 2–11.

7. Morgan, *Puritan Family*, chap. 2. Demos, *Little Commonwealth*, 82–84.

8. Gerda Lerner, "The Lady and the Mill Girl: Changes in the Status of

Women in the Age of Jackson," *Mid-Continent American Studies Journal* 10 (1969): 6.

9. Antoinette Brown Blackwell, "Relation of Woman's Work in the Household to the Work Outside," reprinted in *Up from the Pedestal*, 151.

10. Elizabeth Cady Stanton, "Speech to the 1885 National Suffrage Convention," in *History of Woman Suffrage*, ed. Elizabeth Cady Stanton, Susan B. Anthony, and Matilda Joslyn Gage (Rochester, N.Y.: Susan B. Anthony, 1889), vol. 4, p. 58.

11. Mary Putnam Jacobi, *"Common Sense" Applied to Woman Suffrage* (New York: Putnam, 1894), 138.

12. Elizabeth Cady Stanton, "Introduction," in *History of Woman Suffrage*, vol. 1, p. 22.

13. Ibid., 15

14. Herbert Gutman, "Class, Status, and Community Power in Nineteenth Century American Industrial Cities—Paterson, New Jersey: A Case Study," in *The Age of Industrialism in America*, ed. Frederic C. Jaher (New York: Free Press, 1968), 263–87. For Anthony's prediction on the impact of woman suffrage on women's strikes, see "Woman Wants Bread, not the Ballot," reprinted in *The Life and Work of Susan B. Anthony*, ed. Ida Husted Harper (Indianapolis and Kansas City: Bowen-Merrill, 1898), vol. 2, pp. 996–1003.

15. Elizabeth Cady Stanton, "Solitude of Self," in *History of Woman Suffrage*, vol. 4, pp. 189–91.

16. Stanton, "Introduction," in *History of Woman Suffrage*, vol. 1, p. 18.

17. Elizabeth Cady Stanton, "Self-Government the Best Means of Self-Development," in *History of Woman Suffrage*, vol. 4, 40–42.

18. See Lois B. Merk, "Boston's Historical Public School Crisis," *New England Quarterly* 31 (1958): 196–202.

19. See, for instance, Orestes A. Brownson, "The Woman Question," reprinted in *Up from the Pedestal*, 192–94.

20. "Report of the Committee on Suffrage," in *History of Woman Suffrage*, vol. 2, p. 285.

21. Elizabeth Cady Stanton, "The Family, the State, and the Church," unpublished manuscript speech, Elizabeth Cady Stanton Papers, Manuscript Division, Library of Congress, Washington, D.C.

22. Jacobi, *"Common Sense,"* 108.

23. Mary Earhart, *Frances Willard: From Prayers to Politics* (Chicago: University of Chicago Press, 1944), chap. 10.

24. This process is described in Anne Firor Scott, *The Southern Lady: From*

Pedestal to Politics 1830–1930 (Chicago: University of Chicago Press, 1970), chap. 6.

25. Charlotte Perkins Gilman, *The Home: Its Work and Influence* (New York: McClure, Phillips, & Co., 1903), 325.

26. Susan B. Anthony, "Introductory Remarks," in *Report of the International Council of Women, Assembled by the National Woman Suffrage Association* (Washington, D.C.: Rufus H. Darby, 1888), 31.

3

Politics and Culture in Women's History

This essay concerns the relationship between the history of feminism and the history of women. It rests on two propositions that I believe are closely related: A feminist perspective is necessary to make women's history a vital intellectual endeavor, and women's history should give special attention to the history of the feminist movement. My approach is basically historiographical: What have contemporary women's historians had to say about the history of feminism and how has this affected their interpretations of other matters?

The revival of women's history in the 1960s began with a criticism of the past traditions of feminism, both as an approach to the liberation of women and as a basis for researching women's history. I am thinking here of everything from William O'Neill's *Everyone Was Brave: The Rise and Fall of Feminism in America* and Aileen Kraditor's *Ideas of the Woman Suffrage Movement, 1890–1920* to Gerda Lerner's "The Lady and the Mill Girl: Changes in the Status of Women in the Age of Jackson," Carroll Smith-Rosenberg's "Beauty, the Beast, and the Militant Woman: A Case Study in Sex Roles and Social Stress in Jacksonian America," and Mari Jo Buhle, Ann Gordon, and Nancy Schrom's "Women in American Society: An Historical Contribution."[1] The perspective common to all these works was the belief that the feminist movement that had preceded women's liberation did not have a sufficiently broad understanding of women's oppression and therefore achieved its goals, the most important of which was the vote, without contributing much to the eman-

Originally published in *Feminist Studies* 6 (1980).

cipation of women. Similarly, previous work in the history of women, much of it influenced directly by the women's rights movement, was also criticized for its narrowness and its inability to capture the breadth and complexity of women's historical experiences. Mary Beard's criticism of women's history, that it had misconstrued women's past as the history of unchanging oppression and had seriously underestimated women's active historical involvement, was frequently cited and applauded.[2] The women's history revival criticized its predecessors for limiting themselves to the history of a few individuals and organizations, for ignoring the varieties of oppression experienced by women other than the white middle-class constituents of women's rights, and for mistaking men's images of women for the historical realities of their lives.

Although the women's history revival began with a criticism of traditional feminism and women's history written under its influence, it did so on the basis of a broader feminist perspective. The goal of this revival was a more comprehensive and analytic history of women's oppression that reached beyond questions of political and economic inequality to the total social relations of the sexes. Women's historians of the 1960s and 1970s asked: How did the masses of women experience their lives? What grievances did they articulate? In what ways did they act on their dissatisfactions? What traditions of protest and resistance did they leave us above and beyond the women's rights movement? The answers to these questions have produced a much enriched women's history and a greatly enlarged sense of the relevance of feminism to it. Women's historians have found feminist politics, not just in the women's rights movement, but in the labor movement, the birth control movement, the Socialist party, temperance, and abolitionism.[3] Even more broadly, they have found evidences of protest against male domination and affirmation of sisterhood in domestic novels, benevolent organizations, female friendships, which suggest a very widespread, largely inchoate feminist consciousness among nineteenth-century women. These discoveries greatly strengthen the feminist conception of women's history, which is that the oppression of women and their efforts to understand and overcome it are central themes of women's experience.

The most significant theoretical formulation coming from these discoveries has been the concept of women's culture. The term "women's culture" has been used by historians to refer to the broad-based commonality of values, institutions, relationships, and methods of communication focused on domesticity and morality and particular to late eighteenth- and nineteenth-century women.[4] The concept of women's culture shares a great deal with the concept of slave culture and probably derives in part from it. Reacting to a historical theory of slavery that saw black people only as their masters' ideas of them, historians of slavery have analyzed the social structures and belief systems that slaves formed for themselves and discovered the existence of a semiautonomous slave culture.[5] Although this slave culture did not directly challenge the slave system, it did encourage blacks to resist the masters' power and established limits to their exploitation. It is this "resistance" aspect of slave culture on which historians have focused.

The analogy to women's culture is obvious. Like slaves, nineteenth-century women have been ignored in favor of their images—passive, dependent, content, dedicated to home and family. The investigation of women's culture is a reaction to this, a way to see women creating themselves and not just being created. Here too the emphasis has been on resistance. In women's culture, women developed group solidarity and some degree of psychic autonomy from men. Women's culture itself did not constitute an open and radical break with dominant sexual ideology any more than slave culture openly challenged slavery. Indeed, it was part of the dominant system, sharing most of its assumptions about women and men—separate spheres, women's domesticity, male dominance.

The pressing historical questions about the concept of women's culture center on its relation to feminism. At what point can we say that feminism surfaced out of women's culture? How was feminism in conflict with, as well as a development of, women's culture? What was the impact of feminism, and particularly of the emergence of a women's politics, on the course of women's culture? Women's historians are just beginning to address these questions. In *The Bonds of Womanhood: "Woman's Sphere" in New England, 1780–1835*, Cott stresses that "woman's sphere [was] the basis for a subculture among women" in the 1830s, and that it led to the development of women's consciousness of themselves as a group, which was a necessary prerequisite for the emer-

gence of a feminist movement. Yet, as Cott herself suggests, it is important not to confuse women's culture and feminism, or to assume a simple and direct development out of one into the other.[6] From my own
work on the political ideas of Elizabeth Cady Stanton, I am beginning
to see how women's rights feminism grew out of a critique of what we
are calling women's culture. Stanton was deeply critical of many of
women's traditional values. She thought religion stifled women's minds
and wanted to replace it with a political outlook, a viewpoint foreign to
woman's sphere. She criticized the female ideology of self-sacrifice and
sought to replace it with one of self-development. Above all, she disagreed with the idea that woman had a special mission in society, and she
thought that woman's place should be determined by the same general
principles of individual rights and abstract equality as man's was.

From the point at which the women's rights movement began to develop, it is impossible to understand the history of women's culture without setting it in dialectical relation to feminism. On the one hand, some
defenders of women's culture saw in feminism a serious threat to their
conception of woman's place. In her biography of Catharine Beecher,
Kathryn Sklar writes that Beecher "began the task that was to occupy her
for the rest of her career—that of interpreting and shaping the collective
consciousness of American women" in direct reaction to the feminism of
Sarah and Angelina Grimké, to counter any influence they might have
had on women's thinking. The culmination of this was that Beecher
published one of the first antisuffrage tracts.[7] On the other hand, the
mammoth and powerful Woman's Christian Temperance Union
(WCTU) of the 1870s and 1880s developed out of Frances Willard's
very creative efforts to synthesize the militance and political outlook of
women's rights with the traditional values and intense loyalties of
women's culture.[8]

However, the dominant tendency in the study of women's culture has
not been to relate it to feminism, but to look at it in isolation and to ro-
manticize what it meant for women. Another way to put it is that the
concept of women's culture, the discovery of the humanity and historical activity of all those whom we once dismissed as "true women,"
threatens to satisfy the impulse that led us into women's history; it may

forestall further inquiry into the system that structured women's historical activity and shaped their oppression.

These tendencies can be seen in the pioneering study of women's culture, Carroll Smith-Rosenberg's "The Female World of Love and Ritual: Relations between Women in Nineteenth Century America." Smith-Rosenberg vividly portrays the quality of women's culture and the nature of women's attachment to it and to each other. However, she never really gets outside the female world, to see the larger social and historical developments of which it was a part. She is not concerned with how women's culture arose in history or how it was transformed. Above all, she takes the separateness of the women's world at face value and does not investigate its relation to the dominant male culture. Conflict between the two worlds is underplayed, so much so that the concept of women's oppression begins to seem irrelevant; and Smith-Rosenberg says explicitly that, despite the discrimination, inequality, and misogyny rife in the nineteenth century, women's historical experiences were too rich, the evidence of their power and autonomy too impressive, to call them an "isolated and oppressed subcategory in male society."[9] Nor does she address the limitations of the values of women's culture, the ways that they restrained and confined women, for instance, by being hostile to both politics and sexuality. Such a picture of women's history has little to do with classical women's rights feminism, with its focus on political equality, and elsewhere, Smith-Rosenberg has dismissed the women's rights and woman suffrage movement as "of little importance either to American politics or to American women."[10]

The consequences of interpreting women's social history without reference to feminist politics can be seen very clearly by comparing two recent histories of birth control and women: Daniel Scott Smith's "Family Limitations, Sexual Control, and Domestic Feminism in Victorian America," which ignores the role of political feminism, and Linda Gordon's *Woman's Body, Woman's Right: A Social History of Birth Control in America*, which stresses it. Daniel Scott Smith argues that mid-nineteenth-century American women gained increasing control over marital intercourse, and this enabled them to reduce the number of children they had. He attributes this to the spread of "domestic feminism," by which he means an ideology that encouraged women to win greater freedom and control within their families and through their individual efforts. In addition to helping women to "seize power within the family," domestic feminism functioned among women as a critique of "male, materialistic market society." Clearly Smith's domestic feminism is very close to the concept of women's culture, and indeed some subsequent historians have used it that way.[11] Smith explicitly contrasts domestic feminism with the women's rights movement, which he describes as having a "narrow social base among women" and dismisses because he considers its focus on equality and individuality in public life "limiting as a political ideology" for most nineteenth-century women.[12]

Linda Gordon's approach to the history of birth control and women is very different. Her focus is on the history of political struggles over birth control, and particularly on the rise and fall of a feminist political movement committed to winning reproductive freedom for women. She makes a distinction between the desire and struggle for birth control, which she believes characterizes women's history in all periods, and the rise of a birth control movement at a particular historical moment. She begins her history of birth control where Smith leaves off his, at that point in the nineteenth century when substantial numbers of women began to embrace a birth control ideology. Unlike Smith, Gordon believes that "public" feminism in the women's rights movement had a great deal to do with the spread of these beliefs among average nonpolitical women. Furthermore, she recognizes that the widespread existence of a pro-birth control attitude among women was not sufficient to win them birth control freedom. What was necessary was a feminist political movement committed to that goal and capable of struggling with other forces in the political arena over who would control reproduction and to what ends. She traces the rise of that movement in the 1870s, its transformation into a socialist movement in the early twentieth century, and its ultimate collapse in the 1920s.[13]

Gordon's political focus has subjected her book to much more intense criticism than just about anything else written in women's history. In addition to attacking Gordon because of her explicitly feminist and Marxist point of view, the critics all challenge the prominent role that she gives the political history of birth control. They charge that she has taken the ideas of a few irrelevant birth control ideologues and political activists and offered them as a substitute for what the reviewers believe is the real history of birth control use and ideology among "average" women. Here the critical attacks on Gordon come very close to Daniel Scott Smith's approach, in that they all categorically dismiss any impact that women's rights feminist politics had on the birth control history of the average woman. The critics prefer to concentrate either on the changing character of family and marriage or on technological breakthroughs in contraception to explain why and how women's use of birth control changes.[14]

There is a very sneaky kind of antifeminism here, that criticizes feminism in the name of the common woman and political history in the name of social history. Underlying all the criticisms of Gordon's book is a challenge to the feminist perspective on contemporary society on which it is based. The question Gordon asks is the one posed by the contemporary feminist movement: Why do women today lack real reproductive freedom, especially in light of the modern technological capacity for contraception? Gordon's critics do not accept the validity of this question. For them, the birth control "revolution" is over, because they see it as a matter of "sexual liberation" or "population control," and not as a question over which people have and will struggle politically: women's freedom.

As we have seen, the interest that women's historians have shown in questions of culture parallels similar concerns in black and labor history. So too do my criticisms that questions of culture may have come to replace questions of politics, and that it may be time to return to the study of politics from the more sophisticated perspective which the study of culture has afforded us. In a recent review of the work of Herbert Gutman, David Montgomery has made this observation about tendencies in working-class history and furthermore identifies a lurking inclination to rely on modernization theory, rather than political factors, to explain historical change.[15] Like labor history and black history, women's history was deeply "political" in its origins, arising in connection with contemporary political movements and holding certain political perspectives without any need for apology. As these developments have coalesced into the new field of "social history," many of us have felt some anxiety that these intellectual projects will become "depoliticized" and academic in the worst sense of the word. One way to work against this tendency is to insist that, in our own writing, we give adequate attention to political questions, and thereby insure that the women's history—or black history or working-class history—which we produce retains its focus on social change.

NOTES

1. William O'Neill, *Everyone Was Brave: The Rise and Fall of Feminism in America* (New York: Quadrangle, 1969); Aileen Kraditor, *Ideas of the Woman Suffrage Movement, 1890-1920* (New York: Columbia University Press, 1965); Gerda Lerner, "The Lady and the Mill Girl: Changes in the Status of Women in the Age of Jackson," *Mid-Continent American Studies Journal* 10 (Spring 1969): 5–15; Carroll Smith-Rosenberg, "Beauty, the Beast, and the Militant Woman: A Case Study in Sex Roles and Social Stress in Jacksonian America," *American Quarterly* 23 (October 1971): 562–84; Mari Jo Buhle, Ann D. Gordon, and Nancy Schrom, "Women in American Society: An Historical Contribution," *Radical America* 5 (July-August 1971): 3–66.

2. See Buhle, Gordon, and Schrom, "Women in American Society," p. 4; and Gerda Lerner, "New Approaches to the Study of Women in American History," originally published in 1969 and reprinted in *Liberating Women's History*, ed. Berenice Carroll (Urbana: University of Illinois Press, 1976), p. 350. Also see new research on Beard: Berenice Carroll, "On Mary Beard's *Woman as Force in History*," originally published in 1972 and reprinted in *Liberating Women's History;* also, Ann Lane, ed., *Mary Ritter Beard: A Sourcebook* (New York: Schocken Books, 1977).

3. On feminism in the labor movement, see Nancy Schrom Dye, "Feminism or Unionism? The New York Women's Trade Union League and the Labor Movement," and Robin Miller Jacoby, "The Women's Trade Union League and American Feminism," both in *Feminist Studies* 3, no. 1–2 (Fall 1975): 111–40. On the birth control movement, see Linda Gordon, *Woman's Body, Woman's Right: A Social History of Birth Control in America* (New York: Viking-Grossman, 1976). On feminism in the Socialist party, see Mari Jo Buhle, "Women and the Socialist Party, 1901–1914," originally published in 1970 and reprinted in *From Feminism to Liberation*, ed. Edith Hoshino Altbach (Cambridge, Mass.:

Schenkman Publishing Co., 1971), pp. 65–86. On temperance, see Anne Firor Scott, *The Southern Lady: From Pedestal to Politics, 1830–1930* (Chicago: University of Chicago Press, 1970); and Barbara Epstein, *Politics of Domesticity: Women, Evangelism, and Temperance* (Middletown, Conn.: Wesleyan University Press, 1981). For feminism in the abolitionist movement, see Ellen DuBois, *Feminism and Suffrage: The Emergence of an Independent Women's Movement in America, 1848–1869* (Ithaca, N.Y.: Cornell University Press, 1978); and Blanche Glassman Hersh, *The Slavery of Sex: Feminist Abolitionists in America* (Urbana: University of Illinois Press, 1978). Here and elsewhere, I am using the term "politics," which contemporary feminism has expanded to mean anything that has social (as opposed to individual) origins, in its more limited and classical sense, to mean anything that has to do with the government of community life and institutions, especially the state.

4. The first use of the term I am able to find is in the introduction to Nancy Cott's *Root of Bitterness* (New York: E. P. Dutton & Co., 1972). Also important is Johnny Faragher and Christine Stansell, "Women and Their Families on the Overland Trail to California and Oregon, 1842–1867," *Feminist Studies* 2, no. 2–3 (1975): 150–66. Both Faragher and Stansell and Cott use the term "subculture" rather than "culture." Faragher and Stansell cite: Kathryn Sklar, *Catharine Beecher: A Study in American Domesticity* (New Haven: Yale University Press, 1973); Smith-Rosenberg, "Beauty, the Beast, and the Militant Woman"; Gail Parker, ed., *The Oven Birds* (Garden City: Anchor Books, 1972); and Ann Douglas Wood, "The 'Scribbling Women' and Fanny Fern: Why Women Wrote," *American Quarterly* 23 (Spring 1971): 3–24. Wood, who was one of the earliest contributors to the concept of women's culture, has since reversed her position and written a snide attack on nineteenth-century female sentimentalists, *The Feminization of American Culture* (New York: Alfred A. Knopf, 1977). Other works using the concept of women's culture include: Susan Porter Benson, "Business Heads and Sympathetic Hearts: Women of the Providence Employment Society," *Journal of Society History* 78 (Winter 1978): 302–12; Anne M. Boylan, "Evangelical Womanhood in the Nineteenth Century: The Role of Women in Sunday Schools," *Feminist Studies* 4, no. 3 (October 1978): 62–80; Mary P. Ryan, "The Power of Women's Networks: A Case Study of Female Moral Reform in Antebellum America," *Feminist Studies* 5, no. 1 (Spring 1979): 66–85.

5. Important recent works on slave culture include: John B. Blassingame, *The Slave Community: Plantation Life in the Antebellum South* (New York: Oxford University Press, 1972); Herbert Gutman, *The Black Family in Slavery and*

Freedom, 1750–1925 (New York: Pantheon, 1976); Lawrence Levine, *Black Culture and Black Consciousness* (New York: Oxford University Press, 1977); and Eugene Genovese, *Roll, Jordan, Roll: The World the Slaves Made* (New York: Pantheon, 1974). Stanley Elkins, *Slavery* (Chicago: University of Chicago Press, 1959), is the classical study of slavery that sees slavery only from the viewpoint of the slaveowners, and against which many of these later historians reacted.

6. Nancy Cott, *The Bonds of Womanhood: "Woman's Sphere" in New England, 1780–1835* (New Haven: Yale University Press, 1977), pp. 197–206, and especially p. 205.

7. Sklar, *Catharine Beecher*, p. 132. The antisuffrage tract was *Woman's Profession as Mother and Educator with Views in Opposition to Woman Suffrage*, published in 1872.

8. On the WCTU, see Eleanor Flexner, *Century of Struggle: The Woman's Rights Movement in the United States* (New York: Atheneum, 1968); and Mary Earhart (Dillon), *Frances Willard: From Prayers to Politics* (Chicago: University of Chicago Press, 1944).

9. Carroll Smith-Rosenberg, "The Female World of Love and Ritual: Relations between Women in Nineteenth-Century America," *Signs* 1, no. 1 (Autumn 1975): 9.

10. Carroll Smith-Rosenberg, "The New Woman and the New History," *Feminist Studies* 3, no. 1–2 (Fall 1975): 186.

11. Mary Beth Norton, "The Paradox of Woman's Sphere," in *Women of America: A History*, ed. Carol Berkin and Mary Beth Norton (Boston: Houghton Mifflin Company, 1979), p. 145.

12. Daniel Scott Smith, "Family Limitations, Sexual Control, and Domestic Feminism in Victorian America," in *Clio's Consciousness Raised*, ed. Mary Hartman and Lois Banner (New York: Harper and Row, 1974), especially pp. 119–20, 123–24, 130–32. This article was reprinted from *Feminist Studies* 1, no. 3–4 (Winter-Spring 1973): 40–57.

13. Gordon, *Woman's Body, Woman's Right*, especially pp. 70–71.

14. Hostile reviews include: Edward Shorter, *Journal of Social History* 11 (Winter 1977): 269–74; David Kennedy, *Journal of American History* 64 (December 1977): 23–24; Stanley Lemons, *American Historical Review* 82 (October 1977): 1095; and the bibliographic essay in James Reed, *From Private Vice to Public Virtue* (New York: Basic Books, 1978), p. 439.

15. David Montgomery, "Gutman's Nineteenth Century America," *Labor History* 19 (Summer 1978): 416–29. Genovese, *Roll, Jordan, Roll*, criticizes the tendency to overestimate the potential for resistance carried in slave culture, but

his argument is weakened because it is so often implicit and obscured. Both he and Montgomery are criticized for insufficient attention to political history in articles by British Marxists: Jean Monds, "Workers' Control and the New Economism," *New Left Review,* no. 97 (May 1976): 81–108; and Richard Johnson, "Thompson, Genovese and Socialist Humanist History," *History Workshop Journal,* no. 6 (1978): 79–100.

4

Women's Rights and Abolition
The Nature of the Connection

It is a common error among historians of American feminism to attribute American women's consciousness about the oppression of their sex to the impact of the antislavery movement, particularly to its ultraist Garrisonian element. This argument suggests that, reasoning by analogy, female abolitionists perceived the similarities between their status before the law and that of the chattel slave.[1] Certainly the rhetoric of the prewar women's rights movement abounded in the use of the slave metaphor to describe women's oppression. "Slaves are we, politically and legally," wrote J. Elizabeth Jones in an 1848 address to the women of Ohio.[2] Yet other historical studies have contradicted this hypothesis of a direct connection between antislavery partisanship and awareness of women's oppression by demonstrating the incipient feminism in a wide range of other early nineteenth-century female activities. Since it is undeniably true that antislavery women provided the political leadership for the prewar women's rights movement, we must therefore look for other explanations for the connection between their abolitionism and their historic contribution to American feminism.

Starting in the 1820s and 1830s, American women began to express what might be called caste consciousness in a wide range of contexts. They evidenced a critical awareness of the importance of their femaleness in determining their experiences, began to think of themselves as united by the fact of their sex, and, most important, exhibited consider-

Originally published in *Antislavery Reconsidered*, edited by Michael Fellman and Lewis Perry. Baton Rouge: Louisiana University Press, 1979.

able discontent with their womanly lot. Scholars have discovered such "prepolitical" elements in church-affiliated benevolent societies, the domestic novels written and read by women, pioneers of women's education, and the prewar popular health movement.[3] Caste consciousness and a sense of discontent among women, what we might call protofeminism, seems to have been a phenomenon carried widely through the social fabric and culture of early nineteenth-century America. Many antislavery women experienced it prior to or independent of their abolitionist activity. Lucretia Mott, the matriarch of female abolitionists, was an active member of a female moral reform society in Philadelphia, and Paulina Wright Davis began her public career as an itinerant lecturer on women's physiology. Elizabeth Stanton was a student of Emma Willard, Angelina Grimké considered becoming a pupil of Catharine Beecher, and Lucy Stone, for a short period, studied with Mary Lyon. Willard, Beecher, and Lyon were the early nineteenth-century triumvirate of women's education. As a self-supporting woman, Susan B. Anthony had defended women's right to speak publicly in New York state teacher's conventions well before her first contact with abolitionists.[4]

In some of these contexts, women were beginning to move from a generalized caste consciousness and sense of discontent to a specific program for altering woman's situation, that is, to activism. A more detailed examination of one such attempt, the moral reform societies of the 1830s and 1840s, can suggest the problems women were meeting in translating their protofeminist consciousness into a genuine feminist movement. Contrasting moral reformers with women abolitionists suggests why the latter were able to execute this transformation successfully and therefore to build the women's rights movement.

In her analysis of the feminism of the New York Female Moral Reform Society, Carroll Smith-Rosenberg portrays the society as one manifestation of "a growing self-awareness among middle class American women . . . [and] an ordinarily repressed desire for an expansion of their role." In turn she attributes this widespread female restlessness to the contradiction between the passive, constricted, and static role prescribed for women and a general belief in the possibilities for and desirability of social change in Jacksonian America. Smith-Rosenberg finds many aspects of the society's pursuit of moral purity that seem to have gone beyond contemporary notions of female propriety. On the grounds of their traditionally pietistic prerogatives, female moral reformers developed a militant stance on issues explicitly prohibited to women, such as prostitution, the double standard, and male sexual behavior. They resisted male efforts to supersede their work and, in Smith-Rosenberg's phrase, claimed moral reform as a "self consciously female" endeavor. They projected a nationwide union of women dedicated to purifying American sexual morals. The activities they undertook in pursuit of their goals went well beyond those permitted in woman's sphere to include visiting brothels, managing the society's finances, editing their own journal, and even lobbying for ten years in the New York legislature in behalf of an antiseduction statute.[5]

Yet the Female Moral Reform Society did not continue to develop a feminist program, and evolved instead in the direction of a charity organization. Most of the protofeminist militance which so impresses Smith-Rosenberg had disappeared by 1840. The reasons for this are complex, but an episode early in the society's history permits the identification of two of the major obstacles to the development of feminism within the reform society. In 1838, the society's journal printed an article by Sarah Grimké, then at the height of her notoriety as the first woman in the abolitionist movement to become a public lecturer and agitator. While Smith-Rosenberg interprets this episode as evidence of the moral reform society's sympathy with women's rights, it also indicates important differences between the protofeminism of moral reformers and that of female abolitionists. The journal's readership found Grimké far too radical for their tastes. They seem to have objected, first to her disregard for woman's proper sphere, and second to her anticlericalism. Moral reformers castigated men for usurping women's power but limited their attack to "male tyranny in the HOME department."[6] Grimké's call for women to reject the limitations of home and family and pursue their rights and duties outside the domestic sphere greatly disturbed them. Moreover, they objected to her explicit attack on "priestcraft." As with her, their sense of religious vocation had carried them out of passivity and into new realms of thought and action, but unlike her, they could not distinguish between religion and religious institutions, between their own vocation and the authority of ministers and the church.

Grimké's identification of the priesthood as a source of moral corruption and her charge to women to reinterpret the Bible for themselves were her most specific affronts to moral reformers' sensibilities.

By contrast with the moral reform movement, Garrisonian abolitionism provided women with a political framework that assisted the development of a feminist movement. As Garrisonians, women learned a way to view the world and a theory and practice of social change that they found most useful in elaborating their protofeminist insights. In addition, the antislavery movement provided them with a constituency and a political alliance on which they were able to rely until the Civil War. Thus, American feminism developed within the context of abolitionism less because abolitionists taught women that they were oppressed than because abolitionists taught women what to do with that perception, how to develop it into a social movement.

Two aspects of the way that Garrisonians approached social reality were particularly important to the development of nineteenth-century American feminism: the ability to perceive and analyze entire institutions; and the assumption of absolute human equality as a first principle of morality and politics. Both habits of mind, though seemingly abstract, were derived from the concrete task facing abolitionists, to make slavery a burning issue for northern whites. The women who built the women's rights movement borrowed these approaches and found them eminently useful in overcoming obstacles that had stopped other protofeminists. The habit of institutional analysis permitted Garrisonian women to escape the control of the clergy and move beyond pietistic activism. The principle of absolute human equality freed them from the necessity of justifying all their duties in terms of woman's sphere.

Stanley Elkins has argued that the "anti-institutionalism" of Garrisonians was their basic political weakness. While it is true that Garrisonians refused to act through institutions, it is certainly not true that they were blind to them. On the contrary, Garrisonians broke new ground for the antislavery movement by analyzing and moving to attack at least two basic institutions—organized religion and the institution of slavery itself. Unlike that of many other antislavery people, Garrisonians' indictment of slavery did not rest on specific incidents of cruel treatment and therefore could not be refuted by evidence that many masters were kind and generous to their slaves. Instead, Garrisonians located evil in the institutional arrangements of chattel slavery, which permitted even one case of brutality. Garrisonians criticized the institution of slavery, not the behavior of individuals within it. Similarly, Garrisonians grasped the fact that the churches were human institutions, therefore subject to human criticism.[7] Their ability to comprehend religious institutions and to distinguish them from their own profoundly religious impulses was an impressive achievement for evangelicals in an evangelical age.

The abolitionist women who built the women's rights movement profited from this ability to criticize entire institutions, most specifically from the militant anticlericalism of Garrisonians. This can best be seen in the 1837 conflict between the Grimké sisters and the Congregational clergy of Massachusetts. Like women in moral reform and other pious activisms, the Grimkés had been led by their religious vocation to step outside woman's sphere. At that point, like other benevolent women, they were confronted by clerical authority and ordered to return to more womanly pursuits. Yet the fact that they were Garrisonians enabled them to hold fast to their religious convictions, ignore clerical criticism, and instead indict the churches themselves for being institutional bulwarks of slavery and women's oppression.[8] In the face of the clerical authority that had long restrained women's impulses for a larger life, the Grimkés continued to pursue their feminist inclinations and to lay the groundwork for the women's rights movement a decade later. The Grimkés' successors also relied on the anticlericalism that they had learned as abolitionists. Elizabeth Stanton had wrestled with religious dogma throughout her adolescence and early adulthood, but credited Garrison with her ultimate spiritual liberation.

> In the darkness and gloom of a false theology, I was slowly sawing off the chains of my spiritual bondage, when, for the first time, I met Garrison in London. A few bold strokes from the hammer of his truth, I was free! Only those who have lived all their lives under the dark clouds of vague, undefined fears can appreciate the joy of a doubting soul suddenly born into the kingdom of reason and free thought. Is the bondage of the priest-ridden less galling than that of the slave, because we do not see the chains, the indelible scars, the festering wounds, the deep degradation of all the powers of the God-like mind?[9]

Almost until the Civil War, conflict with clerical authority was the most important issue in the women's rights movement. The 1854 National Women's Rights Convention resolved: "We feel it a duty to declare in regard to the sacred cause which has brought us together, that the most determined opposition it encounters is from the clergy generally, whose teachings of the Bible are intensely inimical to the equality of woman with man." With increasing defensiveness, representatives of the clergy pursued their fleeting authority onto the very platform of the women's rights movement. However, Garrisonian women had learned the techniques of biblical exegesis and absolute faith in their own interpretations in numerous debates over the biblical basis of slavery. They met the clergy on their own ground, skillfully refuting them quote for quote. "The pulpit has been prostituted, the Bible has been ill-used," Lucretia Mott said during an argument with the Reverend Henry Grew at the 1854 National Women's Rights Convention. "It has been turned over and over in every reform. The temperance people have had to feel its supposed denunciations. Then the anti-slavery, and now this reform has met, and still continues to meet, passage after passage of the Bible, never intended to be so used."[10] When ministers with national reputations started to offer their support to the women's rights movement in the late 1850s, the issue of clerical authority began to recede in importance. It was not a major aspect of postwar feminism, because of both changes in the movement and changes in the clergy.

The principle of absolute human equality was the other basic philosophical premise that American feminism borrowed from Garrisonian abolitionism. Because the abolitionists' target was northern racial prejudice and their goal the development of white empathy for the suffering of the slave, the core of their argument was the essential unity of whites with blacks. Although many Garrisonians believed in biological differences between the races, their politics ignored physical, cultural, and historical characteristics that might distinguish blacks from whites. They stressed instead the common humanity and the moral identity of the races. They expressed this approach as a moral abstraction, a first principle, but its basis was the very concrete demands of the agitational task they faced.[11]

Garrisonian feminists appropriated this belief and applied it to women. The philosophical tenet that women were essentially human and only incidentally female liberated them from the sexual ideology that had constrained their predecessors in other reform movements, who had felt it necessary to justify their actions as appropriate to woman's sphere. Abolitionist women did not. Although they continued to believe in the existence of such a sphere, its demands were secondary to those of the common humanity that united women and men, blacks and whites.

As with the issue of clerical authority, this lack of concern for woman's sphere characterized the first episode in abolitionist feminism, the Grimkés' 1837 answer to the Pastoral Letter. In response to the Congregational clergy's demand that she return to "the appropriate duties and influence of women," Sarah Grimké wrote:

> The Lord Jesus defines the duties of his followers in his Sermon on the Mount. He lays down grand principles by which they should be governed, without any reference to sex or condition. . . . I follow him through all his precepts, and find him giving the same direction to women as to men, never even referring to the distinction now so strenuously insisted upon between masculine and feminine virtues. . . . Men and women were *CREATED EQUAL!* They are both moral and accountable beings, and whatever is *right* for man to do, is *right* for woman.[12]

The prewar women's rights movement continued to be distinguished from other movements for the improvement of women's status by its refusal to be sidetracked into the consideration of what was appropriate to woman's sphere. At the fifth national convention, Lucy Stone rejected the notion that the women's rights movement was a matter "of sphere." "Too much has already been said and written about woman's sphere," she contended. "Trace all the doctrines to their source and they will be found to have no basis except in the usages and prejudices of the age. . . . Leave woman, then, to find her own sphere." Similarly, the 1851 convention resolved that "we deny the right of any portion of the species to define for another portion . . . what is and what is not their 'proper sphere'; that the proper sphere for all human beings is the largest and highest to which they are able to attain." The approach of Garrisonian women to the ideology of sexual spheres appears all the more remarkable in light of the fact that the three decades before the Civil War were precisely the years in which that ideology was being elaborated, and that benevolent women played an important part in its elaboration.[13]

As Aileen Kraditor has demonstrated, the Garrisonians' focus on "empathy" had important political limitations, both tactical and analytical. By stressing the moral identity and human equality of blacks and whites, Garrisonians were unable to explain why blacks were regarded and treated so differently from whites. Similarly, the women's rights belief in the moral irrelevance of sexual spheres ignored the reality of women's domestic confinement, which distinguished them from men, structured their relative powerlessness, and gave credence to the doctrine of spheres. Indeed, Garrisonian women ignored the question of woman's sphere while simultaneously believing in its existence. They accepted the particular suitability of women to domestic activities and did not project a reorganization of the division of labor within the home. Like women outside the antislavery movement, they believed that domestic activities were as "naturally" female as childbearing, and as little subject to deliberate social manipulation. This contradiction between the belief in woman's sphere and in its moral irrelevance remained unexamined in the prewar women's rights movement. A convention in Ohio in 1852 simultaneously resolved that "since every human being has an individual sphere, and that is the largest he or she can fill, no one has the right to determine the proper sphere of another," and that "in demanding for women equality of rights with their fathers, husbands, brothers and sons, we neither deny that distinctive character, nor wish them to avoid any duty, or to lay aside that feminine delicacy which legitimately belongs to them as mothers, wives, sisters and daughters."[14] During this early period in the development of an American feminism, the Garrisonian emphasis on the ultimate moral identity of women with men helped the women's rights movement to establish sexual equality as the definition of women's emancipation. The work of examining sexual *inequality*, its origins and the mechanisms that preserved it, remained for the future.

In addition to this philosophical basis, Garrisonianism provided the women's rights movement with a theory of social change, a strategy that gave coherence and direction to efforts for the emancipation of women.

Garrisonians began from the premise that fundamental social change required a change in people's ideas as well as in legal and institutional arrangements. "Great political changes may be forced by the pressure of external circumstances, without a corresponding change in the moral sentiment of a nation," Lydia Maria Child wrote in 1842, "but in all such cases, the change is worse than useless; the evil reappears, and usually in a more exaggerated form." In *Means and Ends in American Abolitionism,* Kraditor has reconstructed the way that Garrisonians worked simultaneously for institutional and ideological change. Their demand for immediate, unconditional abolition was both a concrete reform program and the means to launch an ideological attack on white racism. The Garrisonian scenario called for a long-term educational program, in which the constant exposition of the demand for abolition by a well-trained cadre would bring public opinion up to the high principle of racial equality. Thus, the ultimate achievement of abolition would bring not only a formal adjustment in the legal status of blacks but a revolution in the racial consciousness of whites as well. While not providing for the political mechanisms by which abolition could be achieved, this strategy was well suited to the early years of the antislavery movement, when its primary problem was overcoming political and public indifference.[15] It proved useful for feminists when they faced the same task.

None of the early women's rights leaders held to the Garrisonian program for change more firmly than Elizabeth Stanton. Throughout her long political career, she frequently took the position that anything that focused public attention on women's oppression, anything that *agitated* the issue, was desirable. She wrote in her diary in 1888, "If I were to draw up a set of rules for the guidance of reformers . . . I should put at the head of the list: Do all you can, *no matter what,* to get people to think on your reform, and then, if the reform is good, it will come about in due season." Stanton made no distinction between agitation that generated public sympathy and agitation that generated public antipathy. Either was preferable to the apathy that particularly characterized popular opinion on the woman question in the 1840s and 1850s. Only by heightening the level of intellectual attention to women's oppression, and therefore only by ideological attack, was enduring reform in women's position possible. Stanton understood that other reformers must be ready to translate agitation into concrete reform, but she did not believe that this was her function, nor perhaps the function of the women's rights movement. "I am a leader in thought," she wrote late in her life, when her methods were alien to young feminists, "rather than numbers."[16]

Just as antislavery agitators used the demand for immediate abolition to stimulate change in the racial beliefs of northern whites, Garrisonians in the women's rights movement used the demand for woman suffrage to launch their own ideological campaign. The demand for suffrage served two functions: it was a concrete reform in women's legal status and a way to educate public opinion in the principle of the equal humanity of the sexes. This was possible because, like unconditional abolition, woman suffrage was regarded as an extreme demand, far beyond the willingness of legislators to enact. While many politicians, journalists, social commentators, and influential women outside the movement supported demands for equal property and wage-earning rights and rejected woman suffrage, no one supported woman suffrage and not other equal rights. Woman suffrage was regarded, inside and outside the women's rights movement, as the ultimate legislative demand.

The theory of social change borrowed from Garrisonian antislavery affected the organizational shape of the women's rights movement in the prewar period. Activists saw their primary task as agitating public sentiment on the woman question. Ernestine Rose described it as "breaking up the ground and sowing the seed." Thus, they were not particularly concerned with the deliberate recruitment of new women, with differing levels of commitment to women's rights, into the work. Instead the movement relied on a small group of highly skilled and deeply committed women, willing to shoulder the opprobrium of "strong-mindedness." Nor did those activists feel the need for much coordination of their own agitational efforts. They spread the women's rights faith largely as individuals who undertook canvassing or lecture tours on their own hook. Petition and lobbying campaigns were highly individualistic matters, dependent upon uncoordinated bursts of personal initiative.[17]

The organizational requirements for this kind of political work were minimal. As Kraditor has described it, the Garrisonian concept of a reform organization was a limited one, primarily directed toward providing resources for propagandizing and agitation. Before the Civil War, the women's rights movement had no national or state bodies to guide it. Instead, an informal and constantly changing coordinating committee planned the annual conventions. This process was so spontaneous that in the second half of the 1850s, when several national leaders were simultaneously incapacitated by childbirth, the annual convention was barely arranged in time, and, in 1857, bypassed altogether. These yearly women's rights meetings were oriented to the needs of activists. They concentrated on exchanging information, sharpening rhetorical tools, and revitalizing dedication. The 1852 national convention discussed and rejected a proposal for tighter coordination and the formation of a national women's rights society. Only Clarina Nichols spoke in support of the motion. Angelina Grimké Weld, Elizabeth Oakes Smith, Harriot Hunt, Ernestine Rose, Paulina Wright Davis, and Lucy Stone opposed it, agreeing that formal societies "fetter and distort the expanding mind." All looked with suspicion on any arrangement that placed limits on the individual's prerogatives and activity. Lucy Stone "had had enough of thumb-screws and soul screws ever to wish to be placed under them again." "The present duty is agitation," she concluded.[18]

Formal organization was further impeded by the existence of the American Anti-Slavery Society and its ability to bestow political coherence on the women's rights movement. Articles were printed in antislavery newspapers and tracts were published with antislavery funds. Several of the most effective agitators were paid antislavery agents and spread the women's rights faith as they traveled and lectured on behalf of immediate abolition.[19] Perhaps most important, the women's rights movement relied on the antislavery community for its constituency. The First National Women's Rights Convention was called by antislavery women at an antislavery meeting.[20] Activists expected and got a favorable hearing from Garrisonian abolitionists. The majority of women who joined the women's rights ranks were abolitionists. They had already received a political education. Moreover, their antislavery activity put them outside the pale of respectable womanhood.[21] Already branded as abolitionist extremists, they were not frightened by public hostility or press indictments of long-haired men and short-haired women. They provided the women's rights movement with an audience well suited to the conflict and controversy which its politics invited.

Although primarily a source of strength, the relationship of the women's rights movement to antislavery was also a potential liability. Because of the many resources which abolitionism provided them, women's rights leaders were very dependent on the willingness of the antislavery movement to support and encourage their efforts. Moreover, the partnership between the two reforms was an unequal one, and occasionally women's rights suffered because of its subordinate status. Finally, the availability of a ready-made constituency of antislavery women kept women's rights leaders from learning how to reach the many women who were not active reformers. The fearlessness of female abolitionists protected the women's rights movement from a confrontation with the very real fears of family opposition and public disapproval that lay between it and the majority of women.

The basic precepts, strategic methods, and organizational forms of Garrisonian abolitionism sustained the women's rights movement through its first dozen years. On this basis, women's rights leaders were able to transform insights into the oppression of women which they shared with many of their female contemporaries into a social movement strong enough to have a future. Their self-definition as ultraists helped them to endure and overcome hostility and ridicule. By 1860, they had succeeded in commanding a modicum of political respect, establishing the woman question as a serious political issue, and winning important legislative victories. These achievements, due in large measure to their Garrisonian inheritance, created the conditions for the women's rights movement to assume a new set of political tasks, and therefore to move beyond Garrisonianism to a politics of their own making.

NOTES

1. See for example Andrew Sinclair, *The Better Half* (New York: Harper & Row, 1965), 37.
2. Elizabeth Cady Stanton, Susan B. Anthony, and Matilda Joslyn Gage

(eds.), *History of Woman Suffrage* (6 vols.; Rochester: Susan B. Anthony, 1889), I, 108.

3. See for instance Keith Melder, "Ladies Bountiful: Organized Women's Benevolence in Early Nineteenth Century America," *New York History*, XLVIII (1967), 231–54; Helen Waite Papashvily, *All the Happy Endings* (New York: Harper & Brothers, 1956); and Kathryn Kish Sklar, *Catharine Beecher: A Study in Domesticity* (New Haven: Yale University Press, 1973). See E. J. Hobsbawm, *Primitive Rebels: Studies in Archaic Forms of Social Movement in the Nineteenth and Twentieth Centuries* (New York: W. W. Norton and Co., 1965), for a full exposition of the concept of "prepolitical" activity.

4. Carroll Smith-Rosenberg, "Beauty, the Beast, and the Militant Woman: A Case Study in Sex Roles and Social Stress in Jacksonian America," *American Quarterly*, XXIII (1971), 580; Alice Felt Tyler, "Paulina Kellogg Wright Davis," in Edward T. James, Janet Wilson James, and Paul S. Boyer (eds.), *Notable American Women* (3 vols; Cambridge, Mass.: Harvard University Press, 1971), I, 444–45; Alma Lutz, "Elizabeth Cady Stanton," in *Notable American Women*, III, 342–47; Betty L. Fladeland, "Sarah Moore and Angelina Emily Grimké," in *Notable American Women*, II, 97–99; Louis Filler, "Lucy Stone," in *Notable American Women*, III, 387–90; Alma Lutz, "Susan Brownell Anthony," in *Notable American Women*, I, 51–57.

5. Carroll Smith-Rosenberg, *Religion and the Rise of the American City: The New York City Mission Movement 1812–1870* (Ithaca: Cornell University Press, 1971), 118; Smith-Rosenberg, "Beauty, the Beast, and the Militant Woman," 562–84.

6. Smith-Rosenberg, *Religion and the Rise of the American City*, 116 and passim; Smith-Rosenberg, "Beauty, the Beast, and the Militant Woman," 580–84.

7. Stanley Elkins, *Slavery* (Chicago: University of Chicago Press, 1959); Aileen S. Kraditor, *Means and Ends in American Abolitionism: Garrison and His Critics on Strategy and Tactics* (New York: Pantheon Books, 1967), 20, Chap. IV.

8. "Pastoral Letter of the Massachusetts Congregational Clergy," in Aileen S. Kraditor (ed.), *Up from the Pedestal: Selected Writings in the History of American Feminism* (Chicago: Quadrangle Books, 1968), 50–52; see Sarah Grimké's response to the Pastoral Letter in *Letters on the Equality of the Sexes and the Condition of Woman: Addressed to Mary S. Parker* (Boston: Isaac Knapp, 1837), 16–17.

9. Elizabeth Cady Stanton, "Speech to the 1860 Anniversary of the American Anti-Slavery Society," in Elizabeth Cady Stanton Papers, Manuscript Division, Library of Congress.

10. Stanton, Anthony, and Gage (eds.), *History of Woman Suffrage*, I, 380, 383.

11. Kraditor, *Means and Ends, passim,* especially p. 59.

12. Grimké, *Letters on the Equality of the Sexes*, 16.

13. Stanton, Anthony, and Gage (eds.), *History of Woman Suffrage*, I, 165, 826; Barbara Welter, "The Cult of True Womanhood: 1820–1860," *American Quarterly,* XVIII (1966), 151–74.

14. Kraditor, *Means and Ends*, 243–44; Stanton, Anthony, and Gage (eds.), *History of Woman Suffrage*, I, 817.

15. Lydia Maria Child, "Dissolution of the Union," *Liberator,* May 20, 1842, as quoted in Kraditor, *Means and Ends,* 23; Kraditor, *Means and Ends,* Chap. II.

16. Theodore Stanton and Harriot Stanton Blatch (eds.), *Elizabeth Cady Stanton as Revealed in Her Letters, Diary and Reminiscences* (New York: Harper, 1920), 252; Elizabeth Stanton to Olympia Brown, May 8, 1888, in Olympia Brown Willis Collection, Schlesinger Library, Radcliffe College.

17. Stanton, Anthony, and Gage (eds.), *History of Woman Suffrage*, I, 693; see for example Clarina Nichols's lobbying activities, ibid., 172–74.

18. Kraditor, *Means and Ends,* 165; Eleanor Flexner, *Century of Struggle: The Woman's Rights Movement in the United States* (Cambridge, Mass.: Harvard University Press, 1959), 82; Ida Husted Harper (ed.), *The Life and Work of Susan B. Anthony* (2 vols., Indianapolis and Kansas City: The Bowen-Merrill Company, 1898), I, 171; Stanton, Anthony, and Gage (eds.), *History of Woman Suffrage*, I, 540–42.

19. Both Lucy Stone and Susan B. Anthony were paid agents of the Anti-Slavery Society in the 1850s.

20. Stanton, Anthony, and Gage (eds.), *History of Woman Suffrage*, I, 216.

21. Perhaps the best example of this was Lydia Maria Child, whose abolitionist activities led her to abandon a successful career as a genteel author. See Louis Filler, "Lydia Maria Child," in James, James, and Boyer (eds.), *Notable American Women*, I, 330–33.

5

The Nineteenth-Century
Woman Suffrage Movement
and the Analysis of
Women's Oppression

What is the political significance of studying the history of the feminist movement? Not, I think, to identify revolutionary ancestresses or petit-bourgeois leaders whose errors we can blame for our current oppression. We study the past to learn how to think about the present, to understand how change happens, to see how history creates and restrains the possibilities for people to intervene deliberately in it and change its course. We study the history of radicalism to understand why certain social movements take a particular character in particular periods, to learn how to locate political radicalism in history. Ultimately, we study history so that we can understand the history of which we are a part, and the changes we may be able to bring to it.

This paper is a brief survey of the history of the woman suffrage movement from 1865 to 1875, the decade after the Civil War. There are two major points I want to make about the feminism of this movement. First, I want to assert the basic radicalism of its politics. Suffragists were led by the facts of women's lives to begin to analyze and imagine radical changes in the two major systems that structured women's oppression:

Originally published in *Capitalist Patriarchy and the Case for Socialist Feminism,* edited by Zillah Eisenstein. New York: Monthly Review Press, 1978.

capitalism and male supremacy. Second, I want to locate the limits of the radicalism of the woman suffrage movement in the particular social conditions of nineteenth-century women's lives—specifically, the nature of the sexual division of labor and of women's total dependence on marriage. My object is to situate the woman suffrage movement in its own historical context so that its radicalism can be appreciated and its failures understood.

From one perspective, suffragism in the years immediately following the Civil War was a very radical movement. Its leaders—especially Elizabeth Cady Stanton and Susan B. Anthony—cooperated with Victoria Woodhull and William Sylvis, free love advocates, with the labor movement, and even with the First International. In order to understand the nature of woman's oppression and the possibility of her emancipation, suffragists found themselves drawn more and more toward the most advanced aspects of nineteenth-century political thought. They identified and criticized capitalism as a major source of woman's oppression, addressed themselves to the position of working women, spoke out boldly against the sexual double standard and exploitation of women, and were beginning to identify marriage and the family—even more than political disfranchisement—as the basic source of woman's oppression. Such a politics deserves to be called radical, because of both the breadth to which it aspired and the particular positions it took.

The Reconstruction years were a very active period for reform in general. Even the boldest of abolitionists had not expected the abolition of slavery in their life times, and yet it had happened. This unleashed radical energies and radical visions. If a reform movement could help to liberate an entire race from slavery, then nothing was beyond political agitation, beyond deliberate social change. Particular postwar forces further encouraged suffragists in radical directions. Congressional battles over the Fourteenth and Fifteenth Amendments led them to dissolve their twenty-year alliance with the antislavery movement, which freed them from its domination and was followed by a tremendous explosion of theoretical energy. This rapid development can be seen in the pages of the independent feminist journal *The Revolution*, which Stanton and Anthony edited from 1868 to 1870.

At the same time, the suffragists began to acquire a constituency among American women. This is the period in which suffragism began to take on the character of a social movement—ultimately, although not until much later, to become a mass one. On the one hand, this process of organizing a constituency helped suffrage leaders develop theoretically by connecting the movement to the needs and concerns of nonpolitical American women. On the other hand, the acquisition of a constituency acted to restrain the sexual and economic radicalism to which suffragists were otherwise inclining. The objective social conditions of women's lives in the mid-nineteenth century, their dependence on marriage and the sexually segregated nature of the labor force, constituted the basic framework within which suffragism had to develop.

Suffragists and Capitalism

In the antebellum period, woman suffragists, like other reformers associated with abolitionism, had very little to say about industrial capitalism, the oppression of workers, or the potential power of the labor movement. Their focus was on chattel slavery and on the ruling class of the South. In fact abolitionists—among them such woman suffrage pioneers as Susan B. Anthony and Lucy Stone—seemed to have resented the connections that labor leaders tried to make between chattel and wage-slavery as a diversion from the primary task of eliminating black slavery. (It is only fair to add that labor spokespeople were not foremost in the antislavery ranks and seemed at least as frightened by the possible competition of freed black workers as of the slaveocracy's encroachments on liberty.) In addition, woman suffrage leaders were rarely from the ranks of wage-earners. Some, like Stone and Anthony, were the daughters of small farmers. Others, most notably Stanton, were the children of considerable wealth. The daughter of a major New York landholder, Stanton wrote of her early ideas about poverty: "We believed that all these miserable one-sided arrangements were as much in harmony with God's laws as the revolutions of the solar system; and accepted the results with pious indignation."

What suffragists wrote and said about capitalism in the years immediately after the Civil War stands in stark contrast to this. They admitted that there was antagonism between labor and capital and unequivocally took the part of labor. *The Revolution* covered labor activities, particularly laboring men's conventions in New England and New York. Many of the political and theoretical issues that were of pressing concern to labor leaders—currency reform, land policy, and the formation of a new labor-based reform party—received a great deal of attention from the journal's editors. Its position on the 1868 presidential elections, about which male abolitionists were excessively partisan, was that neither the Democrats nor the Republicans had anything to offer. Anthony wrote, "Both major parties are owned body and soul by the Gold Gamblers of the Nation, and so far as the honest working men and women of the country are concerned it matters very little which succeeds." This clearly reflects the impact of the labor movement and of a working-class perspective.

A speech that Elizabeth Cady Stanton delivered in 1868, entitled "On Labor," further illustrates that suffragists were learning the basic principles of labor reform from its leaders.[1] In this speech Stanton reversed her prewar position and asserted the essential identity of chattel and wage-slavery:

> I find that the same principle degrades labor as upheld slavery. The great motive for making a man a slave was to get his labor or its results for nothing. When we consider that the slave was provided with food and clothes and that the ordinary wages of the laborer provide his bare necessities, we see that in a money point of view they hold the same position. And the owner of one form of labor occupies no higher moral status than the other, because the same motive governs in both cases.

Furthermore, she began the speech with an endorsement of strikes as a method of testing workers' "numbers and purpose" and as a "link in the chain of their final triumph." When we remember that not only did most middle-class reformers consider strikes an illegitimate tactic, but that the issue occasionally divided the ranks of labor itself, we see how much Stanton and other suffragists' economic thought had progressed.

Most of Stanton's speech condemned the suffering of the masses of workers under capitalism. She described for her audience, particularly those "in the full enjoyment of all the blessings that wealth can give" (among which she was clearly included), the conditions of the poor.

> Look around you in the filthy lanes and by-streets of all our cities, the surging multitudes ragged, starving, packed in dingy cellars and garrets where no ray of sunshine or hope ever penetrates, no touch of light or love to cheer their lives. Look in the factories and workshops where young and old work side by side with tireless machines from morn til night, through all the days, the weeks, the months, the years that make up the long sum of life, impelled by that inexorable necessity that knows no law, toil or starvation. . . . Look what these unfortunates suffer in our jails, prisons, asylums; look at the injustice in our courts, for when men must steal or starve, theft may be a virtue that might give the poor man bail as dollars do the rich, for in the scale of justice motive might sometime outweigh the crime. Let us look deep down into the present relations of the human family and see if the conditions of different classes cannot be more fairly established. Under all forms of government, about seven-tenths of the human family are doomed to incessant toil, living in different degrees of poverty, from the man who hopes for nothing but daily bread for himself and family, to the one who aims at education and accumulation. The filth, the squalor, the vice in the conditions and surroundings of the poor are apparent to most careless observers, but the ceaseless anxiety and apprehension of those evils yet to come that pervade all alike in the ascending scale from the lowest to the fortunate few who live on the labor of others add to the sum of human misery an unseen element of torture that can never be measured or understood.

This is very moving prose, but not that unusual: such descriptions were appearing with increasing frequency in the pages of respectable, socially aware magazines and newspapers. The suffering worker was beginning to replace the suffering slave as a staple of liberal social criticism.

In "On Labor" Stanton said more than that the masses suffered from poverty. She also said that they created the wealth which had been stolen from them to make a few very rich. "Is it right that many should be clothed in rags, while the few shine in garments that the poor have woven, in the jewels they have dug from the mines of wealth?" she asked.

This was a material, rather than a moral, critique of the uneven distribution of wealth. Such an analysis reflected the labor theory of wealth that was generally held by nineteenth-century working people. They understood that if something useful had been produced, labor had produced it. This contention reflected the experience of skilled workers, whose perspective and power predominated. They were proud of their economic worth. They—and their employers—knew that without their skills, knowledge, and experience, production could not proceed.

This is what attracted suffragists to the labor movement and to its critical perspective on capitalism. Stanton, Anthony, and others took the part of labor not out of pity for the workers' suffering but out of appreciation for labor's strength. A recognition of the dignity of work and the economic power of skilled labor pointed toward the potential of organized labor as a *political* force, as a source of social change. Stanton wrote in *The Revolution* in 1868, "The one bow of promise we see in the midst of this general political demoralization that all our thinking men deplore today is the determined defiant position of the laboring classes," to which she added, so that we recall the feminist impulse behind all of this political reaching-out, "and the restless craving of women for noble and more serious purposes in life."

From this general perspective on the labor movement, the suffragists developed an interest in working women. Anthony in particular hoped to be able to build what she called "a great movement of working women for the vote." Suffragists gave considerable attention to the low wages, restricted labor market, abysmal working conditions, and general economic vulnerability of wage-earning women. They contended that the ballot would remedy these evils, particularly by increasing the working woman's power during strikes, and they usually argued that working women needed the vote more than other women. But they did not see the working woman primarily as a victim. Instead, they saw her as the woman of the future, as an indication of the direction that women's development as a sex should take toward emancipation. Unlike the rest of the nineteenth-century working woman's defenders, the suffragists believed that women belonged in the labor force and that an ultimate solution to the working woman's oppression was not to return her to her domestic enclave. They championed the working woman on the basis of what they perceived as her strengths, her craft, competence, and productive capacities. Above all, they saw the working woman as aspiring to an honorable independence, which was, after all, what they hoped for from enfranchisement.

All of the characteristics that the suffragists looked for in working women—competence, skill, contribution to the social product, equality with and independence from men—were characteristics of the skilled worker, whose presence and strength shaped the labor movement of the time. For a brief but significant period, Stanton and Anthony worked closely with a group of New York City working women, typesetters. Together, suffragists and typesetters formed a Working Women's Association, an organization that lasted about a year.[2]

The typesetters with whom suffragists allied were very rare among women. They were skilled workers in a field—printing—dominated by male labor. This unique position lay at the center of their feminist impulse and their alliance with the suffragists. The overwhelming majority of working women were much less skilled, earned much less money, and, most importantly, were herded into a very few all-women industries— garment and textile manufacturing and domestic work. Such women lacked the very thing that was the nineteenth-century worker's source of dignity, pride, and sense of self-worth, and which suffragists hoped would provide the basis for working women's feminism, a skill. Put another way, the feminist vision of independence and equality with men had little meaning for women whose wages did not even reach the subsistence level and who had no male coworkers with whom they could demand equality. The skilled, women wage-earners around whom Anthony imagined building a suffrage movement simply did not exist in appreciable numbers. It was this firm division of the labor market into male and female sectors, and the incredibly depressed character of the female sector, that most restrained suffragists.

Rather than women wage-earners, the suffragists found that their demand for the vote and their vision of female independence attracted middle-class women, either those imprisoned in an enforced domesticity or renegades from ladydom who were independent business women, professionals, or artists. Such women formed the major constituency of the suffrage movement until well into the twentieth century, when suffragists once again turned to wage-earning women and the feminist potential among them.

Suffragists and Male Supremacy

We can see similar conflicting impulses for and against the radicalization of suffragists' analysis with respect to the issue of male supremacy, and particularly the sexual oppression of women. In the prewar suffrage movement, demands for basic legal rights, the need to establish the seriousness of women's protests, and the presence of significant numbers of male supporters on feminist platforms preempted any serious examination of heterosexuality, or, as the nineteenth century called it, "the social question." Woman suffrage leaders were themselves divided on the advisability of a public investigation into the "social question," although the majority of them, under the leadership of Stanton, were probably inclined to make such an open investigation.

The break with abolitionists and the founding of *The Revolution* opened new vistas for suffragists. They began to write extensively about the "social question." Whereas the prewar woman suffrage movement hesitated to advocate even liberalized divorce laws, in its first year *The Revolution* published articles on abortion, prostitution, female physiology, sex education, cooperative housekeeping, and the social arrangements of the Oneida community. The positions taken by *Revolution* writers varied. Sometimes, for instance, they condemned the high number of abortions women were having as evidence of their frivolity; at other times they expressed sympathy with women forced because of economic and social inequality into pregnancies they had not invited or did not want. What is important, however, is that all these questions were discussed, with the goal of understanding which social and sexual arrangements would work to women's greatest benefit. *The Revolution*, in other words, was committed to developing a feminist position on the social question. Most often, *Revolution* articles identified the problem as the sexual double standard and called for a militant attack on it. For instance, in an article on prostitution, Sarah Norton suggested that the police "turn their attention to reforming the opposite sex. . . . Prostitution will cease when men become sufficiently pure to make no demand for prostitutes. In any event, the police should treat both sexes alike."

Soon suffragists moved their critique of the double standard out of the pages of *The Revolution* and into more public forums. From 1868 to 1871 Stanton and Anthony organized a series of mass meetings around current sexual scandals, in order to generate a public feminist presence on such issues. The first case, in 1868, was that of Hester Vaughn, a young English immigrant who had been tried and found guilty of infanticide in Pennsylvania. Vaughn had emigrated from England on the promise of marriage, but when she arrived in Philadelphia she found her fiancé married to another woman. Unable to find any other work, she became a domestic servant. After a few months she was seduced by her employer, became pregnant, and was dismissed. She took a room alone, gave birth unattended, and was discovered three days later with her dead infant by her side. She was tried, found guilty, and sentenced to death, the presiding judge remarking that the crime of infanticide had become so prevalent that "some woman must be made an example of." Suffragists organized a mass meeting and distributed free tickets to working women, many of whom came.

The Vaughn case allowed suffragists to demonstrate the connections between the economic, social, and political dimensions of women's oppression. They particularly pointed to the double sexual standard that fixed all blame on Vaughn, first for her illegitimate pregnancy and then for the death of her infant. "What a holocaust of women and children we offer annually to the barbarous customs of our present type of civilization, to the unjust laws that make crimes for women that are not crimes for men," Stanton wrote angrily.

The McFarland/Richardson case followed the Vaughn affair by a year. Daniel McFarland fatally shot Albert Richardson because Richardson was planning to marry McFarland's ex-wife, whom he had so abused that she had divorced him. Abby McFarland married Richardson on his deathbed, Henry Ward Beecher officiating, and most of official New York was incensed at her daring. Stanton, Anthony, and *The Revolution* supported her. Stanton wrote in the journal that Abby McFarland Richardson was like a fugitive slave who has "escaped from a discordant marriage. This wholesale shooting of wives' paramours should be stopped," Stanton insisted. "Suppose women should decide to shoot their husbands' mistresses, what a wholesale slaughter of innocents we should have of it!" McFarland was tried for murder, found innocent on grounds of insanity, and then given custody of his twelve-year-old son. Stanton and Anthony organized another mass meeting of women to protest both the verdict and the custody decision. From the podium Stanton contended that the major issue was whether a husband had the "right of property in the wife"—that is, whether he could compel her to have sexual intercourse at any time. Stanton argued that Abby Richardson's rejection of this "legalized prostitution" had led to her divorce, and she concluded that "even divorce helps to educate other wives similarly situated into higher ideas of purity, virtue, and self-respect." Certainly a far cry from 1860, when the issue of liberalized divorce was kept off the woman suffrage platform.

In addition to these public forums, Stanton brought her forthright analysis of sexual corruption to women in a more direct form. For several years, starting in 1869, she held small meetings—what we might call consciousness-raising sessions—on "marriage and maternity." During the seven or eight months of every year in which she was lecturing around the country, she would speak to mixed audiences on suffrage in the evenings and to women-only audiences in the afternoons on "the new science of marriage and motherhood." She and Anthony even held such a meeting among Mormon women in Salt Lake City, for which offense they were not allowed to return to Utah for many years. She reported that women responded very enthusiastically to these meetings, where she probably urged them to resist intercourse if it was for their husbands' satisfaction only.

By 1870 Stanton had moved beyond a simple condemnation of the sexual double standard and of "legalized prostitution"—unconsenting sexual relations within marriage. She had begun to argue that men's sexual power was the basic source of women's oppression; she came quite close to calling for a feminist attack on marriage. At an unusual, sexually mixed meeting in New York City at which she discussed women's sexual oppression within the marriage institution, she stated, somewhat threateningly: "The men and women who are dabbling with the suffrage movement for women should be at once warned that what they mean logically if not consciously in all they say is next social equality, and next freedom, or in a word free love, and if they wish to get out of the boat, they should for safety sake get out now, for delays are dangerous." Stanton was not the only woman thinking along such lines. Paulina Wright Davis, a long-time feminist activist from Rhode Island, wrote in 1870: "Although equality in education and in industrial avocations may and will be regulated by the ballot, the social relations and rights will not be; they underlie even the ballot, and will only be regulated by purifying the moral sentiment."

Exactly what Stanton and other sexual radicals among the suffragists were putting forward as a program is not clear. At the McFarland/Richardson meeting Stanton urged that women sever unsatisfactory marriage relations by divorce, but later she cautioned against haste in remarriage as "indelicate and indecent." At times, she seemed more to urge women to reject legal marriage than to reform it. This is what the nineteenth century called "free love."

When Stanton's critique of marriage reached this level, her audience began to fall away. A too-public focus on the "compulsory adulteries of the marriage bed," and a call to women to leave it, alienated the women who, at the private parlor talks on marriage and maternity, had responded so enthusiastically. Anthony found that a group of Dayton, Ohio, women whom she was trying to organize "took up the cudgels" in defense of marriage when she criticized the absolute physical control it gave husbands over their wives. At the founding convention of the National Woman Suffrage Association in 1869, new recruits reported that they had "heard people back home say that when women endorsed woman suffrage they endorsed Free Loveism," and asked for a resolution repudiating it. Similarly, at a national meeting of suffragists a year later, the audience refused to resolve in favor of "woman's sole and absolute rights over her own person."

How do we understand this reluctance to commit themselves openly to say in public what they admitted in private about the extent of women's sexual degradation in marriage? To begin with, we must appreciate the number of external obstacles between these women and freedom, how few spiritual and material resources they had, and the opposition they knew they would face, however timid their efforts.

When a small group of Dubuque, Iowa, housewives formed a woman suffrage club in 1869 and concentrated on getting someone to give a July Fourth address on women's right to the ballot, both local and Chicago newspapers called them "radicals" and "free-thinkers." Another group of midwest women had to work several months to win the right to hold offices in a free library association in which they had only been allowed to be members. Like Chinese women less than three decades ago, these women faced the incredibly long road to full freedom with their feet bound.

To end the explanation for nineteenth-century women's sexual and domestic conservatism here, however, would be inadequate. That would leave us with the mistaken impression that building a social movement is always a conservatizing process, in which leaders with a radical vision have to battle their followers' timidity and acceptance of prevailing ideas. The history of American radicalism is full of examples to the contrary, of the rank and file being more radical and daring than its leadership. What is important here is the particular social conditions of the potential membership of the movement at a specific moment in history. Most nineteenth-century women had no alternative to marriage. They could not support themselves through wage labor. The absence of reliable contraception made celibacy or extramarital pregnancy the sexual consequence for a woman who abandoned the institution of marriage. Lacking any real options, women were frequently hostile to what they saw as attacks on the institution of marriage and much more likely to defend than to attack it. The call to the first woman suffrage convention in Iowa in 1870 identified the organizers as "mothers, wives, daughters who believe that the marriage bond is to the social, what the Constitution is to the political union." It seemed to Mary Livermore, an important suffragist who joined the movement in 1869, that "the majority of women will always, as the world stands, be wives, mothers, and mistresses of homes."

Ultimately, it was the conditions of women's lives—specifically their dependence on marriage and the sexual division of labor—that determined the shape of nineteenth-century suffragism. We should understand the inability of nineteenth-century feminists to develop solutions adequate to the oppression of women less as a failure of their political imagination or boldness than as a reflection of the state of historical development of capitalism and of male supremacy.

By the same token, the twin axes of women's oppression are currently in an advanced state of collapse and present contemporary feminists with great revolutionary possibilities. Marriage and the family, to which nineteenth-century women clung, are economically under siege, sexually dysfunctional, and emotionally overloaded. We are certainly no longer tied to them as the only way to organize our personal and social lives. The expansion of capital has transformed women into permanent members of the labor force and is homogenizing the work of all of us into a single level of nonskill. Its continued ability to function without major problems is in doubt.

Thinking about the history of feminism is the same as placing ourselves, our oppressions, and our capacity for liberation in historical perspective. Then we are in a better position to make use of the political prospects with which history presents us.

NOTES

1. For the entire text of this speech, see Ellen DuBois, "On Labor and Free Love: Two Unpublished Speeches of Elizabeth Cady Stanton," *Signs* 1 (1975): 257–68.

2. The story of the Working Women's Association is discussed in Alma Lutz, "Susan B. Anthony for the Working Woman," *Boston Public Library Quarterly* 11 (1959): 33–43; and Israel Kugler, "The Trade Union Career of Susan B. Anthony," *Labor History* 2 (1961): 90–100.

6

Outgrowing the Compact of the Fathers

Equal Rights, Woman Suffrage, and the United States Constitution, 1820–1878

In the midst of the Constitution's bicentennial celebration, it is especially important for historians to recall the radical tradition of equal rights that flourished as a part of nineteenth-century republican thought. Women's rights demands were an important aspect of that popular nineteenth-century republicanism. From its inception to the present, the women's rights movement has pursued rights not explicitly mentioned in the Constitution and has sought to incorporate them into an expanded understanding of its meaning.

From one perspective, the conviction at the heart of radical republicanism, that an expansion of "rights" would help create a more egalitarian society, reached its peak with the enactment—and its nadir with the judicial disposition—of the Reconstruction amendments. However, from a women's rights perspective, the radical republican heritage extends much further. Not only did the struggle for political equality for women reach into the twentieth century, but the drive for the Equal Rights Amendment, as well as intense debate about a whole other realm of rights—sexual and reproductive—keeps the constitutional issue of women's rights alive today.

Originally published in *Journal of American History* 74 (1987).

In this paper on the nineteenth-century movement for women's rights, I have two concerns. One is to integrate women's rights and the other equal rights politics of the nineteenth century—the abolition and black suffrage movements and labor reform—into a comprehensive history of radical republicanism. My other concern is to specify the place, and the possibilities, of the politics of equal rights in women's history. Concepts of rights, individualism, and equality have had a distinct impact on the way that women have understood themselves and have expressed their sense of their proper position in society.

The following overview of the nineteenth-century women's rights movement has three parts. The first part, which covers the antebellum period, establishes that women's rights ideas were linked to other radical equal rights traditions and were widely understood as alternatives to "separate spheres" notions of the subordinate place of women in the social order. With the passage of the Thirteenth Amendment, equal rights politics in general, and the women's rights movement in particular, entered a bolder phase that focused on constitutional change. That is the subject of the second part. During Reconstruction the demand for woman suffrage flourished because it was the most forceful way of expressing—and the most powerful tool for achieving—women's equality with men. At first, women's rights advocates demanded political rights for all without regard to sex or race. Once the Fourteenth and Fifteenth amendments were ratified without woman suffrage, however, they began to argue for the equality not of individuals but of sexes. Thus began a long process by which ideas about the fundamental differences between women and men began to be subsumed within a women's rights framework.

The termination of the constitutional amendment process in 1870 did not immediately signal the end of hopes for women's equal political rights but, instead, heightened struggle over the meaning of the Constitution as amended. That struggle is the subject of the third part. Determined to enforce their egalitarian vision of constitutional rights, women's rights women undertook direct political action. They also began to extend principles of equal rights into the whole realm of "personal rights," of rights over and to one's own body. Women's rights arguments figured significantly in important Supreme Court decisions about the meaning of the Reconstruction amendments. By the mid-1870s equal rights interpretations of the Constitution had been defeated, and the women's rights movement itself began to move in less democratic, more conservative directions. But the possibility of equal rights politics for transforming women's place had not been exhausted, only temporarily stalled.

The Demand for Women's Political Equality, 1820–1860

The term "women's rights"—meaning the equality of women with men—predates the call for woman suffrage by several decades. Women's rights demands, especially those directed against men's economic power over their wives, were nurtured in the British Owenite movement and brought to the United States by Frances Wright. Wright, a leader in the Jacksonian workingmen's movement, was the first public figure in United States history to advocate women's rights. Her lead was followed in this country by Ernestine Rose, a Jewish immigrant from Poland, and by Robert Dale Owen, son of the Owenite movement's leader, Robert Owen. During the 1830s and early 1840s, Rose and Owen advocated a program of women's economic and marital—though not political—rights. They and their comrades lobbied, often successfully, for legal reforms in married women's economic position and for liberalized grounds for divorce, especially for women.[1]

Their women's rights program, with its hostility to the family and its emphasis on women's economic independence, provided an alternative to the ideology of separate spheres that dominated thinking about women's place by 1830. In reaction, separate spheres ideology became more elaborate, more defensive, and more openly political. Catharine Beecher began her influential 1841 treatise on "woman's sphere" by addressing "those who are bewailing themselves over the fancied wrongs and injuries of women in this Nation." The thrust of her argument was to reconcile the general principles of democracy and equal rights with women's "subordinate station" in the family and with their lack of power "in making and administering laws." Beecher quoted Alexis de Tocqueville, who was concerned to refute the "clamor for the rights of woman" in the United States by contrasting it with American women's eager willingness to embrace the limitations of the married state.[2] Despite the intensified debate, however, the impact of the women's rights program during the 1830s and early 1840s was limited, above all because most of its advocates were men who had little faith in women's own capacity for reform activism. Without a way to bring women themselves into politics—in other words, without a program for political rights for women—the political force supporting women's rights had to come from other than women, and would therefore be limited.

The notion of political equality for women was so radical that for a long time it was virtually impossible even to imagine woman suffrage. Within the democratic political tradition, the emphasis on independence as a condition for possession of the suffrage worked to exclude women, who were dependent on men almost by definition. Women had an honored place in early republican thought, but they were never considered men's equals, nor was it regarded as appropriate to demand political rights for them. During the 1820s and 1830s, as popular political passions increased, so did the obstacles to the political inclusion of women.[3] Who besides women could provide the "virtue" needed to protect the republic from the rampant but necessary self-interest of men?

The barrier to the proposition of equal political rights for women was broken within a movement that was not initially political, but within which female activism flourished—abolitionism. Whereas the labor reformers of the 1820s and 1830s advocated women's rights without having much faith in women's own activism, the evangelical movements of the 1830s depended on women's activism.[4] Of the moral reform movements, abolitionism was the most radical and contributed the most to the emerging sensibility of female self-assertion. The abolitionists' indictment of the absolute immorality of slaveholding established a much stronger political language than did workingmen's republicanism for describing the tyrannical abuse of power; women quickly put that language to good use in indicting men's tyranny over them.[5] As arguments against the institution of chattel slavery, abstract ideas about equality and individual rights gained real social meaning. In particular, abolitionists paid attention to the misuses of the slave's body, thus illuminating themes of sexual and marital abuse among free women as well.

In its first decade, radical abolitionism repudiated the political arena as fundamentally corrupt and the Constitution as inherently proslavery; that hostility to politics helped women's activism to flourish within the movement. But, as Eric Foner has made clear, abolitionism had eventually to reconcile itself with popular reverence for the Constitution, with the republican political tradition in its radical form. The rise of political abolitionism in the 1840s temporarily increased women's isolation from politics but eventually lessened it. When the American Anti-Slavery Society split in 1839, political abolitionists, largely male, were on one side, and women abolitionists, mostly Garrisonian, were on the other.[6]

Within a decade, however, that seeming impasse had generated the demand for woman suffrage. The woman who articulated the proposition that women should have the same political rights as men had equally strong links to female and to political abolitionism. She was Elizabeth Cady Stanton, protégé of Lucretia Mott, cousin of Gerrit Smith, and wife of Henry B. Stanton. She came to understand that a fundamental change in women's political status was the key to their comprehensive equal rights. Just as her husband was participating in the development of a political and constitutional approach to antislavery, she was inventing a political and constitutional approach to women's rights. In the summer of 1848, while Henry Stanton was organizing the Free Soil party in Buffalo, New York, Elizabeth Cady Stanton called together the first women's rights convention in Seneca Falls.

The Seneca Falls "Declaration of Sentiments and Resolutions"—an adaptation of the Declaration of Independence—had as its central idea protest against the denial to women of "this first right of a citizen, the elective franchise, thereby leaving her without representation in the halls of legislation, . . . oppressed on all sides." The declaration went on to enumerate the whole range of women's grievances, including women's civil death in marriage, their lack of rights to their own wages, their taxation without representation, and their treatment under divorce and guardianship laws that favored husbands over wives. Despite the comprehensive significance of women's disenfranchisement, which the declaration demonstrated, the convention's participants hesitated before resolving that "it is the duty of the women of this country to secure to themselves their sacred right to the elective franchise."[7] As women they were wary of such a clear-cut assertion of sexual equality, and as aboli-tionists they were suspicious of, and hostile to, politics. But the logic of women's rights led straight to political equality, and the woman suffrage resolution at Seneca Falls—the first formal assertion of the equal rights of women to the political franchise—prevailed.

The demand for political equality could inspire a women's rights movement among women from 1848 on because political democracy was simultaneously a widely held belief and a radical assertion when ap-plied to women. Political equality for women rested on the popular re-publican tradition that insisted on equal rights for all, with the franchise the crowning jewel of individual freedom. Women's rights advocates could speak of their demands in terms of the "rights, for which our fa-thers fought, bled, and died," seeking only to claim women's place in the glorious American political experiment. They enjoyed the confidence of appealing to a virtually hegemonic republican tradition. "We do not feel called upon to assert or establish the equality of the sexes," declared a statement issued by the Second National Woman's Rights Convention in 1851 (though its authors believed fervently in that equality). "It is enough for our argument that natural and political justice . . . alike de-termine that rights and burdens—taxation and representation—should be co-extensive; hence, women as individual citizens . . . liable to be . . . taxed in their labor and property for the support of government, have a self-evident and indisputable right, identically the same right that men have, to a direct voice in the enactment of those laws and the formation of that government." Made possible by the spread of women's reform ac-tivism, the demand for woman suffrage was strengthened by the in-creasing attraction that popular politics began to have for women, as well as for men, during the 1850s.[8] From then on, women's rights began to move into the American political mainstream.

As the demand for woman suffrage became linked with a widely held republican faith, it also expressed the desire of some women for a radi-cally different position in society than women's traditional one. Woman suffrage carried with it the unmistakable message of women's desire for independence, especially from men within the family. "The Right of Suffrage for Women is, in our opinion, the cornerstone of this enter-prise," resolved the 1851 women's rights convention, "since we do not seek to protect woman, but rather to place her in a position to protect herself." A moderate version of the theme of independence emphasized the importance of individual self-development for women, much as Margaret Fuller had in her 1845 manifesto, *Woman in the Nineteenth Century.* The more radical arguments for women's political independence suggested that men's and women's interests were not only distinct but also antagonistic. Elizabeth Cady Stanton could always be counted on to ring that note. She believed that "the care and protection" that men give women was "such as the wolf gives the lamb, the eagle the hare he carries to the eyrie!!"[9]

Underlying both versions of the claim that women needed greater independence from men was the notion of women as individuals. "We believe that woman, as an accountable being, can not innocently merge her individuality in that of her brother, or accept from him the limitations of her sphere," explained Ann Preston at the 1852 Westchester Convention in Pennsylvania.[10] The notion that women's individuality, like men's, was a moral and political absolute ran counter to widely held ideas that women's selflessness, their service to others, was the ethical and emotional core of the family. Moreover, the emphasis on individuality implicitly undermined the first premise of separate spheres ideology: the idea of categorical sexual difference, that is, that all women differed from all men insofar as women were the same as each other. Because of its venerable republican heritage and because of its ability to express women's growing desire for independence and individuality, the demand for woman suffrage attracted many women—especially writers, physicians, and other pioneering professionals—who had never before identified themselves with women's rights.

The new focus on political equality did not narrow the scope of the women's rights movement but enlarged it, particularly to include the issue of wives' subordination to their husbands. Ideologically, the women's rights consensus that centered around woman suffrage emboldened egalitarians like Ernestine Rose and Stanton to elaborate the implications of individual rights principles for the family. Women's position in marriage was criticized, in language borrowed from abolitionism, as a violation of the most elementary individual right, the right to control the uses of one's body. Throughout the 1850s Lucy Stone spoke repeatedly against the common law of marriage because it "gives the 'custody' of the wife's person to her husband, so that he has a right to her even against herself." When contracting her own marriage, she protested against all manifestations of coverture by taking the unheard-of step of refusing her husband's name. During the decade legislative gains gave married women rights to their own earnings and property, rights that constituted a fundamental challenge to the economic inequalities of marriage.[11]

Finally, at the Tenth National Woman's Rights Convention in 1860, Stanton made equal rights criticisms of the marriage relation explicit by reintroducing the old Owenite demand for liberalization of divorce laws. What was important about Stanton's resolutions was not her vehement indictment of the miserable underside of women's married lives— previous women's movements had targeted domestic violence, and Stanton used those traditions in attacking the "legalized prostitution" of coerced marital intercourse and unwilling maternity. What was new was that Stanton based her indictment of women's position in marriage on the supremacy of individual rights, and on the systematic violation in marriage of "the inalienable right of all to be happy," and that she advocated divorce and remarriage, not resignation, as the solution to women's marital misery. The philosophical basis for her position was utilitarian and radically individualist. The relation of marriage had "force and authority," she argued, only to the degree that it made the individuals in it happy. In essence, she contended that marriage had no independent standing as an institution and certainly no moral supremacy over the rights and inclinations of the individuals who entered into it. Inasmuch as women's lives were so much more circumscribed by marriage than were men's, unhappy marriages were infinitely more destructive to wives than to husbands, and on that ground freedom to leave a bad marriage and to form a better one would benefit women more than men.[12]

Participants in the 1860 convention engaged in a heated debate over Stanton's resolutions. Antoinette Brown Blackwell, the first ordained woman minister in the United States, argued that marriage as an institution established the limits of the principles of individual rights—that it was a relation in which the participants incurred "obligations," not only to their children but also to each other, that they could not morally forfeit. As for divorce as a solution to women's marital misery, Blackwell believed that "the advantage, if this theory of marriage is adopted, will not be on the side of woman, but altogether on the side of man." The issue at the heart of the 1860 debate—the fact that women are equally at economic risk in and outside marriage—continues to plague feminists today.[13] But even in the mid-nineteenth century, Stanton's equal rights approach established basic principles that Blackwell had to concede, in particular, the principle of a woman's right to self-determination over her own body.

The debate over divorce reached a stalemate in 1860, with all women's rights leaders agreeing that the issue of women's position in the family belonged on their platform but disagreeing about whether the principle of individual rights was the best guide to resolving it. The issue was not picked up again for over a decade, at which time the women's rights movement was simultaneously exploring the collective grievances of women and insisting, with unparalleled militancy, on equal rights as the only framework for addressing them. Meanwhile the events of the Civil War had given new meaning and possibility to the movement's foremost demand, political rights, from which the subtheme of personal rights was derived. Political equality had been the first principle of the women's rights movement for almost two decades, but it was the historical consequences of the Civil War that began to make it a political possibility.

Women's Rights and Universal Suffrage, 1863–1869

In the wake of the Civil War, equal rights was elevated to the level of constitutional principle. The radical politics of the period focused on constitutional change. Its exponents regarded natural rights in the most egalitarian light, considered the right to vote a natural right, and urged the mobilization of national power and sovereignty to enact and ensure the equal access of all to that right.[14] The faith in constitutional revision and interpretation among believers in equal rights during Reconstruction was virtually unlimited, for if amending the Constitution could abolish slavery, what could it not do? The women's rights movement, already committed to an egalitarian and political version of individual rights, shared deeply in that reverent, yet activist, attitude toward the Constitution. Much as debates over women's rights during the 1840s and 1850s had focused on the meaning of the Bible, in the 1860s and 1870s they focused on the Constitution as their fundamental text.

Thus in 1863 congressional radicals turned to the women's rights movement for support in passing the first of the Reconstruction amendments, the constitutional abolition of slavery. Women's rights leaders, enthusiastic advocates of "*A NEW CONSTITUTION* in which the guarantee of liberty and equality to every human being shall be so plainly and clearly written as never again to be called in question," were eager to help and organized a campaign of popular support, the first such effort on behalf of a proposed constitutional amendment. They collected over four hundred thousand signatures—Robert Dale Owen, now head of the American Freedmen's Inquiry Commission, worked closely with them—and Senator Charles Sumner gave them much of the credit for the ultimate passage of the Thirteenth Amendment.[15]

Once slavery was abolished, the political status of the former slaves became the crucial constitutional question. Black suffrage was the key, both to the freedmen's own future and to the fortunes of the Republican party. Women's rights leaders were determined to take advantage of the constitutional crisis that swirled around black suffrage. In their work on behalf of the Thirteenth Amendment, they took every opportunity to point out that the principle of unconditional emancipation led directly to that of universal enfranchisement. In Stanton's memorable metaphor, the black suffrage issue opened the "constitutional door," and women intended to "avail ourselves of the strong arm and blue uniform of the black soldier to walk in by his side."[16]

Reconstruction strengthened the belief that the right to vote was a natural right. The right to suffrage was either the supreme natural right, as Sumner argued, or the necessary protection of all other natural rights, as George William Curtis contended at the New York Constitutional Convention in 1867. In either case popular suffrage, as the sovereign power, was inherent, not bestowed. "For God gave [the right of suffrage] when he gave life and breath, passions, emotions, conscience, and will," declared Parker Pillsbury. "It was man's inalienable, irrepealable, inextinguishable right from the beginning." As Stanton consistently put it, the republican lesson of the war was that popular sovereignty, the equal political rights of all individuals, preceded and underlay governments and nations, constitutions and laws.[17]

The belief that the right to vote was the individual's natural right made the case for woman suffrage much stronger, more self-evident than it had ever been. "In considering the question of suffrage," Stanton declared in 1867, "there are two starting points: one, that this right is a gift of society, in which certain men, having inherited this privilege from some abstract body and abstract place, have now the right to secure it for themselves and their privileged order to the end of time. . . . Ignoring this point of view as untenable and anti-republican, and taking the opposite, that suffrage is a natural right—as necessary to man under government, for the protection of person and property, as are air and motion to life—we hold the talisman . . . to point out the tyranny of every qualification to the free exercise of this sacred right."[18]

Given those premises, it was only necessary to appeal to the natural rights women held in common with all other persons. Rather than argue that women had a special need or capacity for the franchise, women's rights advocates regarded any mention of race or sex as suspect, as a reference to the inferiority of women and Negroes. "To discuss this question of suffrage for women and negroes, as women and negroes, and not as citizens of a republic," Stanton argued, "implies that there are some reasons for demanding this right for these classes that do not apply to 'white males.'" In the Reconstruction-era approach to women's enfranchisement, race and sex were, in Olympia Brown's words, "two accidents of the body" unworthy of constitutional recognition. "The terms 'male' and 'female' simply designate the physical or animal distinction between the sexes," explained Ernestine Rose, who had always insisted that the distinction of sex was the enemy of women's freedom. "Human beings are men and women, possessed of human faculties and understanding, which we call mind; and mind recognizes no sex, therefore the term 'male,' as applied to human beings—to citizens—ought to be expunged from the constitution and laws as a last remnant of barbarism."[19]

While the Republican party discussed the constitutional disposition of black suffrage, women's rights leaders insisted that the nation be reconstructed not on the basis of special cases designed for "anomalous beings" but on the fundamental principle of universal suffrage. "To bury the black man and the woman in the citizen," they organized the American Equal Rights Association with the goal of incorporating black suffrage and woman suffrage into the overarching demand for universal suffrage.[20]

The Reconstruction-era tendency to regard the difference of sex, and of race, as "incidental" simultaneously advanced and retarded the women's rights movement. Undoubtedly it lent a certain abstraction to the discussion of women's rights, which can be measured by the paucity of discussion of concrete grievances—sexual, economic, domestic—from women's rights platforms in those years. Yet, the emphasis on the equal rights of all individuals carried with it the militant confidence of absolute principle and the intention to abolish female subordination as totally as slavery.

One strength of the Reconstruction-era approach was that it focused more attention on black women than ever before—or after—in the long drive for woman suffrage. A framework that disregards race and sex in favor of our common humanity and individual rights ironically can include, even focus on, black women, whereas a discourse that separates out, and too often counterposes, blacks and women tends to obscure the existence of those persons who are both. No doubt some of the Reconstruction-era emphasis on black women was a way to introduce women's rights into a political dialogue that was largely about race, but it was not all so opportunistic. Sojourner Truth spoke frequently from the women's rights platform in the 1860s and, despite the terrific pressure not to delay the freedmen's enfranchisement, was in favor of holding out for universal suffrage. Frances Dana Gage, a white advocate of women's rights active in the Bureau of Refugees, Freedmen, and Abandoned Lands, appeared often at women's rights conventions where she argued for political rights for black women. Even Stanton, whose capacity for invidious racial distinctions would soon become clear, now directed her arguments to the condition of black women. A few Reconstruction-era women's rights activists began to explore what it might mean to put black, not white, women at the center of the movement's concerns. Women's capacity for resistance, not their weakness, could be emphasized. Thinking of the freedwomen she knew, Gage envisioned "the strength, the power, the energy, the force, the intellect, and the nerve, which the womanhood of this country will bring to bear" once enfranchised.[21]

Given the Republican party's determination to draw the line at black suffrage, however, the political claims of women and of freedmen were increasingly antagonistic. Within reform circles, former allies—Elizabeth Cady Stanton and Wendell Phillips, Susan B. Anthony and Frederick Douglass—divided bitterly over whether to base Reconstruction on black suffrage or on universal suffrage. Each faction staked its claim on different ground. The champions of black suffrage spoke in terms of freedmen's historically specific needs as a group and of the ballot as an instrument for their protection. Douglass's position was that when women were "dragged from their houses and hung upon lamp-posts"— he meant white women—their need for the ballot would be as great as that of the black man.[22]

By contrast, the universal suffrage argument of the women's rights movement was more individualist and lacked the urgent power of contemporary crisis. Possession of the ballot, its proponents claimed, benefited the victims of race and sex discrimination alike by raising the individual out of degradation and dependence. Susan B. Anthony developed that line of argument, frequently linking enfranchisement with the liberating aspects of free wage labor. "I want to inquire whether granting woman the right of suffrage will change anything in respect to the nature of our sexes," Douglass asked her. "It will change the nature of one thing very much, and that is the dependent condition of woman," she answered. "It will place her where she can earn her own bread, so that she may go out into the world an equal competitor in the struggle for life." Anthony, the only self-supporting Reconstruction-era women's rights leader, revived and restated the 1830s artisan republican case for political rights in feminist terms, a tendency reinforced by the women's rights movement's tactical alliance with postwar Democrats.[23]

The failure of the universal suffrage campaign in the face of the political realities of Reconstruction can be read in the language of the Fourteenth Amendment. The amendment included the first reference in the Constitution to the distinction of sex and to the inferiority of women by specifying the number of "male citizens" as the basis of congressional representation. The comparison with the Constitution's three-fifths clause, written eighty years earlier, is obvious. Just as the founders were unwilling to admit that the slave's status contradicted the general principles of natural rights, Reconstruction-era politicians were unwilling to acknowledge the strength of women's political claims. In both cases, language was introduced that insulated the subordinate group's status from constitutional interference. Senator Sumner told Stanton that he "wrote over nineteen pages of foolscap to get rid of the word 'male' and yet keep 'negro suffrage' as a party measure intact; but it could not be done." Women's rights leaders denounced the Fourteenth Amendment as a "desecration." "If that word 'male' be inserted as now proposed," Stanton predicted to her cousin Gerrit Smith, "it will take us a century at least to get it out again."[24]

The Fifteenth Amendment represented a more powerful defense of the freedmen's political rights, but that only underlined the Republicans' refusal to include discrimination by sex with that by race, color, and previous condition of servitude in the constitutional guarantee of political rights. Even Ernestine Rose, an especially strong advocate of equal rights, had to admit at this point that the universal suffrage approach had failed women and that they might do better to find new grounds for their claim for political rights. "Congress has enacted resolutions for the suffrage of men and brothers. They don't speak of the women and sisters," she declared. "I propose to call [our movement] Woman Suffrage; then we shall know what we mean." Women's rights leaders abandoned the American Equal Rights Association and formed a new organization, the National Woman Suffrage Association (NWSA), to assert a new version of their demand.[25]

The impact of the defeat of universal suffrage began to generate new kinds of arguments for women's political rights. Previously the case for suffrage had consistently been put in terms of the individual rights of all persons, regardless of their sex and race. Angered by their exclusion from the Fifteenth Amendment, women's rights advocates began to develop fundamentally different arguments for their cause. They claimed their right to the ballot not as individuals but as a sex. The distinction of sex, they argued, was not irrelevant but central to social organization;

whereas earlier they had opposed its political recognition as a "desecration," now they called for it. The reason women should vote was not that they were the same as men but that they were different. That made for a rather thorough reversal of classic women's rights premises. In an 1869 speech by Stanton, described in the *History of Woman Suffrage* as "a fair statement of the hostile feelings of women toward the amendments," the shift from one kind of argument to the other is obvious. "The same arguments made in this country for extending suffrage from time to time, to white men, . . . and the same used by the great Republican party to enfranchise a million black men in the South, all these arguments we have to-day to offer for woman," Stanton contended, "and one, in addition, stronger than all besides, the difference in man and woman." Stanton had always ridiculed such arguments as "twaddle." Now even she based her case in the contrast between "masculine" and "feminine" elements. "There is sex in the spiritual as well as the physical and what we need to-day in government, in the world of morals and thought, is the recognition of the feminine element, as it is this alone that can hold the masculine in check," she asserted.[26]

The shift from arguments based on the common humanity of men and women to arguments based on fundamental differences between the sexes has had a parallel in virtually every feminist epoch. That makes it all the more important to identify the historically specific character, sources, and impact of such transitions when they occur. The various versions of "womanhood" that began to appear as the women's rights movement's demand shifted from universal suffrage to woman suffrage had their roots in Reconstruction politics as well as in contemporary intellectual trends.

The argument that women should be enfranchised to bring the "feminine element" into government had a decidedly nationalist edge, which reflected the Fifteenth Amendment's transfer of control over the right of suffrage from the state to the national level. Part of the argument for black suffrage was that enfranchising the freedmen would keep the Republican party in power, thus preserving the victories of the war and strengthening the nation. In arguing that the "feminine element" would elevate national life and "exalt purity, virtue, morality, true religion," woman suffrage partisans were trying to match that nationalist argument and go it one better. Enfranchising the freedmen only promised partisan advantage; enfranchising "woman" would uplift the nation at its very heart, the family. An 1869 woman suffrage convention resolved that the "extension of suffrage to woman is essential to the public safety and to the establishment and permanence of free institutions" because "as woman, in private life, in the partnership of marriage, is now the conservator of private morals, so woman in public life, in the partnership of a republican State, based upon Universal suffrage, will become the conservator of public morals." Here the tendency to see in women a fundamentally different social force than in men served a particularly nationalist ideological purpose. "With the black man you have no new force in government—it is manhood still," Stanton argued, "but with the enfranchisement of woman, you have a new and essential element of life and power." Led by Stanton and Anthony, the NWSA distinguished itself among suffrage organizations by its emphasis on national, as opposed to state, action to enfranchise women. Even though it sometimes worked to amend state constitutions, the NWSA's watchword was "national protection for national citizens."[27]

The new suffrage arguments also contained a strong theme of race antagonism, a reaction to the strategic antagonism between black suffrage and woman suffrage. Whereas the advocates of universal suffrage had claimed comradeship between men of the disfranchised and despised classes and all women, woman suffrage advocates now claimed that the enfranchisement of black men created "an aristocracy of sex" because it elevated all men over all women. Woman suffragists criticized the Fifteenth Amendment because "a *man's* government is worse than a *white* man's government" and because the amendment elevated the "lowest orders of manhood" over "the higher classes of women." The racism of such protests was expressed in hints of sexual violence, in the suggestion that women's disfranchisement would mean their "degradation," "insult," and "humiliation."[28] Those overtly racist arguments reflected white women's special fury that men they considered their inferiors had been enfranchised before them.

Beginning in the early 1870s, new trends in social scientific thought also encouraged the move from equal rights arguments to essentialist ones. Of particular importance to women's rights partisans was the special role attributed to "woman" by positivists such as Auguste Comte, in the organicist solutions they proposed for social conflict. "The great questions now looming upon the political horizon can only find their peaceful solution by the infusion of the feminine element in the councils of the nation," declared an 1872 woman suffrage resolution. "Man, representing force, would continue . . . to settle all questions by war, but woman, representing affection, would, in her true development, harmonize intellect and action, and weld together all the interests of the human family."[29]

Such new intellectual currents, decidedly scientific and secular, merged with much older and more conservative ideas about sexual difference and female nature. Isabella Beecher Hooker, half-sister of the renowned advocate of female domesticity, Catharine Beecher, began to assume a leadership role among suffragists in 1870. She used the arguments her sister had developed in opposition to women's rights thirty years before to argue *for* political equality for women. She stressed the importance of political equality for mothers because it would permit them to better carry out their responsibilities to their children. "Mothers for the first time in history are able to assert . . . their right to be a protective and purifying power in the political society into which [their] children are to enter." Other suffrage leaders of the period made allied arguments. Phebe Hanaford, an ordained minister, called for woman suffrage on religious grounds, because of the "moral influence that the participation of women in government would have upon the world." Paulina Wright Davis, once a moral reform activist, urged woman suffrage as an antidote to men's corruption, sexual and political alike.[30] "Motherhood," "purity," Christian civilization, and women's duties—all were notions that had traditionally been posed against the demand for women's rights; now they were being assimilated into it.

By the end of the 1870s, such arguments would dominate woman suffrage ideology. The impact of that ideological change was complex. The demand for woman suffrage, in that it claimed the vote for women as women, permitted the cultivation of sex-consciousness far more than had the equal rights and universal suffrage approach. The call for woman suffrage, therefore, was much more effective in forging women into a group with a common status and with a common demand—a group that would form the popular basis for a women's rights movement. Yet the emphasis on sexual difference steered the women's rights movement away from its egalitarian origins; the movement would ultimately become more compatible with conservative ideas about social hierarchy.

Woman Suffrage and the Meaning of the Reconstruction Amendments, 1870–1878

By inscribing the freedmen's political rights firmly in the Constitution, the ratification of the Fifteenth Amendment threatened to bring the process of constitutional revision, and the strategic possibilities of winning women's political rights, to an end. When the amendment passed Congress in February 1869, it created what looked like a strategic dead end for woman suffrage. Then in October, a husband and wife team of Missouri suffragists, Francis Minor and Virginia Minor, came up with a different approach to the Reconstruction amendments: an activist strategy for winning woman suffrage that relied on what was already in the Constitution, rather than requiring an additional amendment.[31]

The Minors argued that the Constitution, properly understood, already provided for women's political rights; women were already enfranchised and had only to take the right that was theirs.[32] Their argument rested on the link in the pending Fifteenth Amendment between national supremacy and equal political rights. Although the first section of the Fourteenth Amendment had defined national citizenship, the second section had left suffrage under control of the individual states. The Fifteenth Amendment shifted that control to the national level, thus intensifying the nationalizing aspect of the Fourteenth Amendment and extending its scope to the franchise. Much of the subsequent woman suffrage case was based on that relationship between the two amendments.

The Minors believed that the initial premises of the Constitution, greatly strengthened by the Reconstruction amendments, supported their case. They cited the Constitution's preamble to substantiate their claim that popular sovereignty preceded and underlay constitutional authority. To establish the supremacy of national citizenship, they cited various provisions of Article I, the supremacy clause of Article VI, and the first section of the Fourteenth Amendment. The weakest point of their argument—but also its linchpin—was the assertion that suffrage was a right of national citizenship. The Fifteenth Amendment was still pending, but they found an alternate constitutional basis in a frequently cited 1823 case, *Corfield v. Coryell*, which had found the elective franchise to be one of the "privileges and immunities" protected by Article IV.[33]

Although the Minors' constitutional argument was new, their underlying assumptions were consistent with the Reconstruction-era approach to women's rights. Their argument perfectly expressed the era's radical political philosophy that this article has been tracing: a combination of natural rights, popular democracy, national sovereignty, and extreme reverence for the Constitution. But the Minors provided a new, militant, activist stance for woman suffragists, a stance that rested on the premise that women had merely to take a right that was already theirs. That approach, which came to be called the "New Departure," became the strategic basis for suffragists' actions during most of the 1870s.[34] In many ways, the New Departure period was one of the most radical in the history of women's rights, both in its tactical militancy and in its larger vision of female emancipation. From the larger perspective of constitutional history, the New Departure became part of the conflict over the meaning of the Reconstruction amendments, a struggle that extended far beyond the courts, although that is where it was resolved.

The tactics that the Minors advocated were a combination of direct action and litigation. "I am often jeeringly asked," Virginia Minor explained, "'If the Constitution gives you this right, why don't you take it?'" So she urged women to try to vote and, if they were stopped, to sue those officials who refused to register them. In fact, women in the spiritualist center of Vineland, New Jersey, had successfully voted as early as 1868; that they attempted to vote and were permitted to do so by election officials suggests how widespread, even popular, the assumptions that underlay the New Departure were. The passage of the Enforcement Act to strengthen the Fifteenth Amendment in May 1870 seems to have encouraged many more women—in California, New Hampshire, Michigan, and elsewhere—to regard the right to vote as already theirs.

That year black women went to the polls in South Carolina, encouraged to do so by federal government agents.[35]

In early 1871, the NWSA drew up a resolution formally advising women of their "duty . . . to apply for registration at the proper times and places, and in all cases when they fail to secure it to see that suits be instituted in the courts having jurisdiction and that their right to the franchise shall secure general and judicial recognition." A group of women in the District of Columbia tried, but were not permitted, to register in 1871. Susan B. Anthony and fifteen of her friends in Rochester, New York, succeeded in voting in 1872, only to be arrested a few weeks later for violating the Enforcement Act, the very law that they believed protected their rights. As the number of women attempting to vote grew, their cases began to move through the judicial system.[36]

Then a second direction was opened up in the New Departure strategy. In January 1871 Victoria Woodhull, already a notorious figure and one heretofore not associated with the organized woman suffrage movement, appeared before the House Judiciary Committee to speak on behalf of political equality for women. Woodhull had been invited to address the committee by one of its members, Benjamin Butler, a Massachusetts Republican who was seeking to lead his party into the 1870s under the twin banners of labor reform and woman suffrage. Woodhull had her own links to the radical labor movement through her leadership in the International Workingmen's Association. Like the Minors, Woodhull argued that women were already enfranchised under the Constitution. But instead of calling for the courts to vindicate her constitutional interpretation, she proposed that Congress pass a declaratory act clarifying the constitutional right of all United States citizens, including women, to vote. In other words, she proposed a way to pursue the New Departure that was more overtly political than the Minors' tactics of direct action and litigation.[37]

Woodhull's constitutional argument that the right to vote was inherent in national citizenship was even stronger than the Minors'. Woodhull asserted that the newly ratified Fifteenth Amendment established the "right of any citizen of the United States to vote," a right that could not be abridged by state law "neither on account of sex or otherwise." In a speech supporting the Woodhull memorial, Judge A. G. Riddle agreed that the Fifteenth Amendment must be understood to assume "the right of the citizen to vote as already existing, and it specifies classes, as persons of color, of certain race, and of previous servitude, as especially having the right to vote." He did not believe it should be read as authorizing the disfranchisement of classes not mentioned—that is, women. As a right of national citizenship, the suffrage was subject to the same protections as all other such rights.[38]

With other advocates of the New Departure, Woodhull believed that the relationship between the Fourteenth and Fifteenth amendments made voting a right of national citizenship. Her constitutional case had other elements to it, which bore the mark of her own distinctive thought. "Women, white and black, belong to races, although to different races," she explained, and "the right to vote can not be denied on account of color." Therefore, "all people included in the term color have the right to vote, unless otherwise prohibited." She also contended that "women, white and black, have from time immemorial groaned under what is properly termed in the Constitution 'previous condition of servitude.'" Thus, when the Thirteenth Amendment abolished slavery, it also abolished the subordinate condition of women.[39]

Inasmuch as she was cooperating with Butler, Woodhull's sudden emergence as an advocate of woman suffrage was a product of an intense struggle within the Republican party over its future now that the freedmen had been enfranchised and, what was essentially the same thing, over the meaning of the Reconstruction amendments. Some Republicans initially supported Woodhull's initiative. After her memorial, Republican leaders in the House gave suffragists a room in the Capitol from which to lobby, a move Anthony suspected was a "Republican dodge." However, the dominant Republican faction did not support Woodhull and used her memorial as an opportunity to voice its opposition to the New Departure to the courts, where various New Departure cases were pending. In response to the New Departure's expansive and egalitarian construction, the House Judiciary Committee's Majority Report, authored by John Bingham, argued that the Fourteenth Amendment neither elevated national over state citizenship nor added anything new to it but merely strengthened the federal government's ability to protect already existing "privileges and immunities." Moreover, the report disagreed with Woodhull's interpretation of the Fifteenth Amendment, that it implied a prohibition on any limitation to the suffrage other than those explicitly indicated.[40]

Woodhull is, of course, remembered more as a sexual radical than as a constitutional scholar of woman suffrage, but the two politics have the same philosophical roots. Her leadership in the women's rights movement during the 1870s reveals the link between women's political equality and the women's rights critique of women's subordination in marriage, a connection not openly made since the 1860 debate on divorce. Woodhull's "free love" ideas were based on the same philosophy of individual rights as her suffrage arguments. She asserted that individuals had the inalienable right to make and to dissolve sexual relations as they desired. The right of sexual self-determination was derived from what Woodhull characterized as "our theory of government, based upon the sovereignty of the individual." Her most famous declaration of "free love" was expressed in constitutional terms and infused with natural rights assumptions. "Yes, I am a Free Lover," she responded to a heckler at one of her speeches. "I have an *inalienable, constitutional* and *natural* right to love whom I may, . . . to *change* that love *every day* if I please, . . . and it is *your duty* not only to *accord* [my right], but, as a community, to see that I am protected in it."[41]

Applied to marriage, to sexuality and reproduction, "the sovereignty of the individual" began to take on a corporeal dimension, to become the right of the individual to determine the uses of her or his body. According to a controversial 1871 suffrage resolution that reflected Woodhull's influence, "the right of self ownership [is] the first of all rights." (Paulina Wright Davis delivered that resolution, and there was a great flap after the convention as to whether she "knew" what she had "said.")[42] The new emphasis on rights to one's "person" was an inevitable development of the individual rights tradition once it had been taken into a women's movement and women had brought it to bear on their deep discontent with their sexual and reproductive lives within marriage.

In Woodhull's writings and speeches, "self sovereignty" remained relatively abstract, but in Stanton's accomplished hands it turned into a much more concrete program for women's sexual rights. In addition to her advocacy of divorce law liberalization, Stanton came to imagine that women might have rights with respect to their maternity. To describe such rights—which in the 1870s had no name but which would later be called "birth control" and, even later, "reproductive rights"—Stanton used the term "self sovereignty." Beginning in 1871 she convened small groups of women—including one in Salt Lake City—to urge that wives "learn and practice the true laws of generation" in order to have fewer children. "We are to be the sovereigns of the world but woman must first understand her true position," Stanton explained. "Woman must at all times be the sovereign of her own person." "Whenever we stay in a town two days I talk one afternoon to women alone," she wrote to a friend. "The new gospel of fewer children and a healthy, happy maternity is gladly received."[43]

The free love issue was raised first by Woodhull's opponents, notably in the *Christian Union*, which Henry Ward Beecher edited. Rather than take on her constitutional case for women's political equality, her critics attacked her personal life and claimed that, as a divorced and sexually active woman, she was too disreputable to speak for her sex. Stanton clearly understood the political functions of such attacks. Woodhull, she wrote, "has done a work for women that none of us could have done. She has faced and dared men to call her names that make women shudder. She has risked and realized the sort of ignominy that would have paralyzed any of us who have longer been called strong-minded." "We have had women enough sacrificed to this sentimental, hypocritical prating about purity," Stanton wrote to Lucretia Mott. "This is one of man's most effective engines for our division and subjugation."[44] The attacks did destroy Woodhull, and both her political credibility and her sanity were eventually ruined. On the eve of the 1872 presidential election, she was arrested by federal marshals for violating the just-passed Comstock law. Less than a month later, Susan B. Anthony was also arrested by federal marshals—for "criminal voting," an act based on the same ideas as those advocated by Woodhull. In retrospect, those events demonstrate what was not yet clear to the New Departure suffragists: federal power could as easily be the enemy as the protector of individual rights, depending on political forces.

Meanwhile, following the lead of the 1871 Bingham report of the House Judiciary Committee, Republican judges began to rule against cases brought by New Departure suffragists. The first major New Departure case to reach the courts was the suit brought by Sara Spencer and seventy other women against election officials in the District of Columbia for refusing to register their votes. In October 1871 Judge Cartter of the Washington, D.C., United States District Court found against the women. His ruling was based more on ideological grounds than on constitutional ones, and it indicated how the general fear of political democracy was working against woman suffrage and against the expansive and egalitarian interpretation of the Reconstruction amendments with which it had associated itself. "The claim, as we understand it," Cartter explained, "is, that [women] have an inherent right, resting in nature, and guaranteed by the Constitution, in such wise that it may not be defeated by legislation. . . . The right of all men to vote is as fully recognized in the population of our large centres and cities as can well be done. . . . The result in these centres is political profligacy and violence verging upon anarchy. . . . The fact that the practical working of the assumed right would be destructive of civilization is decisive that the right does not exist."[45]

The next stage in the judicial history of the New Departure was *Bradwell v. State* in which Myra Bradwell challenged the Illinois Bar's refusal to admit her to practice before it. The case was brought to the United States Supreme Court by Matthew Carpenter, Republican senator from Wisconsin. Carpenter argued for Bradwell's right to practice law just as suffragists were arguing for women's right to vote—on the grounds that the Fourteenth Amendment pledged the national government to protect women's rights equally with those of all other citizens. There was considerable historical irony in Carpenter's brief. Although he used the structure of New Departure arguments, Carpenter went to great lengths to distinguish Bradwell's right to practice law, which he argued was one of the rights protected under the Fourteenth Amendment, from women's right to vote, which he argued was not. He made the distinction in order "to quiet the fears of the timid and conservative."[46]

The Court's ruling on *Bradwell* came in conjunction with its first major interpretation of the Fourteenth Amendment, the famous *Slaughterhouse* cases. In the *Slaughterhouse* cases, the Court declared, by a bare five to four majority, that the amendment created no new national rights and did not establish national citizenship as supreme over state citizenship. Those were virtually the same arguments that Representative Bingham had made in the House Judiciary Committee's Majority Report rejecting Woodhull's petition. Then the Court moved on to the *Bradwell* case, and with only Chief Justice Salmon P. Chase dissenting, applied the same principle to reject the argument that Bradwell's right to be admitted to the bar was protected by the Fourteenth Amendment.[47]

A few months after the *Slaughterhouse* and *Bradwell* decisions, Anthony's case, *United States v. Anthony*, was heard before the United States Circuit Court in Canandaigua. (Anthony had so thoroughly canvassed her home county of Monroe, explaining her case to potential jurors, that the venue of the trial had to be changed.) Judge Ward Hunt, a Roscoe Conkling appointee, earned himself a special place of infamy in the annals of women's rights by depriving Anthony of her constitutional rights and directing the jury to find her guilty. Hunt rejected Anthony's arguments that national citizenship was supreme over state citizenship and that voting was a right of national citizenship, and he cited the *Bradwell* and *Slaughterhouse* decisions to support his opinion. Regarding the Fifteenth Amendment, he argued that it applied only to disfranchisement on grounds it "expressly prohibited" and that it did not imply a prohibition of discrimination by sex. Anthony saw that the implications of such opinions reached beyond woman suffrage to the whole framework of political rights. She predicted with stunning accuracy that "if we once establish the false principle, that United States citizenship does not carry with it the right to vote in every state in this Union, there is no end to the petty freaks and cunning devices that will be resorted to, to exclude one and another class of citizens from the right of suffrage."[48]

Hunt kept Anthony's case from going to the Supreme Court. Appropriately, the case that allowed the Supreme Court to rule once and for all on the New Departure was Virginia Minor's suit against the Missouri election official who refused to accept her ballot. Since the claim that the

Fourteenth Amendment created a national citizenship that superseded state citizenship had already been dismissed in the *Slaughterhouse* and *Bradwell* cases, *Minor v. Happersett* focused exclusively on voting as a right of citizenship. The suit treated that assertion as so obvious, so basic to the entire meaning of the Civil War and Reconstruction, as to be virtually unchallengeable: "We claim, and presume it will not be disputed, that the elective franchise is a privilege of citizenship within the meaning of the Constitution of the United States." Yet the Court was "unanimously of the opinion that the Constitution of the United States does not confer the right of suffrage upon any one."[49]

In 1875, much as Anthony had predicted, the Court began to undermine the voting rights of the freedmen along lines that reflected its dismissal of New Departure interpretations of the Fifteenth Amendment with respect to woman suffrage. In *United States v. Reese* and in *United States v. Cruikshank,* the Court deprived black men of their right to vote by narrowing the prohibitions of the Fifteenth Amendment, first to disfranchisement that was the direct result of state action, and then to racial disfranchisement only when the grounds were explicitly stated. The judicial fate of the woman suffrage New Departure had laid the legal groundwork for those decisions in several ways. The precedent of rejecting the constitutional arguments for woman suffrage by interpreting the Fifteenth Amendment as intended to forbid only disfranchisement by race made it much easier to disfranchise the freedmen on grounds, such as education, income, or residence, that were surrogates for race. Furthermore, the Court's decisions in the New Departure cases severed the Fourteenth and Fifteenth amendments—they separated the right to vote from federal powers of enforcement and from the affirmative statement of national citizenship in the Fourteenth Amendment. That left voting rights dependent solely on the Fifteenth Amendment and, therefore, much more vulnerable. In *Minor v. Happersett,* the Court ruled conclusively that the right of suffrage was not a necessary attribute of national citizenship, and from there it was a very short step to permitting the whole range of indirect devices for de facto disfranchisement of the freedmen.[50]

Afterword

In 1878, three years after the defeat of its New Departure strategy by the Court's decision in the *Minor* case, the NWSA began pursuing a different strategy for winning women's political rights: a constitutional amendment, patterned after the Fifteenth Amendment, exclusively to prohibit disfranchisement by sex. Earlier an amendment had been proposed that included both a general assertion that "the Right of Suffrage in the United States shall be based on citizenship, and shall be regulated by Congress," and the specific prohibition against "any distinction or discrimination whatever founded on sex." The 1878 amendment, which was eventually adopted as the Nineteenth Amendment, did not make any general assertions about the right to vote but simply prohibited disfranchisement by sex. The small difference of wording indicated a much larger difference of political atmosphere; it revealed the reformulation of the demand for woman suffrage to coincide with an age in which political democracy was contracting rather than expanding. Not only had many reformers, woman suffragists included, turned against black voters, seeing them as a source of ignorance and corruption, but white workers, angry over their own subordination, had also shown their capacity for violence and social disorder.[51] To what larger political propositions could woman suffrage be attached in such an era?

At the NWSA's 1878 Tenth Washington Convention, where the new woman suffrage amendment was introduced, Reconstruction-era assertions that all individuals deserved the vote, irrespective of sex or race, were mixed with categorical arguments about what women as women could be expected to do with the vote, both to protect themselves and to benefit the larger society. But it was the essentialist arguments that fit best with the new, antidemocratic spirit behind woman suffrage. That link was expressed by Elizabeth Boynton Harbert, a representative of the new generation of suffragists. Harbert emphasized two themes in her speech at the 1878 convention: that "the ballot in the hands of women would prove a help, not a hindrance" in lowering taxes and reasserting the power of property; and that women had a distinct "mother instinct for government" that was the best reason for trusting them with the vote. The two arguments were fundamentally linked inasmuch as women could be relied on to represent the forces of order and stability in government as in the family. Other suffragists of the late 1870s made similar connections. Characteristically, they based their arguments on woman's special capacity to halt the growing power of "vice," a concept that expressed the fear of working-class power by mixing it with the powerful spectre of unleashed sexuality.[52]

Harbert's speech contrasted with an impassioned speech, entitled "National Protection for National Citizens," that Stanton gave at the same convention. Although the convention was meant to inaugurate a grand campaign for the proposed woman suffrage amendment, Stanton delivered a stubborn defense of the New Departure, particularly of the principle of popular sovereignty, which held that political rights were inherent, not bestowed. To her what was at stake in the NWSA's rejection of the New Departure was not simply woman suffrage but a larger egalitarian interpretation, both of the Constitution and of national purpose. Stanton's interpretation of the Constitution emphasized the power of the federal government, especially its power to enforce equal rights. Federal action could realize true equality because its impact was "uniform" and "homogeneous" on all citizens; it had the power to level. Against that egalitarian definition of national supremacy, Stanton contrasted the growing use of national power "to oppress the citizens of the several States in their most sacred rights," for instance by undermining the separation of church and state.[53]

Stanton certainly understood that her interpretation of the Constitution as a document that committed the nation to the protection of equal rights had been defeated. In the future, the Constitution would be used to defend the rights of property, not persons. But for that reason, the defeat of equal rights constitutionalism would necessarily be temporary. "A century of discussion has not yet made the constitution understood," Stanton asserted. "It has no settled interpretation. Being a series of compromises, it can be expounded in favor of many directly opposite principles." Above all, she took heart because "the numerous demands by the people for national protection in many rights not specified by the constitution, prove that the people have outgrown the compact that satisfied the fathers."[54]

NOTES

1. Celia Morris Eckhardt, *Fanny Wright: Rebel in America* (Cambridge, Mass., 1984), 1–3, 282–83; Barbara Taylor, *Eve and the New Jerusalem: Socialism and Feminism in the Nineteenth Century* (New York, 1983), 1–18, 65–70.

2. Catharine E. Beecher, *A Treatise on Domestic Economy, for the Use of Young Ladies at Home, and at School* (Boston, 1841), 4, 6–7, 9.

3. Linda K. Kerber, *Women of the Republic: Intellect and Ideology in Revolutionary America* (Chapel Hill, 1980), 11–12; Ellen Carol DuBois, *Feminism and Suffrage: The Emergence of an Independent Women's Movement in America, 1848–1869* (Ithaca, 1978), 40–47; Ellen Carol DuBois, "Radicalism of the Woman Suffrage Movement: Notes toward the Reconstruction of American Feminism," *Feminist Studies*, 3 (Fall 1975), 63–71.

4. Sean Wilentz, *Chants Democratic: New York City & the Rise of the American Working Class, 1788–1850* (New York, 1984), 248; Mary P. Ryan, *Cradle of the Middle Class: The Family in Oneida County, New York, 1790–1865* (New York, 1981), 105–44; Carroll Smith-Rosenberg, "Beauty, the Beast, and the Militant Woman: A Case Study in Sex Roles and Social Stress in Jacksonian America," *American Quarterly*, 23 (Oct. 1971), 562–84; Nancy A. Hewitt, *Women's Activism and Social Change: Rochester, New York, 1822–1872* (Ithaca, 1984), 97–138.

5. See especially the writings of Angelina Grimké and Sarah Grimké. Sarah, for example, repudiated the "flattering language of man since he laid aside the whip as a means to keep woman in subjection." Sarah M. Grimké, *Letters on the Equality of the Sexes and the Condition of Woman: Addressed to Mary S. Parker, President of the Boston Female Anti-Slavery Society* (Boston, 1838), 17.

6. Eric Foner, *Free Soil, Free Labor, Free Men: The Ideology of the Republican Party before the Civil War* (New York, 1970), 73–102; Aileen S. Kraditor, *Means and Ends in American Abolitionism: Garrison and His Critics on Strategy and Tactics, 1834–1850* (New York, 1967), 39–77.

7. "Declaration of Sentiments and Resolutions," in *The Concise History of Woman Suffrage*, ed. Mari Jo Buhle and Paul Buhle (Urbana, 1978), 94–98.

8. "Syracuse National Convention, Syracuse, New York, September 8–10, 1852," in *Concise History of Woman Suffrage*, ed. Buhle and Buhle, 117; "Second National Convention, Worcester, Massachusetts, October 15–16, 1851," in ibid., 112; Lori D. Ginzberg, "'Moral Suasion Is Moral Balderdash': Women, Politics, and Social Activism in the 1850s," *Journal of American History*, 73 (Dec. 1986), 601–22.

9. "Second National Convention," 112; Margaret Fuller Ossoli, *Woman in the Nineteenth Century and Kindred Papers Relating to the Sphere, Condition and Duties of Woman* (Boston, 1855), 96; Elizabeth Cady Stanton, "Address at Seneca Falls," in *Elizabeth Cady Stanton, Susan B. Anthony: Correspondence, Writings, Speeches*, ed. Ellen Carol DuBois (New York, 1981), 33.

10. Elizabeth Cady Stanton, Susan B. Anthony, and Matilda Joslyn Gage, eds., *History of Woman Suffrage*, vol. I: *1848–1861* (Rochester, 1881), 364.

11. "Syracuse National Convention," 123; "Second National Convention," 107; Henry B. Blackwell and Lucy Stone, "Protest," in *Concise History of Woman Suffrage*, ed. Buhle and Buhle, 151–52; Norma Basch, *In the Eyes of the Law: Women, Marriage, and Property in Nineteenth-Century New York* (Ithaca, 1982), 162–99.

12. Smith-Rosenberg, "Beauty, the Beast, and the Militant Woman"; "Debates on Marriage and Divorce, Tenth National Woman's Rights Convention, May 10–11, 1860" in *Concise History of Woman Suffrage*, ed. Buhle and Buhle, 170–89.

13. "Debates on Marriage and Divorce," 182. For a modern feminist study of the negative consequences of divorce law liberalization for women, see Leonore Weitzman, *The Divorce Revolution: The Unexpected Social and Economic Consequences for Women and Children in America* (New York, 1985), 357–401.

14. David Montgomery, *Beyond Equality: Labor and the Radical Republicans, 1862–1872* (New York, 1967), 80–81; Judith Baer, *Equality under the Constitution: Reclaiming the Fourteenth Amendment* (Ithaca, 1983), 59.

15. Elizabeth Cady Stanton, Susan B. Anthony, and Matilda Joslyn Gage, eds., *History of Woman Suffrage*, vol. II: *1861–1878* (Rochester, 1881), 85.

16. Elizabeth Cady Stanton, "'This Is the Negro's Hour,'" in *Concise History of Woman Suffrage*, ed. Buhle and Buhle, 219. Elizabeth Cady Stanton used the same "door" metaphor, but with racist overtones, to ask whether "the representative women of the nation . . . had better stand aside and see 'Sambo' walk into the kingdom first," (ibid.).

17. "Woman's Rights Convention, New York City, May 10, 1866, including Address to Congress adopted by the Convention," in *Concise History of Woman Suffrage*, ed. Buhle and Buhle, 226; Stanton, Anthony, and Gage, eds., *History of Woman Suffrage*, II, 206, 281, 291.

18. Stanton, Anthony, and Gage, eds., *History of Woman Suffrage*, II, 185.

19. Ibid., 185, 241, 356.

20. Ibid., 174, 185.

21. Ibid., 193, 197, 211–13, 274.

22. DuBois, *Feminism and Suffrage*, 53–104; "Debates at the American Equal Rights Association Meeting, New York City, May 12–14, 1869," in *Concise History of Woman Suffrage*, ed. Buhle and Buhle, 258.

23. Ida Husted Harper, ed., *The Life and Work of Susan B. Anthony* (3 vols., Indianapolis, 1898–1908), I, 324; Stanton, Anthony, and Gage, eds., *History of Woman Suffrage*, II, 404.

24. Elizabeth Cady Stanton, *Eighty Years and More: Reminiscences, 1815–1897* (New York, 1898), 242; Alma Lutz, *Created Equal: A Biography of Elizabeth Cady Stanton* (New York, 1940), 134.

25. "Debates at the American Equal Rights Association Meeting," 273.

26. Elizabeth Cady Stanton, "Address to the National Woman Suffrage Convention, Washington, D.C., January 19, 1869," in *Concise History of Woman Suffrage*, ed. Buhle and Buhle, 249–56; William Leach, *True Love and Perfect Union: The Feminist Reform of Sex and Society* (New York, 1984), 147; Stanton, Anthony, and Gage, eds., *History of Woman Suffrage*, II, 318.

27. Stanton, Anthony, and Gage, eds., *History of Woman Suffrage*, II, 384; "Resolutions and Debate, First Annual Meeting of the American Equal Rights Association, New York City, May 10, 1867," in *Concise History of Woman Suffrage*, ed. Buhle and Buhle, 240; Elizabeth Cady Stanton, Susan B. Anthony, and Matilda Joslyn Gage, eds., *History of Woman Suffrage*, vol. III: *1876–1885* (Rochester, 1886), 73–77.

28. Stanton, "Address to the National Woman Suffrage Convention," 252; Stanton, Anthony, and Gage, eds., *History of Woman Suffrage*, II, 359, 387.

29. Leach, *True Love and Perfect Union*, 292–322; Stanton, Anthony, and Gage, eds., *History of Woman Suffrage*, II, 493. See also Elizabeth Cady Stanton, "Proposal to Form a New Party, May, 1872," in *Elizabeth Cady Stanton, Susan B. Anthony*, ed. DuBois, 167.

30. Isabella Beecher Hooker, Susan B. Anthony, et al., *An Appeal to the Women of the United States by the National Woman Suffrage and Educational Committee* (Hartford, 1871); Stanton, Anthony, and Gage, eds., *History of Woman Suffrage*, II, 398, 436.

31. Stanton, Anthony, and Gage, eds., *History of Woman Suffrage*, II, 407–10.

32. Ibid. For further discussion of the Minors' arguments, see Louise R. Noun, *Strong Minded Women: The Emergence of the Woman Suffrage Movement in Iowa* (Ames, 1969), 168–69.

33. Stanton, Anthony, and Gage, eds., *History of Woman Suffrage*, II, 407–10; *Corfield v. Coryell*, 6 F. Cas. 546 (E.D. Pa. 1823) (No. 3, 230).

34. On the New Departure, see Stanton, Anthony, and Gage, eds., *History of Woman Suffrage*, II, 407–520, 586–755. See also Harper, ed., *Life and Work of Susan B. Anthony*, I, 409–48.

35. Stanton, Anthony, and Gage, eds., *History of Woman Suffrage*, II, 410, III, 585; Paulina W. Davis, comp., *A History of the National Woman's Rights Movement for Twenty Years, . . . from 1850 to 1870* (New York, 1871), 23; Eleanor Flexner, *Century of Struggle: The Woman's Rights Movement in the United States* (Cambridge, Mass., 1975), 371.

36. Harper, ed., *Life and Work of Susan B. Anthony*, I, 178, 409–65; Stanton, Anthony, and Gage, eds., *History of Woman Suffrage*, II, 407–520.

37. Stanton, Anthony, and Gage, eds., *History of Woman Suffrage*, II, 443–48; Dale Baum, "Woman Suffrage and the 'Chinese Question': The Limits of Radical Republicanism in Massachusetts, 1865–1876," *New England Quarterly*, 56 (March 1983), 60–77; Emanie Sachs, *"The Terrible Siren": Victoria Woodhull (1838–1927)* (New York, 1927), 146.

38. Stanton, Anthony, and Gage, eds., *History of Woman Suffrage*, II, 444, 448–58, esp. 455.

39. Ibid., 445. The argument that women, as part of races, have the rights of races, combines the powerful ring of common sense and tremendous naïveté for the legal niceties; thus it suggests that Victoria Woodhull had a role in writing her own argument and was not merely reading words written for her by Benjamin Butler or other male politicians and lawyers. That is the one of many common and unsubstantiated assertions made by historians about Woodhull. See, for example, Elisabeth Griffith, *In Her Own Right: The Life of Elizabeth Cady Stanton* (New York, 1984), 149.

40. Harper, ed., *Life and Work of Susan B. Anthony*, I, 381; Stanton, Anthony, and Gage, eds., *History of Woman Suffrage*, II, 461–64.

41. Victoria C. Woodhull, *A Speech on the Principles of Social Freedom, Delivered in New York City, November 20, 1871, and Boston, January 3, 1872* (London, 1894), 23–24.

42. *Woodhull and Claflin's Weekly*, May 27, 1871, 3.

43. "For Women Only," *Des Moines Daily Register*, July 29, 1871; Elizabeth Cady Stanton to Martha Coffin Wright, June 19, 1871, box 60, Garrison Family Collection (Sophia Smith Collection, Smith College, Northampton, Mass.).

44. Paxton Hibben, *Henry Ward Beecher: An American Portrait* (New York,

1927), 235; "Lady Cook and Victoria Woodhull," *Chicago Daily Socialist*, March 21, 1911 (the author wishes to thank Mari Jo Buhle for the citation; for another version of the quotation, see Lutz, *Created Equal*, 228); Stanton to Lucretia Mott, April 1, 1872, Elizabeth Cady Stanton Papers (Vassar College, Poughkeepsie, N.Y.).

45. Stanton, Anthony, and Gage, eds., *History of Woman Suffrage*, II, 597–99.

46. *Bradwell v. State*, 16 Wallace 130 (1873); quoted in Stanton, Anthony, and Gage, eds., *History of Woman Suffrage*, II, 615–22.

47. *Slaughterhouse Cases*, 16 Wallace 36 (1873); William E. Forbath, "The Ambiguities of Free Labor: Labor and the Law in the Gilded Age," *Wisconsin Law Review* (no. 4, 1985), 767–89; Stanton, Anthony, and Gage, eds., *History of Woman Suffrage*, II, 622–26. While arguing for the relevance of the Fourteenth Amendment to the Bradwell case, Sen. Matthew Carpenter submitted a brief to the Court *against* the relevance of the amendment in the *Slaughterhouse Cases* because he opposed a construction so "broad that it would invalidate desirable government regulation." *Slaughterhouse Cases*, 21 U.S. Supreme Court Reports Lawyer's Edition, 399–401 (1873).

48. *United States v. Anthony*, 24 F. Cas. (C.C.N.D.N.Y. 1873) (No. 14, 459); quoted in Stanton, Anthony, and Gage, eds., *History of Woman Suffrage*, II, 641, 675–79.

49. *Minor v. Happersett*, 21 Wallace 162 (1875); quoted in Stanton, Anthony, and Gage, eds., *History of Woman Suffrage*, II, 717–42, esp. 719, 742. Chief Justice Salmon P. Chase, the lone dissenter in *Bradwell v. State*, had died and had been replaced by Chief Justice Morrison R. Waite.

50. *United States v. Reese*, 92 U.S. 214 (1876); *United States v. Cruikshank*, 92 U.S. 542 (1876).

51. Stanton, Anthony, and Gage, eds., *History of Woman Suffrage*, II, 333, III, 14, 25, 75. For comments on the railroad strikes of 1877, both for and against the strikers, see ibid., III, 72–73.

52. Stanton, Anthony, and Gage, eds., *History of Woman Suffrage*, III, 73–77; Steven M. Buechler, *The Transformation of the Woman Suffrage Movement: The Case of Illinois, 1850–1920* (New Brunswick, 1986), 108–17; Christine Stansell, *City of Women: Sex and Class in New York, 1789–1860* (New York, 1986), 203–9.

53. Stanton, Anthony, and Gage, eds., *History of Woman Suffrage*, III, 80–92.

54. Ibid., 87–88.

7

Taking the Law into Our Own Hands

Bradwell, Minor, and Suffrage Militance in the 1870s

Among the most contested elements of the Constitution have been the Reconstruction amendments, and a crucial aspect of that contest has been the relation of the Fourteenth Amendment to women's rights. This essay addresses the early history of women's rights claims to the Fourteenth and Fifteenth Amendments. It explores the legal arguments with which woman suffragists approached the Reconstruction amendments, the popular support and militant activism they inspired, and the role that the defeat of women's rights claims played in the larger history of Reconstruction constitutionalism. This mid-nineteenth-century episode in women's rights history was extremely brief, but it reverberates richly with many important and perplexing issues facing feminist thinkers and activists today. At various moments during which I worked on this essay, I felt that this material provided the historical key to current debates within feminism over "equality," over "rights," and over "politics."

Here, in the post–Civil War years, we can see proponents of women's rights as they move from universal to particularistic arguments, providing us with the Gilded Age equivalent of the shift from "equality" to "difference" in the feminism of our own time. While many of my contem-

Originally published in *Visible Women*, edited by Nancy Hewitt and Suzanne Lebsock. Urbana: University of Illinois Press, 1990.

poraries emphasize the abstract and "male" character of such universalistic categories as "person" or "citizen," I have chosen to stress the many costs to the women's rights tradition of moving away from such frameworks—however "hegemonic" they may seem to our postmodern consciousness—which have helped situate women's emancipation in the larger context of humanity's freedom.[1]

Here, too, we can trace the course of the demands of a disempowered group based on the venerable but problematic constitutional concept of "rights." Of late, "rights arguments" have been criticized, not only by conservatives but also by those on the left, for the assumption that entitlement inheres "naturally" in individuals, flourishing in a "private" realm that must be protected from interference, by others and by the state. Such a concept of "rights," it is argued, masks the workings of power and favors those already privileged by existing social and political structures—men, white people, and the propertied.[2] But this episode in women's rights, perhaps the entire tradition, treats rights quite differently: as something to be won and exercised collectively rather than individually; as the object of political struggle as much as of judicial resolution; as that which government affirmatively establishes rather than negatively shields; and above all as that which has greatest meaning not to the powerful, who already enjoy their entitlements, but to the powerless, who have yet to have their full place in society recognized.

Finally, this episode has implications for the character and place of the "political" in women's history. While women's historians have deepened our knowledge of the public activism of women, even—or especially—before their enfranchisement, much of this scholarship has followed what is called (in shorthand) "the separate spheres" model. Women, it is argued, have had—and may still have—their own political culture distinct from men's, and they have chosen to work for their own and society's betterment by embracing different institutions, following different rules, and adhering to different political values.[3] This essay suggests that to the degree that nineteenth-century women abandoned a political terrain also occupied by men—of partisan power and judicial contest—they were driven from it by defeat and forced to pursue politics by other, more indirect means. This essay considers women as they attempted to march into power directly, through the main political entrance, rather than indirectly, through the backdoor of the nursery or kitchen.

Most histories of women's rights—my own included—have emphasized the initial rage of women's rights leaders at the Radical Republican authors of the Fourteenth and Fifteenth Amendments. In 1865 Elizabeth Cady Stanton was horrified to discover what she called "the word male" in proposals for a Fourteenth Amendment. The second section of the amendment defines the basis of congressional representation as "male persons over the age of twenty-one" and in doing so makes the first reference to sex anywhere in the Constitution. The passage of the Fifteenth Amendment in 1869, a much more powerful constitutional defense of political equality, only deepened the anger of women's rights advocates because it did not include sex among its prohibited disfranchisements.[4]

In 1869 the crisis split suffragists into two camps—the National Woman Suffrage Association, which protested the omission of women from the Reconstruction amendments, and the American Woman Suffrage Association, which accepted the deferral of their claims. This part of the story is well known to students of woman suffrage, as is the National Association's concentration, through most of its twenty-one-year life (in 1890 it amalgamated with the American Association), on securing a separate amendment enfranchising women. Inasmuch as the form that federal woman suffrage ultimately took was precisely a separate constitutional amendment—the Nineteenth, ratified in 1920—this strategy is taken as the entirety of woman suffragists' constitutional claims. Yet, in the first few years after the passage of the Fourteenth and Fifteenth Amendments, suffragists in the National Association camp energetically pursued another constitutional approach. They proposed a broad and inclusive construction of the Fourteenth and Fifteenth Amendments, under which, they claimed, women were already enfranchised. This constitutional strategy, known at the time as the New Departure, laid the basis for the subsequent focus on a separate woman suffrage amendment, even as it embodied a radical democratic vision that the latter approach did not have.[5]

*

While the Fourteenth Amendment was in the process of being ratified, woman suffragists concentrated on its second clause, because of the offensive reference to "male persons." This phrase was included by the amendment's framers because in 1867 there was an active movement demanding the franchise for women, and it would no longer do to use such gender neutral terms as "person" to mean only men.[6] Yet such explicit exclusions of particular groups from the universal blessings of American democracy were not at all in the egalitarian spirit of the age. Perhaps it was for this reason that in writing the first section of the Fourteenth Amendment, which defines federal citizenship, the framers could not bring themselves to speak of races or sexes but instead relied on the abstractions of "persons" and "citizens." In other words, the universalities of the first section of the Fourteenth Amendment, where federal citizenship is established, run headlong into the sex-based restrictions of the second section, where voting rights are limited. Those Reconstruction Era feminists angered at the restrictive clause quickly recognized these contradictions and became determined to get women's rights demands included in the broadest possible construction of the terms "persons" and "citizens" in the first section, to use, in other words, the first section to defeat the second.

After the Fifteenth Amendment was finally ratified, the suffragists of the National Association therefore shifted from the claim that the Reconstruction amendments excluded women and began to argue instead that they were broad enough to include women's rights along with those of the freedmen. This strategic turn, known within woman suffrage circles as the New Departure,[7] was first outlined in October 1869 by a husband and wife team of Missouri suffragists, Francis and Virginia Minor. They offered an elaborate and elegant interpretation of the Constitution to demonstrate that women already had the right to vote. Their construction rested on a consistent perspective on the whole Constitution, but especially on a broad interpretation of the Fourteenth Amendment.[8]

The Minors' first premise was that popular sovereignty preceded and underlay constitutional authority. In exchange for creating government, the people expected protection of their preeminent and natural rights. This is a familiar element of revolutionary ideology. Their second premise was to equate the power of the *federal* government with the defense of individual rights, to regard federal power as positive.[9] Historically, the federal government had been regarded as the enemy of rights; the Bill of Rights protects individual rights by enjoining the federal government from infringing on them. In the wake of the devastating experience of secession, the Fourteenth Amendment reversed the order, relying on federal power to protect its citizens against the tyrannical action of the states. The Minors thus argued in good Radical Reconstruction fashion that national citizenship had finally been established as supreme by the first section of the Fourteenth Amendment: "the immunities and privileges of American citizenship, however defined, are national in character and paramount to all state authority."

A third element in the Minors' case was that the benefits of national citizenship were equally the rights of all. This too bore the mark of the Reconstruction Era. In the words of the amendment, "all persons born or naturalized in the United States" were equally entitled to the privileges and protections of national citizenship; there were no additional qualifications. In the battle for the rights of the black man, the rights of all had been secured. The war had expanded the rights of "proud white man" to all those who had historically been deprived of them, or so these Radical Reconstructionists believed.[10] In other words, the historic claim of asserting *individual* rights was becoming the modern one of realizing *equal* rights, especially for the lowly.

Finally, the Minors argued that the right to vote was one of the basic privileges and immunities of national citizenship. This was both the most controversial and the most important part of the New Departure constitutional construction. Popular sovereignty had always included an implicit theory of political power. The Minors' New Departure argument took this article of popular faith, reinterpreted it in light of Reconstruction Era egalitarianism, and gave it constitutional expression to produce a theory of universal rights to the suffrage. The New Departure case for universal suffrage brought together the Fourteenth Amendment, which nationalized citizenship and linked it to federal power, and the Fifteenth Amendment, which shifted the responsibility for the suffrage from the state to the national government.[11] This theory of the suffrage underlay much of the case for black suffrage as well, but because the drive for black suffrage was so intertwined with Republican partisan interest, it was woman suffrage, which had no such political thrust behind it, that generated the most formal constitutional expression of this Reconstruction Era faith in political equality.

The New Departure was not simply a lawyer's exercise in constitutional exegesis. Reconstruction was an age of popular constitutionalism. Although presented in formal, constitutional terms, what the Minors had to say had much support among the rank and file of the women's rights movement. The underlying spirit of the Minors' constitutional arguments was militant and activist. The basic message was that the vote was already women's right; they merely had to take it. The New Departure took on meaning precisely because of this direct action element. Many women took the argument to heart and went to the polls, determined to vote. By 1871 hundreds of women were trying to register and vote in dozens of towns all over the country.[12] In 1871 in Philadelphia, to take one of many examples, Carrie Burnham, an unmarried tax-paying woman, got as far as having her name registered on the voting rolls. When her vote was refused, she formed the Citizens Suffrage Association of Philadelphia, dedicated not only to the defense of women's political rights but also to the greater truth that the right to vote was inherent, not bestowed. If the contrary were true, if the right to vote were a gift, this "implied a right lodged somewhere in society, which society had never acquired by any direct concession from the people." Such a theory of political power was patently tyrannical.[13]

That the first examples of women's direct action voting occurred in 1868 and 1869, before the Minors made their formal constitutional argument, suggests that the New Departure grew out of a genuinely popular political faith. In 1868 in the radical, spiritualist town of Vineland, New Jersey, almost two hundred women cast their votes into a separate ballot box and then tried to get them counted along with the men's. "The platform was crowded with earnest refined intellectual women, who feel it was good for them to be there," *The Revolution* reported. "One beautiful girl said 'I feel so much stronger for having voted.'"[14] The Vineland women repeated the effort for several years, and the ballot box eventually became an icon, which the local historical society still owns. From Vineland, the idea of women's voting spread to nearby towns, including Roseville, where, despite the American Association's official disinterest in the New Departure, Lucy Stone and her mother tried—but failed—to register their votes.

On the other side of the continent, Mary Olney Brown also decided she had the right to vote because the legislature of Washington Territory had passed an act giving "all white American citizens above the age of twenty-one years the right to vote." She wrote to other "prominent women urging them to go out and vote at the coming election . . . [but] I was looked upon as a fanatic and the idea of woman voting was regarded as an absurdity." "Many [women] wished to vote. . . ," she decided, "[but] had not the courage to go to the polls in defiance of custom." Finally, in 1869, she went to the polls with her husband, daughter, and son-in-law. Election officials threatened that she would not be "treated as a lady."

> Summoning all my strength, I walked up to the desk behind which sat the august officers of election, and presented my vote. . . . I was pompously met with the assertion, "You are not an American citizen; hence not entitled to vote." . . . I said . . . "I claim to be an American citizen, and a native-born citizen at that; and I wish to show you from the fourteenth amendment to the constitution of the United States, that women are not only citizens having the constitutional right to vote, but also that our territorial election law gives women the privilege of exercising that right." . . . I went on to show them that the . . . emancipation of the Southern slaves threw upon the country a class of people, who, like the women of the nation, owed allegiance to the government, but whose citizenship was not recognized. To settle this question, the fourteenth amendment was adopted.

Whereupon, the local election official, "with great dignity of manner and an immense display of ignorance," insisted "that the laws of congress don't extend over Washington territory" and refused her vote. When Brown was refused again, two years later, she concluded,

> It amounts to this: the law gives women the right to vote in this territory, and you three men who have been appointed to receive our votes, sit here and arbitrarily refuse to take them, giving no reason why, only that you have decided not to take the women's votes. There is no law to sustain you in this usurpation of power.[15]

Top: In 1893 Colorado became the first state to put woman suffrage into its constitution. These middle class and "respectable" Denver women are comfortably and proudly voting alongside men. (Courtesy of Denver Public Library)

Left: Borrowed from British abolitionists, this emblem of female abolitionism was much used in the United States. The supplicant figure suggests the inequality underlying the appeal to the bonds of sisterhood. (Courtesy of Smithsonian Institute)

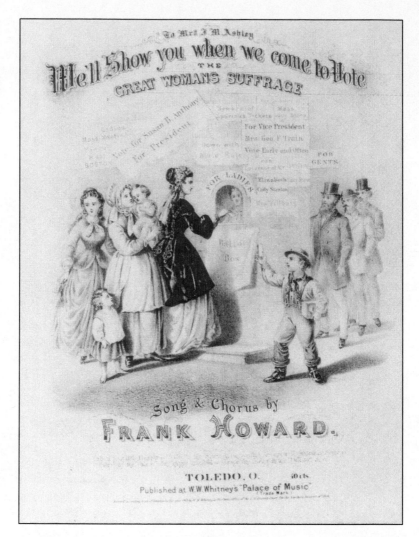

By 1869 the notion of women's voting was gaining popular attention, and the names of Elizabeth Cady Stanton and Susan B. Anthony had become recognizable. The separate polling place for "the ladies" is a reference to the enfranchisement that year of women in Wyoming Territory. (Courtesy of Lester S. Levy Collection of Sheet Music, Special Collections, Milton S. Eisenhower Library, the Johns Hopkins University)

Victoria Woodhull and her sister Tennessee Claflin attempting to cast their ballots in New York City in 1871. A year before Susan B. Anthony succeeded in voting in Rochester, Woodhull and Claflin were among those who tried to vote around the country. They were following the direct action suffrage strategy known as the New Departure. (Courtesy of the Smithsonian Institute)

Above: Along with other suffrage leaders (see Anthony to her left), Elizabeth Cady Stanton spoke before the Senate Committee on Privileges and Elections on behalf of a constitutional amendment prohibiting disenfranchisement by sex. The amendment, sponsored by Senator Aaron Sargent, of California, was known as the "Sixteenth Amendment;" forty years later, when ratified, it became the Nineteenth Amendment. This illustration is from the *Daily Graphic,* January 16, 1878. (Courtesy of the Library of Congress) *Opposite:* Elizabeth Cady Stanton, 1871, studio portrait. (Courtesy of Seaver Center for Western History Research, Natural History Museum of Los Angeles County)

Elizabeth Cady Stanton in 1871, aged 56.

Susan B. Anthony was preaching woman suffrage in California as early as 1871. She went back in 1895 and again the next year, but despite her efforts, the state suffrage referendum for which she worked was defeated in 1896 by fourteen thousand votes. Seventy-five-year-old Susan B. Anthony is at the center; the horse she is riding was named Moses. Two persons to her right is Anna Howard Shaw. (Courtesy of the Huntington Library, San Marino, California)

This unusually informal photograph shows Anthony and Shaw late in June 1895 in Portland, Oregon, where they had been invited by veteran Oregon suffragist Abigail Scott Duniway. Oregon enfranchised its women in 1912. (Courtesy of the Oregon Historical Society)

In 1910 Washington became the fifth state to amend its state constitution to enfranchise women, inaugurating a series of successful state referenda over the next four years. (Courtesy of the Washington State Historical Society)

In 1911 California suffragists waged a brief, sophisticated campaign that made "the golden state" the sixth star in the suffrage flag. This unnamed woman, one of the handful of American-born Chinese women at the time, is registering to be enfranchised. (Courtesy of the Huntington Library, San Marino, California)

Harriot Stanton Blatch, daughter of Elizabeth Cady Stanton, modernized suffrage activism in the early twentieth century. In 1907 she organized the Equality League of Self–Supporting Women in New York City, a suffrage society made up of wage-earning and professional working women. The woman behind her is the trade union suffragist Rose Schneiderman. (Courtesy of Archives of Labor and Urban Affairs, Wayne State University)

These suffragists, proudly bearing a banner declaring themselves women workers, participated in the giant parade in New York City in May 1912. All suffragists, regardless of class, were encouraged to wear white and to buy the same inexpensive suffrage hat to make their ranks look uniform and disciplined. (Courtesy of Schlesinger Library, Radcliffe College)

Charlotte Perkins Gilman, suffragist and feminist, speaking to a street-corner audience in New York City from the back of an automobile. New techniques such as stump speaking and mass parades distinguished the twentieth-century "votes for women" movement. Gilman was known for her feminist sociology of the family and for her belief in the emancipating capacities of wage labor for women. (Courtesy of Bryn Mawr College)

In 1910 the Equality League of Self–Supporting Women was renamed the Women's Political Union (WPU) and in 1913 succeeded in getting the New York legislature to authorize a referendum on woman suffrage for November 1915. Throughout the summer of 1914, the WPU campaigned among upstate voters from Buffalo to Nyack from this "portable headquarters." (Courtesy of Rhoda Barney Jenkins)

Elizabeth Freeman, center, a veteran British suffragette, was one of the WPU's prize paid organizers, much in demand among working-class audiences. She joins other "suffrage newsgirls" to advertise one of the several suffrage papers in New York City, perhaps the WPU's weekly, *The Women's Political World*. (Courtesy of the Library of Congress)

This float tableau, in a parade in Cleveland in 1914, depicts the familiar symbol of the suffrage herald, lifting up the woman wage earner and triumphing over conventionality and degradation. (Courtesy of Western Reserve Historical Society, Cleveland, Ohio)

The International Woman Suffrage Alliance (IWSA) was founded in 1902 and led by Carrie Chapman Catt. In 1912, the IWSA met in Stockholm, Sweden. (Courtesy of Schlesinger Library, Radcliffe College)

News of the efforts of women to register and vote spread through formal and informal means. Women's rights and mainstream journals reported on them, but information also might have been passed by word of mouth through networks of activists. Many sisters and friends, often in different states, turn up in the stories of New Departure voting women. In her account, Mary Olney Brown tells of her sister, who was inspired by her efforts to try to vote in a nearby town. Brown's sister took a different approach and was more successful. Eager to vote in a school election, she and her friends prepared a special dinner for election officials. "When the voting was resumed, the women, my sister being the first, handed in their ballots as if they had always been accustomed to voting. One lady, Mrs. Sargent, seventy-two years old, said she thanked the Lord that he had let her live until she could vote."[16]

The voting women of the 1870s often went to the polls in groups. They believed in the suffrage as an individual right, but an individual right that would be achieved and experienced collectively. The most famous of these voting groups was the nearly fifty local activists, friends, and relatives who joined Susan B. Anthony in attempting to vote in Rochester, New York, in 1872. Virginia Minor herself was swept up in this collective activism. When she and some of her friends, all suffrage activists and Republican partisans, tried to register in St. Louis and were refused, she sued.

The congressional passage of the Enforcement Act in May 1870 to strengthen the Fifteenth Amendment greatly accelerated women's direct action voting. The Enforcement Act was meant to enforce the freedmen's political rights by providing recourse to the federal courts and penalties against local election officials who refused the lawful votes of citizens. Women who wanted to vote saw the act as a way to use the power of the federal government for their own benefit. Benjamin Quarles reports that freedwomen in South Carolina were encouraged by Freedmen's Bureau officials to attempt to vote by appealing to the Enforcement Act.[17] Some election officials responded to the Enforcement Act by accepting women's votes. When Nanette Gardner went to vote in Detroit in 1871, the ward official in her district was sympathetic to her protest and accepted her vote. The same man accepted Gardner's vote again in 1872, and she presented him with "a beautiful banner of white satin, trimmed with gold fringe on which was inscribed . . . 'To Peter Hill, Alderman of the Ninth Ward, Detroit. . . . By recognizing civil liberty and equality for woman, he has placed the last and brightest jewel on the brow of Michigan.'"[18]

Most local officials, however, refused to accept women's votes. While Nanette Gardner voted successfully in Detroit, her friend Catherine Stebbins (the daughter of one of the Rochester voters) was turned away in the next ward. When Mary Brown's vote was refused in Olympia, she concluded that politicians more powerful than the local committeemen had decided to resist women's direct action efforts to vote and that "money was pledged in case of prosecution." In Santa Cruz, California, when Ellen Van Valkenberg was similarly turned back at the polls, she became the first woman to sue an election official under the Enforcement Act for refusing her vote.[19] By 1871 numerous New Departure woman suffrage cases were making their way through the federal courts.

Meanwhile, the New Departure gained an advocate who moved it from the local level into national politics: Victoria Woodhull. In January of 1871 Woodhull appeared before the House Judiciary Committee to make the constitutional case for women's right to vote. No woman had ever before been invited to address a committee of the U.S. Congress. Her appearance was sponsored by Massachusetts Republican Benjamin Butler, who may have helped her outline her constitutional case. The deeply felt conviction about women's rights underlying her argument was undoubtedly her own, however. Her memorial asked Congress to pass legislation clarifying the right of all women to vote under the new Reconstruction amendments.[20] The major difference between Woodhull and the Minors was tactical; she urged women to turn to Congress to resolve the question, while they relied on the courts.

Like all New Departure advocates, Woodhull embraced the premise that popular sovereignty was absolute: "the sovereign power of this country is perpetual in the politically-organized people of the United States, and can neither be relinquished nor abandoned by any portion of them." Her case for woman suffrage was simple and, from a Radical Reconstruction perspective, virtually unassailable: inasmuch as the first section of the Fourteenth Amendment made no reference to sex, women along with men were citizens of the United States, and foremost among the "privileges and immunities" of national citizenship was the right to vote.[21] Like the Minors, Woodhull argued that the Fourteenth Amendment established the supremacy of national over state citizenship and the obligation of the federal government to protect the rights of all citizens equally.

Woodhull also argued from the Fifteenth Amendment, which she interpreted broadly, that voting is "a Right, not a privilege of citizens of the United States."[22] She directly confronted the most obvious objection to this interpretation, that the Fifteenth Amendment specifically prohibits only disfranchisements by race, color, and previous condition. First, she argued, the amendment's wording does not bestow the right to vote but assumes it to be preexisting. Although it explicitly prohibited certain disfranchisements, Woodhull argued that it could not be read to implicitly permit others. Second, the Fifteenth Amendment forbids disfranchisement "under three distinct conditions, in all of which," Woodhull argued, "woman is distinctly embraced." In other words, "a race comprises all the people, male and female." Woodhull here seems to grasp what many modern white feminists are still struggling to understand, that counterposing the discriminations of race and sex obscures the experience of those who suffer both, that is, black women. Finally, Woodhull argued for her broad construction of the right of suffrage on the grounds of what she called "the blending of [the Constitution's] various parts," that is, the relation between the Fourteenth Amendment, which nationalizes citizenship and links it to the power of the federal government, and the Fifteenth Amendment, which shifts the responsibility for the suffrage from the state to the national government.[23]

The first official reaction to the New Departure came in response to Woodhull's memorial. The House Judiciary Committee issued two conflicting reports on the constitutional issues she raised.[24] Here we begin to see that debate over the feminists' particular constitutional arguments was inseparable from questions of the larger meaning of the Reconstruction amendments. The Majority Report rejected Woodhull's claims. Its author was John Bingham, one of the framers of the Fourteenth Amendment. Although Bingham conceded that women enjoyed the privileges of U.S. citizenship along with men, he disagreed that the Fourteenth Amendment added anything new to the content of national citizenship or altered the relationship between national and state citizenship. The Minority Report, signed by William Loughridge of Iowa and Benjamin Butler of Massachusetts, supported Woodhull's memorial and the generous and radical interpretation of the amendments on which it relied. The Minority Report interpreted the Fourteenth Amendment broadly, arguing that it was intended "to secure the natural rights of citizens as well as their equal capacities before the law." The Majority Report rejected Woodhull's argument that the Fifteenth Amendment shifted responsibility for the suffrage from the state to the national level, while the Minority Report agreed that the Fifteenth Amendment "clearly recognizes the right to vote, as one of the rights of a citizen of the United States."[25] "Thus it can be seen," Woodhull observed archly, "that equally able men differ upon a simple point of Constitutional Law."[26]

The mere fact of a congressional hearing was a victory for woman suffrage leaders, and the language of constitutional principle was an improvement over the semisexual innuendo with which their claims were often met.[27] The favorable Minority Report meant that some of the leaders of the Republican party supported women's rights claims on the Constitution. In 1871 two committee rooms in the Capitol were put at the disposal of the suffragists to facilitate their lobbying efforts.[28] "Could you feel the atmosphere of . . . Congress, to-day, you would not doubt what the end must be, nor that it will be very soon," Isabella Beecher Hooker wrote.[29] The National Woman Suffrage Association urged women to put pressure on their congressmen to support the Butler Report, as well as to continue trying to vote and to work through the courts.[30]

It was in this context, as Republicans struggled over the claims of the New Departure and suffragists grew hopeful, that the issue of "free love" was raised. The sexual discourse that soon surrounded the New Departure played a role in shaping the political context and therefore the constitutional outcome. Woodhull is generally remembered in the history books not for her powerful constitutional arguments but for her shady sexual reputation. These sexual issues, however, were introduced not by

Woodhull but by her opponents, who saw in them a way to divert attention from the constitutional arguments she made. Republican newspapers, notably the *New York Tribune*, accused Woodhull of multiple marriages, bigamy, and advocacy of free love.[31] Suffrage leaders allied with Woodhull were either accused of sharing her "free love" sentiments or warned against the consequences of associating with disreputable women. As in other times, when politicians cannot face the genuine issues before them, the importance of "character" was asserted. "Men judge men's conventions not more by the formal platform they present than by . . . the character of those who are prominent in the proceedings," a New York periodical solemnly warned.[32]

Rather than react defensively to the attacks on her, Woodhull embraced the "free love" opprobrium with which she was charged. To her, the principles at the heart of sexual life were the same as those at the heart of political life, and the true basis of marriage was the same as the true basis of republican government: individual rights. Groping for a way to express her conviction that women, whether married or unmarried, must have unqualified control over their own reproductive and sexual lives, she used the language of Reconstruction constitutionalism to proclaim the doctrine of rights to and over one's own person. "Yes I am a Free Lover," Woodhull responded to a heckler at one of her speeches. "I have an *inalienable, constitutional* and *natural* right to love whom I may, . . . to *change* that love *every day* if I please, . . . and it is *your duty* not only to *accord* [me my right], but, as a community, to see that I am protected in it."[33]

Such sex radicalism was not the predominant strain in nineteenth-century feminist circles. Most of the New Departure leaders (with the significant exception of Elizabeth Cady Stanton) were closer to the Victorian stereotype than Woodhull was, and they believed that the sex impulse must be tamed, not constitutionally secured. Nonetheless, even these "pious" women defended their alliance with Woodhull and rejected the conventional moral divide that separated "good" women from "bad." "God has raised up Woodhull to embody all questions of fellowship in political work [among] women irrespective of character," declared Isabella Beecher Hooker.[34] Instead of joining in a crusade against the immorality of women, New Departure suffragists began to attack the "hypocrisy" of men. Woodhull had been "raised up of God," Paulina Wright Davis claimed, to expose the perfidy of "a class that no one dares touch," men who said one thing and did another, men in power.[35] They shifted accusations of immorality not only from women to men but also from sexuality to politics. The true prostitutes, Woodhull asserted, were Republican leaders, who sold out principles for party power and wealth.[36]

In late 1871, in the midst of this increasingly sexualized political context, the first New Departure cases began to reach the dockets of the federal courts. One was the case of Sara Spencer and seventy other women from the District of Columbia, who sued election officials under the Enforcement Act for refusing to permit them to vote. The District of Columbia was a deliberate choice for testing the New Departure argument. There, as advocates of black suffrage had first realized in 1867, the power of the federal government over the suffrage was not complicated by questions of dual sovereignty and states rights.[37]

In October Judge Cartter of the Supreme Court of the District of Columbia ruled against Spencer. Cartter conceded that the Fourteenth Amendment included women along with men in the privileges and immunities of national citizenship; however, he rejected the democratic theory of suffrage on which the case rested. To concede that voting was a right was, in his opinion, to open the door to anarchy and would "involve the destruction of civil government." "The right of all men to vote is as fully recognized in the population of our large centres and cities as can well be done," wrote Cartter. "The result . . . is political profligacy and violence verging upon anarchy."[38] The larger context of the opinion, therefore, was anxiety about democratic politics, and Cartter's concern for the proper position of women in society was secondary. This was true of the entire New Departure debate (and perhaps of judicial disposition of women's rights claims more generally); it was conducted primarily in terms of "rights," not woman's sphere. What was claimed or denied for women was claimed or denied for all citizens, especially those previously excluded from rights due them. Whether this was because the question of woman's place was subsumed in a more general struggle for political democracy or because sex-prejudice was still unspeakable in constitutional terms, the consequence was the same: denying women the rights they claimed under general provisions weakened those provisions in general.

The observation that general questions of constitutional rights had overtaken the specific discourse on woman's place is even clearer in the next major New Departure decision, the *Myra Bradwell* case. *Bradwell* was the first case touching on the New Departure to reach the Supreme Court. In 1869 Myra Bradwell, a Chicago feminist and pioneering woman lawyer, was refused admission to the Illinois bar. The grounds on which the state supreme court refused her application, along with the initial brief that Bradwell submitted in response, were concerned entirely with coverture, that is, with the question of the disabilities of married women before the law. By the time Bradwell brought her case before the U.S. Supreme Court in October 1871, she had changed the terms radically. Her case was no longer about coverture but had been reformulated in entirely New Departure terms. Her brief argued that her right to practice law was a citizen's right and that Illinois's action in refusing her was prohibited by the Fourteenth Amendment. As for coverture, she asserted that "the great innovation of the XIV Amendment . . . sweeps away the principles of the common law," so that even reforms of married women's property rights were no longer necessary. The *Bradwell* case is one of the few concerning women's rights commonly included in the history of constitutional law, but in my opinion it is not correctly situated, since it is usually cited to illustrate judicial assumptions about woman's place rather than the constitutional issues of citizenship on which it was actually argued and decided.[39]

Bradwell's case was closely watched by suffragists as an indication of how much support to expect from the Republican party. Bradwell was represented before the Supreme Court by Senator Matthew Carpenter, one of the major second-generation leaders of the Republican party. While Carpenter took up Bradwell's case and argued it in strong Fourteenth Amendment terms, he prefaced his case with an equally strong argument about why the right to vote was not covered by the Reconstruction amendments. He insisted, in other words, on a distinction between civil and political rights. While the federal government protected civil rights, women's as well as men's, Carpenter argued, the suffrage remained under the control of the states, beyond the lawful interference of federal power.[40]

Suffragists were understandably confused by the way Carpenter argued Bradwell's case. Was it an indication that Republican leaders were in favor of the New Departure or against it? Stanton allowed herself to be encouraged; if women were covered along with men under the Fourteenth Amendment, wasn't the fundamental point of equal rights won?[41] Victoria Woodhull, however, saw it differently; she argued that women might be admitted to the benefits of the postwar amendments only to find those amendments so narrowed that they bestowed virtually nothing at all, certainly not political rights. She charged that Republicans, "frightened by the grandeur and the extent" of the amendments they had enacted, had retreated to the enemies' doctrine of states' rights, where their own greatest achievements would ultimately be undone.[42]

The Supreme Court held back its decision on *Bradwell* until after the election. To trace the final judicial disposition of the suffragists' constitutional arguments, we have to understand what was at stake in this election and what a Republican victory would mean. The election of 1872 was a crisis for the Republicans.[43] In June 1872 an important group of reformers split off from regular Republicans to run an independent presidential campaign. These political rebels, the Liberal Republicans, based their revolt on the old opposition between central government and individual rights. From the perspective of feminists, who were also looking for a political alternative to the regular Republicans, the terms of the bolt were particularly disappointing. Feminists had learned from freedmen to see the federal government not as a threat to their rights but as the agency for winning them.

To add insult to injury, the Liberal Republicans picked as their candidate Horace Greeley, a man who had made his opposition to woman suffrage clear many years before. Infuriated by the nomination of Greeley, many New Departure suffragists campaigned actively for Ulysses Grant in 1872.[44] The regular Republicans cultivated their support, sending them about the country on official speaking tours and inserting a timid little reference to "additional rights" for women in their platform, a plank so insignificant that suffragists called it a "splinter." Holding off a decision on *Bradwell* was consistent with this temporary friendliness. Anthony expected that if Republicans won, they would reward women with the suffrage by recognizing the New Departure claims. She was so sure that when she came home from her last speaking tour on election day, she gathered together friends and relatives and went down to her local polling place to submit her vote for Grant. Although the local Republican official accepted the votes of fifteen of the demonstrators, including Anthony,[45] a few weeks later a U.S. marshal came to her house and arrested her for violation of federal law—the Enforcement Act.

Anthony's arrest was a signal that the Republicans were ready to dispose of the New Departure. Because she was the most famous woman suffragist in the nation, there is good reason to suspect her arrest had been authorized at the highest level of government. The conduct of her trial several months later reinforces this suspicion. The trial was moved from her home county, where she had lectured extensively to educate potential jurors, to another venue. The judge was no small-town jurist but a recent appointee to the U.S. Supreme Court. He refused to submit the case to the jury, instead directing a guilty verdict from the bench, a practice that was later found unconstitutional. Years later, Anthony's lawyer observed, "There never was a trial in the country with one half the importance of Miss Anthony's. . . . If Anthony had won her case on the merit it would have revolutionized the suffrage of the country. . . . There was a prearranged determination to convict her. A jury trial was dangerous and so the Constitution was deliberately and openly violated." Anthony was not even permitted to appeal.[46]

In general, the outcome of the election cleared the way for the Republican party to retreat from the radical implications of the postwar amendments. There is a link between the judicial dismissal of the feminists' New Departure and the larger repudiation of the postwar amendments. It is embodied in the fact that the Supreme Court's opinions on *Bradwell* and on the *Slaughterhouse* cases were delivered on the same day in 1873. *Slaughterhouse* is generally considered the fundamental Fourteenth Amendment Supreme Court decision. The case involved a group of Louisiana butchers who challenged a state law regulating their occupation on the grounds that it violated their rights as federal citizens (to practice their vocation—the same issue as *Bradwell*) and that the Fourteenth Amendment established the supremacy of national over state citizenship.[47]

Six months after the election, the Court delivered negative opinions in both cases, interpreting the Fourteenth Amendment very narrowly and finding it inapplicable in both cases. The case that the Court lingered over was *Slaughterhouse*.[48] By a bare majority, it ruled that the amendment's intent was only to ensure "the freedom of the slave race" and that it did not transfer the jurisdiction over fundamental civil rights from state to federal government. The opinion in *Bradwell* covered much less territory but did so by a larger majority. The Court merely rejected the claim that the right to practice law was one of the privileges and immunities of federal citizenship protected by the amendment. Beyond that, the Court simply commented that "the opinion just delivered in the Slaughterhouse Cases . . . renders elaborate argument in the present case unnecessary."[49] We should not be misled by this preemptory dismissal, however. The very interpretation under which the *Slaughterhouse* cases had been decided, that the Fourteenth Amendment was limited to matters of race and did not elevate national over state citizenship, had first been articulated in 1871 in the Majority Report of the House Judiciary Committee, rejecting Victoria Woodhull's claim that the Fourteenth Amendment guaranteed her right to vote.

The Supreme Court ruled conclusively against the New Departure two years later, in 1875. The case in which it did so was *Minor v. Happersett*, brought, appropriately enough, by Virginia Minor, the woman who had first argued that as a citizen of the United States, she was constitutionally protected in her right to vote. Like Anthony, Minor had tried to vote in the 1872 election, but when her vote was refused, she brought suit under the Enforcement Act. The Missouri courts ruled against her, and she appealed to the U.S. Supreme Court on the grounds that constitutional protections of the citizen's right to vote invalidated any state regulations to the contrary. The Court ruled unanimously against her. Since the *Slaughterhouse* and *Bradwell* cases had disposed of the first element of the New Departure, that the Fourteenth Amendment established the supremacy of national citizenship, the decision in Minor concentrated on the second assertion, that suffrage was a right of citizenship. On this, the Court ruled starkly that "the Constitution of the United States does not confer the right of suffrage upon any one."[50]

Here, too, there was an intimate link between the fate of woman suffragists' constitutional claims and that of the Reconstruction amendments in general. The day after the Court delivered its opinion in *Minor*, it heard arguments in *United States v. Cruikshank*. In this case and in *United States v. Reese*, black men for the first time brought suit under the Enforcement Act for protection of their political rights under the Fourteenth and Fifteenth Amendments, and the Court ruled against them. In the process of ruling against the plaintiffs, the Court found the Enforcement Act, under which both feminists and freedmen had sought protection, unconstitutional. Citing the recent decision in *Minor*, the Court ruled that inasmuch as the Constitution did not bestow the suffrage on anyone, the federal courts were outside their jurisdiction in protecting the freedmen's political rights.

The rejection of woman suffrage arguments on the grounds that the Fifteenth Amendment was only intended to forbid disfranchisement by race paved the way for a reading of the Fifteenth Amendment that was so narrow it did not even protect the freedmen themselves. In its decision in *United States v. Reese*, the Court argued that the plaintiff, although a black man, had not proved that his vote was denied on the grounds of race and so was not covered by constitutional protections. Eventually, of course, the freedmen were effectively disfranchised on grounds of income, residence, and education, all surrogates for race. Anthony had anticipated this connection. At her own trial, she predicted that the general narrowing of the Reconstruction amendments would follow on the heels of the repudiation of women's claims of equal rights under them. "If we once establish the false principle, that United States citizenship does not carry with it the right to vote in every state in this Union," she said, "there is no end to the petty freaks and cunning devices that will be resorted to to exclude one and another class of citizens from the right of suffrage."[51]

Three years after the *Minor* defeat, suffragists began their pursuit of a separate constitutional amendment to prohibit disfranchisement on account of sex. At many levels, this was a less radical strategy. With the defeat of the New Departure, winning the vote for women was no longer tied to an overall democratic interpretation of the Constitution. To the degree that the struggle for women's votes was not strategically linked to the general defense of political democracy, that its goal was "woman suffrage" not "universal suffrage," elitist and racist tendencies faced fewer barriers, had freer reign, and imparted a more conservative character to suffragism over the next half-century.

Yet, despite this very important strategic shift, the New Departure period left a deep mark on the history of feminism. From time to time, some suffragist would see possibilities in the existing propositions of the Constitution and propose some clever legal mechanism for exploiting them.[52] Even direct action voting never completely died away. Twenty years after the *Minor* decision, Elizabeth Grannis of New York City made her eighth attempt to register to vote.[53] Certainly the larger spirit of militant direct action resurfaced in a spectacular way in the last decade of the American suffrage movement. The deepest mark of the New Departure, however, was to make women's rights and political equality indelibly constitutional issues. As Susan B. Anthony wrote, she "had learned . . . through the passage of the Fourteenth and Fifteenth Amendments that it had been possible to amend [the Constitution] in such a way as to enfranchise an entire new class of voters."[54] The *Minor* case, the historian Norma Basch has observed, "drew the inferiority of women's status out of the grooves of common law assumptions and state provisions and thrust it into the maelstrom of constitutional conflict. The demand for woman suffrage . . . acquired a contentious national life."[55]

NOTES

1. The literature generated by the contemporary feminist debate on equality versus difference is enormous. Two excellent analyses by historians are Linda Gordon, "On Difference," *Genders* 10 (Spring 1991): 91–111; and Joan Scott, "Deconstructing Equality-versus-Difference; or the Uses of Poststructuralist Theory for Feminism," *Feminist Studies* 14 (Spring 1988): 33–50. Jean Bethke Elshtain criticizes the appropriateness of "androgynous" concepts for feminist analysis; see, for instance, "Against Androgyny," *Telos* 47 (1981): 5–21. In a re-

cent article, Lise Vogel explores the implications of this debate for feminist legal scholarship: "Debating Difference: Feminism, Pregnancy, and the Workplace," *Feminist Studies* 16 (Spring 1990): 9–32.

2. For a sampling of critical legal studies scholarship on the limitations of rights thinking, see Mark Tushnet, "An Essay on Rights," *Texas Law Review* 62 (May 1984): 1386, and Peter Gabel, "The Phenomenology of Rights Consciousness and the Pact of Withdrawn Selves," ibid., 1563–99. Frances Olsen develops the implications of this perspective for feminism; see "Statutory Rape: A Feminist Critique of Rights Analysis," *Texas Law Review* 63 (October 1984): 387–42. From the perspective of a woman of color, Patricia Williams criticizes this dismissal of rights consciousness; see "Alchemical Notes: Reconstructed Ideals from Deconstructed Rights," *Harvard Civil Rights Civil Liberties Law Review* 22 (Spring 1987): 401–33. From the perspective of political philosophy, Nancy Fraser considers the translation of "needs claims" into "rights claims"; see "Struggle Over Needs: Outline of a Socialist-Feminist Critical Theory of Late-Capitalist Political Culture," in *Women, the State, and Welfare*, ed. Linda Gordon (Madison: University of Wisconsin Press, 1990), 199–225.

3. Paula Baker made this argument most forcefully for the pre-1920 period; see "The Domestication of Politics: Women and American Political Society, 1780–1920," *American Historical Review* 89 (June 1984): 620–47. The implications of her argument for the existence of a separate women's political culture after 1920 are ambiguous. Susan Ware, in her biography of Molly Dewson (*Partner and I: Molly Dewson, Feminism, and New Deal Politics* [New Haven, Conn.: Yale University Press, 1987]), adapts Baker's argument to the post-1920 era. For a complex and interesting overview of the historical literature on woman's sphere and women's political involvement, see Lori Ginzberg, "Introduction," in *Women and the Work of Benevolence* (New Haven, Conn.: Yale University Press, 1990). In her focus on the continuing importance of women's voluntary organizations in the post-suffrage period, Anne Firor Scott is inclined to accept the importance of a distinct women's political culture after, as well as before, the Nineteenth Amendment; see her *Natural Allies: Women's Associations in American History* (Urbana: University of Illinois Press, 1991).

4. Ellen Carol DuBois, *Feminism and Suffrage: The Emergence of an Independent Women's Movement in America, 1848–1869* (Ithaca, N.Y.: Cornell University Press, 1978); Elizabeth Cady Stanton, *Eighty Years and More: Reminiscences, 1815–1897*, ed. Ellen Carol DuBois (Boston: Northeastern University Press, 1993 [1898]), 242. In the context of women's history, emphasizing the opposition of woman suffrage leaders to the Fourteenth and Fifteenth Amendments has highlighted the collapse of the prewar abolitionist unity of women's

rights and black rights and the rise of a new racism in the woman suffrage movement.

5. The constitutional issues raised by the New Departure became, like virtually every other political issue, an element in the American/National split. To distinguish itself from the National Association and the New Departure constitutional strategy it advocated, the American Association advocated a separate woman suffrage constitutional amendment throughout the early 1870s. Ironically, this proposal for what would have then been a Sixteenth Amendment had first been made by Elizabeth Stanton in 1869 as a protest against the "manhood suffrage" of the Fifteenth Amendment, then still pending. But just as the original National proposal for a woman suffrage amendment was primarily a protest against the black suffrage amendment rather than a strategy in its own right, so the American's advocacy of it was primarily a protest against the New Departure approach. Full-fledged advocacy of a separate woman suffrage amendment did not begin until the late 1870s, when it became the trademark demand of the National. The American, again seeking to distinguish itself from its rival, focused its energies on state suffrage campaigns. See Elizabeth C. Stanton, Susan B. Anthony, and Matilda J. Gage, eds., *History of Woman Suffrage*, vol. 2 (Rochester, N.Y.: Susan B. Anthony, 1881), 350–55, 802–17 (hereafter cited as HWS).

6. Stanton, *Eighty Years and More*, 242.

7. HWS, vol. 2, 407–520; Ida Husted Harper, ed., *Life and Work of Susan B. Anthony*, vol. 1 (Indianapolis: Bowen-Merrill, 1898), 409–48.

8. HWS, vol. 2, 407–10; on the Minors, see Louise R. Noun, *Strong Minded Women: The Emergence of the Woman Suffrage Movement in Iowa* (Ames: Iowa State University Press, 1969), 168–69.

9. David Montgomery notes the importance of this Reconstruction Era shift in attitude to the positive state in *Beyond Equality: Labor and the Radical Republicans, 1862–1872* (New York: Random House, 1967), 80–81.

10. On this aspect of Reconstruction Era constitutional thought, see Judith A. Baer, *Equality under the Constitution: Reclaiming the Fourteenth Amendment* (Ithaca, N.Y.: Cornell University Press, 1983).

11. While the Fifteenth Amendment was still pending, the Minors found an alternative constitutional basis for their claim that suffrage was a natural right, in the frequently cited 1820 case *Corfield v. Coryell*, which included the franchise as one of the privileges and immunities protected in Article IV.

12. In New Hampshire in 1870, Matilda Ricker tried to vote (HWS, vol. 2, 586–87). In New York in 1871, Matilda Joslyn Gage tried to vote in Fayetteville, and a group of women, led by Louise Mansfield, tried to vote in Nyack

(HWS, vol. 3, 406; Isabelle K. Savelle, *Ladies' Lib: How Rockland Women Got the Vote* [New York: Rockland Historical Society, 1979], 13–16); in New York City, Victoria Woodhull and Tennessee Claflin tried to vote (Johanna Johnston, *Mrs. Satan* [New York: Popular Library, 1967], 110). In Connecticut, Anna Middlebrook and nineteen others tried to vote in Bridgeport, and Louise Mateen led a group in Hadlyone (*Woodhull and Claflin's Weekly*, April 22, 1871, 5). In Hyde Park, Illinois, also in 1871, Catherine Waite, wife of an important Republican politician, tried to vote (HWS, vol. 2, 601, and vol. 3, 571–72); and in California, her sister-in-law, Mrs. Van Valkenburg, tried in the same year (HWS, vol. 3, 766).

13. HWS, vol. 3, 461–62; see also HWS, vol. 2, 600–601.

14. Eleanor Flexner, *Century of Struggle: The Woman's Rights Movement in the United States* (Cambridge, Mass.: Belknap Press, 1959), 168, citing *The Revolution*, November 19, 1868, 307. On the links between spiritualism and women's rights, see Anne Braude, *Radical Spirits: Spiritualism and Women's Rights in Nineteenth Century America* (Boston: Beacon, 1991).

15. HWS, vol. 3, 780–86.

16. Ibid., 784.

17. Benjamin Quarles, "Frederick Douglass and the Woman's Rights Movement," *Journal of Negro History* 25 (June 1940): 35.

18. HWS, vol. 3, 523–24.

19. Ibid., 766.

20. Ibid., vol. 2, 443–48.

21. "The Constitution defines a woman born or naturalized in the United States, and subject to the jurisdiction thereof, to be a citizen. It recognizes the right of citizens to vote." Ibid., 445.

22. Victoria C. Woodhull, *Constitutional Equality: A Lecture Delivered at Lincoln Hall, Washington, D.C., February 16, 1871* (New York: Journeymen Printers Co-operative Association, 1871).

23. HWS, vol. 2, 445–46. The comment on "blending" was made in Woodhull's arguments in support of her congressional memorial. These are available in Victoria Woodhull, *The Argument for Woman's Electoral Rights under Amendments XIV and XV of the Constitution of the United States* (London: G. Norman and Son, 1887), 44.

24. Both reports can be found in HWS, vol. 2, 461–82.

25. Ibid., 469, 478. In support of their interpretation, they cited the federal district court's decision in what was called the *Crescent City* case, later renamed the *Slaughterhouse* cases.

26. Woodhull, *Constitutional Equality*, 4.

27. Martha Wright complained to Elizabeth Stanton about a congressman who "said rudely to Mrs. Davis & Mrs. Griffing, 'You just call on us because you like to,'" to which Mrs. Griffing answered, "'We call on you, because it is the only way known to us, to present our appeal to you,' & Mrs. Davis said 'You must remember that we are your constituents.'" Wright to Stanton, December 29, 1870, Garrison Family Collection, Smith College, Northampton, Mass.

28. HWS, vol. 2, 489.

29. Isabella Beecher Hooker to the Editor, *Independent*, February 11, 1871, reprinted in *Woodhull and Claflin's Weekly*, March 4, 1871, 10.

30. Ibid.; *An Appeal to the Women of the United States by the National Woman Suffrage and Educational Committee* (Hartford, Conn.: National Woman Suffrage Association, April 19, 1871).

31. Woodhull's response to the charges can be found in the *New York World*, May 22, 1871, 3. A close study of "free love" attacks on Frances Wright in the 1820s would probably show a similar pattern.

32. "The Voice of Apollo Hall," *Every Saturday*, June 17, 1871, 554.

33. Victoria C. Woodhull, *The Principles of Social Freedom, Delivered in New York City, November 20, 1871* (New York: Woodhull, Claflin and Company, 1871), 23–24.

34. Isabella Beecher Hooker to Anna E. Dickenson, April 22, [1871], box 9, Dickenson Papers, Library of Congress, Washington, D.C.

35. Paulina Wright Davis to Woodhull, May 29, 1871, Victoria Woodhull Martin Collection, Southern Illinois University, Carbondale.

36. Victoria C. Woodhull, "The Speech of Victoria C. Woodhull before the National Woman's Suffrage Convention at Apollo Hall, May 11, 1871," reprinted in Woodhull, *The Argument for Woman's Electoral Rights*, 137.

37. HWS, vol. 2, 587–99. Spencer's lawyer was Arthur Riddle, former congressman from Ohio and one of Woodhull's advisers. Riddle emphasized the relationship between the Fourteenth and Fifteenth Amendments. The Fifteenth Amendment, he contended, was only important inasmuch as it invalidated what he called "the mischief" of the second section of the Fourteenth. Inasmuch as the right to vote is assumed to exist by the Fifteenth Amendment, it was actually conferred by the first section of the Fourteenth.

38. Ibid., 598.

39. Ibid., 622. The opinion in *Bradwell* that is usually cited is not the terse dismissal of the Fourteenth Amendment argument that settled the case but an individual concurring opinion by Justice Bradley that addressed the coverture issues that Bradwell had removed from her argument.

40. HWS, vol. 2, 618.

41. Elizabeth Cady Stanton, "Argument before the Senate Judiciary Committee," January 11, 1872, reprinted in *Woodhull and Claflin's Weekly*, January 27, 1872, 7; see also Stanton to Woodhull, December 29, [1872], Stanton Miscellaneous Papers, New York Public Library, New York.

42. Woodhull anticipated that if a narrow construction of the Fifteenth Amendment was adopted, if the southern states were only forbidden to disfranchise the freedmen "because they belonged to the African race, they might have invented any other reason and excluded them in spite of Congress. If this doctrine prevail, I do not see why the States may not . . . find reasons to exclude every negro in them from the ballot." Victoria Woodhull, *Carpenter and Cartter Reviewed: A Speech before the National Suffrage Association at Lincoln Hall, Washington, D.C., January 10, 1872* (New York: Woodhull, Claflin and Company, 1872), 20.

43. Montgomery, *Beyond Equality*, 379–86.

44. "We must make it hot for the Cincinnatians for their neglect to recognize us." Anthony to Stanton, July 10, 1872, box 38, National American Woman Suffrage Association Papers, Library of Congress.

45. Nancy A. Hewitt, *Women's Activism and Social Change: Rochester, New York, 1822–1872* (Ithaca, N.Y.: Cornell University Press, 1984), 211. Anthony to Stanton, November 5, 1872, Harper Papers, Huntington Library, San Marino, Calif.: "Well I have been & gone & done it!! positively voted the republican ticket strait this A.M. at 7 o'clock & *swore my vote in at that.* Was registered on Friday & 15 other women followed suit in this ward. Then on Sunday others some 20 or thirty other women *tried to register*, but all save two were refused. All my three sisters voted. Rhoda De Garmo too. Amy Post was rejected & she will immediately bring action against the registrars. . . . I hope the morning's telegrams will tell of many women all over the country trying to vote. It is splendid that without any concert of action so many should have moved here. . . . If only *now all the woman suffrage women* would work to this end, of *enforcing the existing constitutional* supremacy of *national law* over state law, what strides we might make this very winter. But I'm awful tired—for five days I have been on the constant run, but to splendid purpose, so all right. I hope you voted too."

46. Harper, ed., *The Life and Work of Susan B. Anthony*, vol. 1, 423–53. The case was heard before Judge Ward Hunt, appointed to the Supreme Court in December 1872 at the suggestion of Roscoe Conkling. Charles Fairman, *History of the Supreme Court*, vol. 7 (New York: Macmillan, 1987), 224. Hunt voted with the majority in the *Slaughterhouse* cases. Anthony was sure that Conkling

was responsible for his decision against her. Harper, ed., *The Life and Work of Susan B. Anthony*, vol. 1, 441.

47. Moreover, Matthew Carpenter, who had been Myra Bradwell's counsel, was counsel for the *defendants* in the *Slaughterhouse* cases. On the surface, this appears inconsistent: Carpenter argued for the applicability of the Fourteenth Amendment in *Bradwell*, but he argued against it in *Slaughterhouse*. I think there is a consistency in his position, though, especially when we remember how much of his argument in *Bradwell* was against the inclusion of the suffrage in the "privileges and immunities" of the Fourteenth Amendment; the consistency resides in Carpenter's determination, on behalf of the Republican leadership, to control and limit the breadth of the Fourteenth Amendment. Fairman, *History of the Supreme Court*, vol. 7, 285. Carpenter's argument in *Slaughterhouse* can be found in 21 Court Reporters Lawyers Edition, 399–401 (1872).

48. 16 Wall. 36 (1873). The language of the *Slaughterhouse* opinion frequently identifies races with men; for instance, since "the laws were administered by the white man alone . . . a race of men distinctively marked as was the negro" could not expect justice. I presume such language was not accidental but reflected the coexistence of arguments that women were persons also, or, as Victoria Woodhull had said, that "races contain both men and women."

49. 16 Wall. 130 (1873).

50. HWS, vol. 2, 734–42.

51. Ibid., 641.

52. The most important of these was Catherine McCullough's successful argument that the Constitution permitted states legislatively to enfranchise voters for presidential electors. This argument for "presidential suffrage" seems to have begun with Henry Blackwell in the 1890s. In 1914 Illinois passed a "presidential suffrage" law, giving women votes in the 1916 presidential election. See Steven W. Buechler, *The Transformation of the Woman Suffrage Movement: The Case of Illinois, 1850–1920* (New Brunswick, N.J.: Rutgers University Press, 1986), 174–76.

53. Unidentified clipping, vol. 12, p. 75, Susan B. Anthony Memorial Library Collection, Huntington Library, San Marino, Calif.

54. HWS, vol. 4, 10.

55. Norma Basch, "Reconstructing Female Citizenship" (paper delivered at Women and the Constitution Conference, American University and the Smithsonian, October 1987).

8

Seeking Ecstasy on the Battlefield

Danger and Pleasure in Nineteenth-Century
Feminist Sexual Thought

with Linda Gordon

It is often alleged that female sexuality is a more complex matter than men's, and, if so, a major reason is that sex spells potential danger as well as pleasure for women. A feminist politics about sex, therefore, if it is to be credible as well as hopeful, must seek both to protect women from sexual danger and to encourage their pursuit of sexual pleasure.

This complex understanding of female sexuality has not always characterized the feminist movement. In general feminists inherit two conflicting traditions in their approach to sex. The strongest tradition, virtually unchallenged in the mainstream women's rights movement of the nineteenth century, addressed primarily the dangers and few of the possibilities of sex. Another perspective, much less developed despite some eloquent spokeswomen by the early twentieth century, encouraged women to leap, adventurous and carefree, into sexual liaisons, but it failed to offer a critique of the male construction of the sexual experience available to most women. It is no use to label one side feminist and the other antifeminist, to argue by name-calling. We cannot move ahead unless we grasp that both traditions are part of our feminism.

Neither feminist tradition is adequate to our needs today. Both were thoroughly heterosexist in their assumptions of what sex is. Even the

Originally published in *Feminist Studies* 9 (1983).

nineteenth-century women who experienced intense emotional and physical relationships with each other did not incorporate these into their definition of what was sexual.[1] Certainly women had relationships with other women that included powerful sexual components, but the feminists who are the subject of this paper did not theorize these relationships as sexual. Furthermore, both feminist lines of thought—that emphasizing danger and that emphasizing pleasure—were often moralistic. They condemned those whose sexual behavior deviated from their standards, not only sexually exploitive men but also women who did not conform.

Still, without an appreciation of these legacies and the processes of thought and experience that produced them, we cannot have much historical insight into our own concerns. Without a history, political movements like ours swing back and forth endlessly, reacting to earlier mistakes and overreacting in compensation, unable to incorporate previous insights and transcend previous limitations. Today we observe some of that pendulum-like motion. In reaction to the profound disappointments of what has passed for "sexual liberation," some feminists are replicating an earlier tradition, focusing exclusively on danger and advocating what we believe to be a conservative sexual politics.

We use a label like "conservative" cautiously. Such terms, like "left" and "right," come to us from class politics. When applied to sex and gender, they fit less comfortably. The oppressions of women, the repressions of sex, are so many and so complex, by virtue of their location in the most intimate corners of life, coexisting even with love, that it is not always obvious in which direction a better world lies. We use the term "conservatism" to characterize strategies that accept existing power relations. We are suggesting that even feminist reform programs can be conservative in some respects if they accept male dominance while trying to elevate women's "status" within it. In this case, we believe that the nineteenth-century feminist mainstream accepted women's sexual powerlessness with men as inevitable, even as it sought to protect women from its worst consequences. Its appraisal of women's sexual victimization was not, on balance, offset by recognition of women's potential for sexual activity and enjoyment. We think our judgment will be justified by the historical description which follows. Through that description we hope to

show, too, that despite the stubborn continuities of women's sexual oppression, there have also been momentous changes in the last 150 years,
changes that require different strategies today.

The feminist movement has played an important role in organizing
and even creating women's sense of sexual danger in the last 150 years.
In that movement, two themes more than others have encapsulated and
symbolized women's fears: prostitution and rape. There is a certain parallel construction between the nineteenth-century focus on prostitution
and the modern emphasis on rape as the quintessential sexual terror. It
is remarkable, in fact, how little emphasis nineteenth-century feminists
placed on rape per se. It is as if the norms of legal sexual intercourse were
in themselves so objectionable that rape did not seem that much worse!
Instead feminists used prostitution as the leading symbol of male sexual
coercion. While rape is an episode, prostitution suggests a condition that
takes hold of a woman for a long time—possibly for life—difficult to escape. The symbolic emphasis in prostitution is on ownership, possession, purchase by men, while in rape it is on pure violence. Rape can
happen to any woman, while prostitution involves the separation of
women into the good and the bad, a division with class implications, as
we shall see, even when the division is blamed on men.

Lest it seem trivializing to the real sufferings of women as prostitutes
or rape victims to treat experiences as symbols or metaphors, let us emphasize again our subject: we are looking at how feminists conceptualized different sexual dangers, as a means of organizing *resistance* to sexual oppression. We want to look at how these feminist strategies
changed, so that we can examine historically how we conduct feminist
campaigns around sexual issues today.

In different periods, feminists emphasized different aspects of prostitution. In the 1860s and 1870s, for example, they focused on the economic pressures forcing women into sexual commerce, while in the Progressive Era their primary theme was "white slavery," the physical coercion of women into the trade. Despite these shifts, however, aspects of
their approach to prostitution were consistent. First, they exaggerated its
magnitude.[2] They did so because their definition of prostitute included
virtually all women who engaged in casual sex, whether or not they were
paid. Second, feminists consistently exaggerated the coerciveness of

prostitution. In their eagerness to identify the social structural forces encouraging prostitution, they denied the prostitute any role other than that of passive victim. They insisted that the women involved were sexual innocents, helpless young women who "fell" into illicit sex. They assumed that prostitution was so degrading that no woman could freely choose it, not even with the relative degree of freedom with which she could choose to be a wife or a wage earner. Thus the "fallen woman" was always viewed as a direct victim, not only of male dominance in general, but of kidnapping, sexual imprisonment, starvation, and/or seduction in particular.[3] These attitudes toward prostitution were not exclusive to feminists, but were also part of the ideological outlook of many male reformers, including some antifeminists. Our point here, however, is that feminists not only failed to challenge this oversimplified and condescending explanation of prostitution, but also made it central to their understanding of women's oppression.

The feminists' exclusive emphasis on the victimization of the prostitute ultimately prevented their transcending a sexual morality dividing women into the good and the bad.[4] They wanted to rescue women from prostitution, and to admit prostitution's victims into the salvation of good womanhood; but they clung fast to the idea that some kinds of sex were inherently criminal, and they were confounded by the existence of unrepentant whores. Furthermore, their equation of prostitution with any illicit sex indicates that a crucial element of their fear was loss of respectability. The power of prostitution rested on the common understanding that once a woman had sex outside of marriage she was "ruined," and would become a prostitute sooner or later. This potential loss of respectability was not imaginary, but a real, material process with sanctions that varied by culture and class. For middle-class and many white working-class women, the loss of purity—we would call it getting a bad reputation—damaged prospects for marriage. It led to a total loss of control over one's own sexuality, as once "used" by a man, women became free game for that entire sex.

Maintaining respectability was an especially severe problem for black women, fighting to free their entire race from a slave heritage that tended to place them at the disposal of white men's sexual demands. Thus the black women's movement conducted a particularly militant campaign for respectability, often making black feminists spokespeople for prudery in their communities.[5] White feminists assimilated the horror of black slavery to their fears of prostitution. They understood the sexual tyranny of slavery as central, and as a form of prostitution; among their most powerful antislavery writings were images of beautiful, pure black womanhood defiled; and white feminist abolitionists found it difficult to accept the possibility of willing sex between black women and white men.[6]

The fear of prostitution represented also a fear of direct physical violence, but in a displaced manner. In the nineteenth century, as today, women encountered sexual and nonsexual violence most often at home. Rape in marriage was no crime, not even generally disapproved; wifebeating was only marginally criminal. Incest was common enough to require skepticism about the idea that it was tabooed. Although feminists occasionally organized against domestic violence, they did not make it the object of a sustained campaign, largely because they were unable to challenge the family politically.[7] The focus on prostitution was a focus on extrafamilial violence. Nineteenth-century feminists came closer to intrafamily matters in the temperance campaign. Their criticisms of drinking were laced through with imagery of the bestial, violent quality of male sexuality, but blaming alcohol also allowed a displacement of focus, an avoidance of criticizing men and marriage directly.[8]

Certain dangers in marriage had to be faced. One was venereal disease, and this too was assimilated to the central imagery of prostitution, for men who patronized prostitutes could then transmit disease to their wives. In keeping with the division of women between good and bad, feminists implicitly considered prostitution as the source of venereal disease. The communicability and incurability of these diseases proved to them that absolute monogamy was women's only source of safety amid the sexual dangers.[9] (One is reminded of conservative response to herpes today.) Feminists also opposed the sexual demands of self-centered husbands on their wives, which law and convention obligated women to meet. But instead of protesting "marital rape," as we do, they criticized what they called "legalized prostitution" in marriage.[10]

Sex posed another serious danger in marriage—unwanted conception. Given the equation of sex with intercourse, and the lack of access to reliable contraception, desire to control conceptions often resulted in the antisexual attitudes of women.[11] Despite a great reverence for motherhood, an unexpected pregnancy was often threatening. For poor women, for virtually all black women, having children meant introducing them into social and economic circumstances where their safety and well-being could not be guaranteed. Even for prosperous women, mothers' economic dependence on men was extreme. Single motherhood was an extremely difficult situation in the absence of any regular welfare or childcare provisions. Mothers were frequently forced to remain with abusive men for fear of losing their children. Indeed, prostitution was sometimes seen as an option for a single mother, for at least she could do it while she remained at home with her children![12] A bitter irony surrounds the place of motherhood in the sexual system of nineteenth-century feminism: clearly it was women's greatest joy and source of dignity; for many women it was what made sexual intercourse acceptable. But at the same time motherhood was the last straw in enforcing women's subordination to men, the factor that finally prevented many from seeking independence. What was conceived as women's greatest virtue, their passionate and self-sacrificing commitment to their children, their capacity for love itself, was a leading factor in their victimization.

Of the many factors constructing the feminist fear of prostitution perhaps none is so hard for contemporary feminists to understand as religion. But we would miss the dilemma that these women faced in dealing with sex if we did not thoroughly appreciate their religious culture. Those actively rebelling against established religion were as influenced by it as the dutiful church members or Christian reform activists. All had been raised on the concept of sin, especially sexual sin. They all shared the view that there could be high and low pleasures, and the guilt they felt about indulging in the low was not just psychological self-doubt. It was a sense of self-violation, of violation of the source of their dignity.[13]

We are arguing here that the feminist understanding of sexual danger, expressed so poignantly in the fear of prostitution, must be seen as part of a sexual system in which they were participants, sometimes willing and sometimes unwilling, sometimes conscious and sometimes unaware.[14] Their very resistance often drew them into accommodation with aspects of this oppressive system. What is surprising is the extent of

resistance that actually challenged this sexual system. Some women labeled "loose," who might or might not have been prostitutes, rejected
the notion that their disreputable sexual behavior was something to be
ashamed of or something that had been forced upon them.[15] There were
young sexual "delinquents" who took pleasure and pride in their rebel-
lion.[16] There were women who passed as men in order to seize male sexual (and other) prerogatives, and to take other women as wives.[17] Even
respectable, middle-class married women had orgasms more than they
were supposed to. One survey had 40 percent of women reporting orgasms occasionally, 20 percent frequently, and 40 percent never, pro-
portions which may not be so different than those among women
today.[18] About the present, it is angering that so many women do not experience orgasm; about the past, it is impressive—and analytically important—that so many women did. In other words, our nineteenth-century legacy is one of resistance to sexual repression as well as victimization by it.

Despite resistance, the weight of the nineteenth-century feminist concern was with protection from danger. This approach, usually known as
"social purity," reflected an experienced reality and was overwhelmingly
protectionist in its emphasis.

The major target of the feminist social purity advocates was the double standard. Their attack on it had, in turn, two aspects: seeking greater
safety for women and more penalties for men. Their object was to
achieve a set of controls over sexuality, structured through the family, enforced through law and/or social morality, which would render sex, if
not safe, at least a decent, calculable risk for women. Social purity feminists railed against male sexual privileges, against the vileness of male
drunkenness and lust, and they sought with every means at their disposal
to increase the costs attached to such indulgences.[19]

The most positive achievements of social purity feminism were in the
homes and communities of the middle-class women most likely to be its
advocates. Here, efforts to make marriage laws more egalitarian, upgrade
women's property rights, and improve women's educational and professional opportunities altered the balance of power between wife and husband. Social purity thought emphasized the importance of consensual

sex for women, and insisted that even married women should not be coerced into any sexual activities they did not choose freely; inasmuch as
they believed that sexual drive and initiative were primarily male, they
understood this as women's right to say no. Through organizations like
the Woman's Christian Temperance Union, feminists propagandized for
these standards, with tirades against the threat to civilization caused by
immorality, and with energetic moral and sex education programs.[20]
And they succeeded in changing culture and consciousness. Without
knowing precisely how much peoples' lives conformed to this standard,
we can say that the ideal of marital mutuality and a woman's right to say
no were absorbed into middle-class culture by the turn of the century.
There is mounting evidence that, for reasons not yet clear, immigrant
and poor women did not establish the same standards of marital mutuality, but fought for power within their families differently, by accepting
certain patriarchal prerogatives while asserting their power as mothers
and housewives.[21] The negative consequences of social purity's single-
minded focus on sexual danger come into focus when we look at their
vigorous campaign against prostitution. Over time the repressive tendencies of this campaign overwhelmed its liberatory aspects and threw a
pall over feminism's whole approach to sexuality. The beginning of
women's reform work on prostitution in the early nineteenth century
was a big step forward in the development of feminism. That "respectable" women took the risk of reaching out, across a veritable gulf of
sexual sin, to women stigmatized as whores, was a declaration of female
collectivity that transcended class and moralistic divisions. The reformers visited and talked with prostitutes, conducted public discussion of
the issue, and established homes into which prostitutes could "escape."
In doing so they were opening a crack in the wall of sexual "innocence"
that would eventually widen into an escape route for women of their
class as well. The attitudes that we today perceive as a patronizing desire
to "help," were initially a challenge to the punitive and woman-hating
morality that made sexual "ruin" a permanent and irredeemable condition for women.[22]

   In the 1860s and 1870s feminists reactivated themselves into a militant and successful campaign to halt government regulation of prostitution. The system of regulation, already in existence in France and parts

of England, forced women alleged to be prostitutes to submit to vaginal examinations and licensing; its purpose was to allow men to have sex with prostitutes without the risk of venereal disease. Feminist opposition not only drew from their anger at men who bought female flesh, but also reaffirmed their identification with prostitutes' victimization. Feminists asserted that all women, even prostitutes, had a right to the integrity of their own bodies.[23]

But, after a relatively easy victory over government regulation, social purity feminists began to press for the abolition of prostitution itself. They sponsored legislation to increase the criminal penalties for men clients, while continuing to express sympathy with the "victimized" women. The catch was that the prostitutes had to agree that they were victims. The "white slavery" interpretation of prostitution—that prostitutes had been forced into the business—allowed feminists to see themselves as rescuers of slaves.[24] But if the prostitutes were not contrite, or denied the immorality of their actions, they lost their claim to the aid and sympathy of the reformers. "The big sisters of the world [want the] chance to protect the little and weaker sisters, by surrounding them with the right laws for them to obey for their own good," one feminist explained, unwittingly capturing the repressive character of this "sisterhood."[25] The class nature of American society encouraged these middle-class feminists to conduct their challenge to the double standard through other women's lives, and to focus their anger on men other than their own husbands and fathers.

Another attack on prostitution which sometimes turned into an attack on women was the campaign to raise the age of sexual consent.[26] In many states in the nineteenth century this had been as low as nine or ten years for girls. The feminist goals were to deny the white slavers their younger victims, to extend sexual protection to girls, and to provide punishments for male assailants. Like most of these feminist sexual causes, this one had in it a radical moment: it communicated an accurate critique of the limitations of "consent" by women in a male-dominated society. Yet, by late in the century, when urban life and the presence of millions of young working girls changed the shape of family and generational relations, age-of-consent legislation explicitly denied women the right to heterosexual activity until they were adults, or—and note that this qualification applied at any age—married. In fostering this hostility to girls' sexual activity, the feminists colluded in the labeling of a new class of female offenders: teenage sex delinquents. Sex delinquency was soon the largest category within which young women were sent to reformatories.[27] These moralistic reformers, some of them feminists, allowed the criminal justice system to take over the task of disciplining teenage girls to conform to respectable morality.

This inability to see anything in prostitution but male tyranny and/or economic oppression affected not only "bad" women, but the "good" ones as well. Feminists' refusal to engage in a concrete examination of the actuality of prostitution was of a piece with their inability to look without panic at any form of sexual nonconformity. We do not suggest that prostitutes were necessarily freer than other women sexually. Our point is that feminists remained committed to the containment of female sexuality within heterosexual marriage, despite the relative sexual repressiveness that marriage meant for women at that time.[28] "Are our girls to be [as] free to please themselves by indulging in the loveless gratification of every instinct . . . and passion as our boys?" the social purity feminist Frances Willard asked her audience in 1891; and we can imagine that they answered with a resounding "No!"[29]

Feminist politics about sex became more conservative in the period up to World War I because women's aspirations and possibilities outstripped the feminist orthodoxy. Growing feminist organizational strength, and the ability to influence legislation, combined with the class and racial elitism of the world in which the feminists moved, further strengthened their conservative political tendencies. Social purity feminists not only accepted a confining sexual morality for women, but they also excluded from their sisterhood women who did not or could not go along. The prostitute remained, for all their sympathy for her, the leading symbol of the woman excluded, not only from male-bestowed privilege, but also from the women's community.[30]

Yet, just as there was behavioral resistance to the sexually repressive culture of the nineteenth century, so too there was political resistance within the women's movement. Although a decidedly minority viewpoint, a thin but continuous stream of feminists insisted that increased sexual activity was not incompatible with women's dignity and might even be in women's interests. We refer to this as the "pro-sex" tendency within the feminist tradition. It began with the free love and utopian movements of the 1820s through the 1840s. These radicals challenged the identification of sexual desire as masculine; and even though they remained for the most part advocates of the strictest monogamy, they challenged the coercive family and legal marriage as the channels for sexuality.[31] In the 1870s the free lover Victoria Woodhull appeared as a spokesperson from within the women's movement, idealizing as "true love" sex that involved mutual desire and orgasms for both parties.[32] At the same time Elizabeth Cady Stanton, a revered, if maverick, heroine, also asserted the existence of women's sexual desires.[33] In the 1880s and 1890s a few extremely visionary free love feminists began to formulate the outlines of a sexuality not organized around the male orgasm. Alice Stockham, a physician and suffragist, condemned the "ordinary, hasty and spasmodic mode of cohabitation . . . in which the wife is a passive party" and envisioned instead a union in which "the desires and pleasure of the wife calls forth the desire and pleasure of the husband."[34] Still, on the whole, these nineteenth-century feminists were only relatively "prosex," and most of them shared with social purity advocates a belief in the need to control, contain, and harness physiological sex expression to "higher" ends. Furthermore, even this limited sex-radical tradition was so marginal to American feminism that when the twentieth-century feminist Margaret Sanger searched for a more positive attitude to sex, she had to go to Europe to find it.

The only issue within mainstream nineteenth-century feminism where "pro-sex" ideas had a significant impact was divorce. Led by Cady Stanton, some feminists argued that the right to divorce and *then to remarry*—for that was the crucial element, the right to another sexual relationship after leaving a first—was a freedom important enough to women to risk granting it to men as well. Still, most feminists took a strict social purity line and opposed divorce for fear it would weaken marriage and expose women to even greater sexual danger.[35]

Ironically, one sexual reform strongly supported by social purity advocates became the vehicle by which a new generation of feminists began to break with the social purity tradition. This was birth control.[36] Nineteenth-century feminists had argued this as "voluntary motherhood," the right of women to refuse intercourse with their husbands if they did not want to conceive. Voluntary motherhood was a brilliant tactic because it insinuated a rejection of men's sexual domination into a politics of defending and improving motherhood. Consistent with its social purity orientation, voluntary motherhood advocates rejected contraception as a form of birth control for fear it would allow men to force even more sex upon their wives and to indulge in extramarital sex with even greater impunity. In the early twentieth century, by contrast, an insurgent feminist support for contraception arose, insisting that sexual abstinence was an unnecessary price for women to pay for reproductive self-determination, and that sexual indulgence in the pursuit of pleasure was good for women.

That this new generation of feminists could break with social purity was possible in part because they were no longer controlled by their fear of becoming, or being labeled, prostitutes. They no longer saw the prostitute as only a victim; they began to break the association between sexual desire and prostitution. Indeed they embraced and romanticized sexual daring of all sorts.[37] The specter of the white slaver no longer haunted them, and they were willing to take risks. They ventured unchaperoned into theaters and bars, lived without families in big cities, and moved about the city to discover the lives of those across class and race boundaries where their mothers would not have gone. Some of their names you recognize—Emma Goldman, Margaret Sanger, Crystal Eastman, Elizabeth Gurley Flynn, even Louise Bryant—but there were many more. Above all, they asserted a woman's right to be sexual. They slept with men without marrying. They took multiple lovers. They became single mothers. Some of them had explicitly sexual relationships with other women, although a subsequent repression of evidence, along with their own silences about homosexuality, make it hard for us to uncover this aspect of their sexual lives.[38]

In many ways these women were beginning to explore a sexual world which we are determined to occupy. But as pioneers they could explore only part of it, and they did not imagine changing its overall boundaries. Even when it contradicted their own experience, they continued to accept a male and heterosexual definition of the "sex act." They were, so to speak, upwardly mobile, and they wanted integration into the sexual world as defined by men. The man's orgasm remained the central event, although now it was preferable if a woman had one at the same time; stimulation other than intercourse was considered foreplay; masturbation was unhealthy. And sex, all the more desirable now because of the transcendent possibilities they attributed to it, remained bound up with the structure of gender: it could only happen between a man and a woman.[39] These feminists criticized male dominance in the labor force and in the public arena, but they did not seem to notice how it shaped sex. They fought for women's freedom, but they rarely criticized men.

Once the organized women's rights movement began to fade, women who advocated this "pro-sex" politics were more and more alienated from a larger community of women; they seemed to feel that to enter the world of sex, they had to travel alone and leave other women behind. This rejection of women occurred both because the dominant tradition of feminism was so antisexual, and because their own understanding of sex was so heterosexual. They were part of a generation that branded intense female friendships as adolescent.[40] The tragedy was that in rejecting a community of women which they experienced as constricting and repressive, they left behind their feminist heritage.

At the same time these pioneering sex radicals offer us a positive legacy in their willingness to take risks. It would be easier if we could progress toward sexual liberation without sufferings, if we could resolve the tension between seeking pleasure and avoiding danger by some simple policy; but we cannot. We must conduct our sexual politics in the real world. For women, this is like advancing across a mined field. Looking only to your feet to avoid the mines means missing the horizon, and the vision of why the advance is worthwhile; but if you see only the future possibilities, you may blow yourself up.

If this is warlike imagery, it is not bravado. The dangers are substantial, women are assaulted and killed. But each act of violence against women would be multiplied in its effect if it prevented us from seeing where we have won victories, and if it induced us to resign ourselves to restriction of our sexual lives and constriction of our public activities.

Seen in this light, the contemporary focus on rape and other sexual violence against women represents an advance over the earlier campaign against prostitution. Through this new conceptualization of the problem of sexual danger, feminists have rejected the victim blaming that was inherent in the notion of the "fallen woman"; we know that any of us can be raped. Our critique of sexual violence is an institutional analysis of the whole system of male supremacy which attempts to show the commonalities of women, as potential agents as well as victims. Thus the campaign against rape comes out of our strength as well as our victimization. Whether the actual incidence of rape has increased or decreased, the feminist offensive against it represents an escalation of our demands for freedom. We have redefined rape to include many sexual encounters that nineteenth-century feminists would have considered mere seduction, and for which they might have held the woman responsible; we have included in our definition of rape what was once normal marital intercourse. We have denied impunity to any man: we will bring charges against boyfriends, fathers, and teachers; we will label as sexual harassment what was once the ordinary banter of males asserting their dominance. We declare our right—still contested, viciously—to safety not only in our homes, but in the streets. We *all* intend to be streetwalkers.

It is vital to strategy building to know when we are winning and when losing, and where. Failing to claim and take pride in our victories leads to the false conclusion that nothing has changed. When the campaign against rape is fought as if we were the eternal, unchanged victims of male sexuality, we run the risk of reentering the kind of social purity world view that so limited the nineteenth-century feminist vision.[41] It is important to offer our comprehensive critique of misogyny, violence, and male dominance without ceding the arena of sexuality itself to the men, as the nineteenth-century feminists did.

We have tried to show that social purity politics, although an understandable reaction to women's nineteenth-century experience, was a limited and limiting vision for women. Thus we called it conservative. Today, there seems to be a revival of social purity politics within feminism, and it is concern about this tendency that motivates us in recalling its history. As in the nineteenth century, there is today a feminist attack on pornography and sexual "perversion" in our time, which fails to distinguish its politics from a conservative and antifeminist version of social purity, the Moral Majority and "family protection movement." The increasing tendency to focus almost exclusively on sex as the primary arena of women's exploitation, and to attribute women's sexual victimization to some violent essence labeled "male sexuality," is even more conservative today, because our situation as women has changed so radically. Modern social purists point to one set of changes. The rise of sexual consumerism, and the growing power of the mass media to enforce conformity to sexual norms, are debilitating for women's sexual freedom. As feminists, we are learning to be suspicious of a sexual politics that simply calls for "doing your own thing," and to ask whether women's desires are represented in these visions of sexual "freedom." We must not make the same mistake as the early twentieth-century sexual libertarians who believed that ending sexual inhibition in itself could save women. Instead, we have to continue to analyze how male supremacy and other forms of domination shape what we think of as "free" sexuality.

But there have been liberating developments as well, that we can ill afford to ignore. Women have possibilities for sexual subjectivity and self-creation today that did not exist in the past. We have a vision of sexuality that is not exclusively heterosexual, nor tied to reproduction. We have a much better physiological understanding of sexual feeling, and a vision of ungendered parenting. We have several strong intellectual traditions for understanding the psychological and social formation of sexuality. Perhaps most important, we have today at least a chance at economic independence, the necessary material condition for women's sexual liberation. Finally, we have something women have never enjoyed before—a feminist past, a history of 150 years of feminist theory and praxis in the area of sexuality. This is a resource too precious to squander by not learning it, in all its complexity.

NOTES

1. These "homosocial" relationships are documented and analyzed in Lillian S. Faderman, *Surpassing the Love of Men: Romantic Friendship and Love between Women from the Renaissance to the Present* (New York: William Morrow & Co., 1981); Carroll Smith-Rosenberg, "The Female World of Love and Ritual: Relations between Women in Nineteenth-Century America," *Signs* 1 (Autumn 1975): 1–29; Blanche Wiesen Cook, "Female Support Networks and Political

Activism: Lillian Wald, Crystal Eastman, Emma Goldman," *Chrysalis* 3 (1977): 43–61.

We distinguish here between behavior recognized as sexual by its actors and behavior not so recognized, aware that some historians will not agree. Furthermore, we are also emphasizing the importance of conscious sexual thought, theorizing, and politicizing for the feminist effort to transform women's sexual experience. We do so aware that, in the past decade, in an exciting renaissance of feminist historical scholarship, women's history scholars have chosen to focus more on behavior and culture than on political ideology. In the history of American feminism, for reasons that are undoubtedly important to explore, the initial focus for explicitly sexual politics was on the relations between women and men. The history and chronology of feminist conceptualization of what we today call lesbianism is different and we do not address it here, but Carroll Smith-Rosenberg and Esther Newton do so in their paper "The Mythic Lesbian and the New Woman: Power, Sexuality and Legitimacy," delivered at the Fifth Berkshire Conference on the History of Women, June 1981, Poughkeepsie, New York.

2. For instance, in 1913, a suffrage newspaper estimated that there were 15,000 to 20,000 prostitutes in New York City, who serviced 150,000 to 225,000 male customers daily; this would work out to roughly 1 out of every 100 females in all five boroughs and 1 out of every 10 males. See *Women's Political World* (2 June 1913): 7. Using a more precise definition of prostitution, for example, women who supported themselves solely by commercial sex, a member of New York City's Vice Commission estimated less than one-half that number (Frederick Whitten to Mary Sumner Boyd, 17 March 1916, National American Woman Suffrage Association Collection, New York Public Library).

3. The historical literature on nineteenth-century and early twentieth-century reformers' views of prostitution is extensive. The best recent study is Judith R. Walkowitz, *Prostitution and Victorian Society: Women, Class, and the State* (Cambridge: Cambridge University Press, 1980); much less aware of issues concerning gender, see Mark Connelly, *Response to Prostitution in the Progressive Era* (Chapel Hill: University of North Carolina Press, 1980).

4. Marian S. Goldman, *Gold Diggers and Silver Miners: Prostitution and Social Life on the Comstock Lode* (Ann Arbor: University of Michigan Press, 1981), chap. 7. Also see Elizabeth Jameson, "Imperfect Unions: Class and Gender in Cripple Creek, 1894–1904," in *Class, Sex, and the Woman Worker*, ed. Milton Cantor and Bruce Laurie (Westport, Conn.: Greenwood, 1977).

5. *Black Women in White America: A Documentary History*, ed. Gerda Lerner

(New York: Pantheon, 1972), 150–72; Cynthia Neverdon-Morton, "The Black Woman's Struggle for Equality in the South, 1895–1925," in *The Afro-American Woman: Struggle and Images,* ed. Sharon Harley and Rosalyn Terborg-Penn (Port Washington: Kennikat, 1978), 55–56.

After attending the 1914 convention of the National Association of Colored Women, white feminist Zona Gale wrote of black women's effort to work "against the traffic in women (which I hope I shall never again call the 'white slave' traffic)." See *Life and Labor* "National Association of Colored Women's Biennial," 4 (September 1914): 264.

6. For examples of feminist abolitionists' focus on sexual abuse in their attacks on slavery, see Lydia Maria Child, "Appeal in Favor of That Class of Americans Called Africans," in *America Through Women's Eyes,* ed. Mary R. Beard (New York: Macmillan, 1933), 164; and Elizabeth Cady Stanton, "Speech to the [1860] Anniversary of the American Anti-Slavery Society," in *Elizabeth Cady Stanton, Susan B. Anthony: Correspondence, Writings, Speeches,* ed. Ellen C. DuBois (New York: Schocken, 1981), 84.

The reluctance of white feminist abolitionists to acknowledge the possibility of affection and/or voluntary sex between black women and white men can be seen in the initial response of Angelina and Sarah Grimké to the discovery that their brother had fathered a child by a slave woman. They assumed that Thomas Grimké had raped the woman, but their nephew Archibald, who had been raised as a slave, objected that this was untrue and cast his parents and the circumstances of his birth in a sordid light.

7. Linda Gordon, *Woman's Body, Woman's Right: A Social History of Birth Control in America* (New York: Viking, 1976), chaps. 5 and 6; William L. O'Neill, *Everyone Was Brave: A History of Feminism in America* (Chicago: Quadrangle, 1971).

8. Barbara Leslie Epstein, *The Politics of Domesticity: Women, Evangelism, and Temperance in Nineteenth-Century America* (Middletown: Wesleyan University Press, 1981), 100–114; Ruth Bordin, *Woman and Temperance: The Quest for Power and Liberty, 1873–1900* (Philadelphia: Temple University Press, 1981), 7, 26.

9. Walkowitz, chap. 3; Gordon, 106; E. M. Sigsworth and T. J. Wyke, "A Study in Victorian Prostitution and Venereal Disease," in *Suffer and Be Still: Women in the Victorian Age,* ed. Martha Vicinus (Bloomington: Indiana University Press, 1972); Connelly, chap. 4.

10. For example see Elizabeth Cady Stanton, "Speech to the McFarland-Richardson Protest Meeting" (1869), in *Elizabeth Cady Stanton, Susan B. An-*

thony, 129; Clara Cleghorne Hoffman, "Social Purity," and Lucinda B. Chandler, "Marriage Reform," in *Report of the International Council of Women* (Washington, D.C.: R. H. Darby, 1888), 283, 285.

11. See Gordon, chap. 5, "Voluntary Motherhood."

12. Evidence of these problems abounds in case records of social service agencies used by Linda Gordon in "Child-Saving and the Single Mother: A View from the Perspective of the Massachusetts Society for the Prevention of Cruelty to Children, 1880–1920," *American Quarterly* 37, 2 (1985): 173–92.

13. For an exceptionally good account of the religious culture of nineteenth-century women and the conflicts it generated, see Kathryn Kish Sklar, *Catharine Beecher: A Study in American Domesticity* (New Haven: Yale University Press, 1973); the major nineteenth-century feminist opponent of women's religious traditions was Elizabeth Cady Stanton; see *Elizabeth Cady Stanton, Susan B. Anthony,* pt. 3.

14. In taking this approach, we are drawing on two recent schools of historical interpretation: feminist historians, for instance, Nancy Cott, Gerda Lerner, and Ann Douglas, who emphasize the role of women as active agents of cultural change, but who have concentrated on domesticity rather than sexuality; and male theorists of sexuality, notably Michel Foucault, who regard sexuality as a socially constructed, historically specific cultural system, but leave women out of their accounts.

15. Ruth Rosen and Sue Davison, eds., *The Maimie Papers,* (Old Westbury, N.Y.: Feminist Press, 1977).

16. Estelle B. Freedman, *Their Sisters' Keepers: Women's Prison Reform in America, 1830–1930* (Ann Arbor: University of Michigan Press, 1981); Rosalind Rosenberg, *Beyond Separate Spheres: Intellectual Roots of Modern Feminism* (New Haven: Yale University Press, 1982), chap. 5 and p. 228. Sheldon Glueck and Eleanor T. Glueck, *Five Hundred Delinquent Women* (New York: Alfred A. Knopf, 1934), chap. 5; Mabel Ruth Fernald et al., *A Study of Women Delinquents in New York State* (New York: Century, 1920), chap. 12.

17. Jonathan Katz, *Gay American History: Lesbians and Gay Men in American History* (New York: Crowell, 1976), pt. 3; Erna O. Hellerstein et al., eds., *Victorian Women: A Documentary Account of Women's Lives in Nineteenth-Century England, France, and the United States* (Stanford: Stanford University Press, 1981), 185–89.

18. Carl Degler, *At Odds: Women and the Family in America from the Revolution to the Present* (New York: Oxford, 1980), 262–63. Beatrice Campbell, "Feminist Sexual Politics: Now You See It, Now You Don't," *Feminist Review* no. 5 (1981): 1–18. For a contemporary assessment of women's orgasms, see Shere

Hite, *The Hite Report: A Nationwide Study on Female Sexuality* (New York: Macmillan, 1976). Despite conceptual problems, Hite's study points to women's continuing problems with having orgasms, at least in partnered sex.

19. David J. Pivar, *Purity Crusade: Sexual Morality and Social Control, 1868–1900* (Westport, Conn.: Greenwood, 1973); Degler, chap. 12; Walkowitz, chap. 12; Gordon, chap. 6; "Social Purity Session," *Report of the International Council of Women,* 251–84.

20. Epstein, 125–37; Bordin, chap. 6.

21. For a good summary of black and immigrant family life, in contrast to middle-class families, see Degler, chap. 4 and *passim*. For specific evidence of poor women's weaker marital position vis-a-vis their husbands' sexual demands, see Eli S. Zaretsky, "Female Sexuality and the Catholic Confessional," Special Issue on Women, Sex, and Sexuality, *Signs* 6 (Autumn 1980): 176–84; and Ruth Hall, ed., *Dear Dr. Stopes: Sex in the 1920s* (New York: Penguin, 1978), chaps. 1 ("The Lower Classes") and 2 ("The Upper Classes"). Note that we deliberately avoid expressing this difference as a contrast between middle- and working-class families. We suspect that greater male sexual dominance is not so much a matter of proletarian experience as it is of peasant authoritarian background and women's extreme economic dependence.

22. Carroll Smith-Rosenberg, "Beauty, the Beast, and the Militant Woman: A Case Study in Sex Roles and Social Stress in Jacksonian America," *American Quarterly* 23 (October 1971): 562–84; Mary P. Ryan, "Power of Women's Networks: A Case Study of Female Moral Reform in Antebellum America," *Feminist Studies* 5 (Spring 1979): 66–85; Barbara Berg, *The Remembered Gate: Origins of American Feminism* (New York: Oxford, 1978).

23. Walkowitz, pt. 2; Pivar, chap. 2; Degler, 284–88; John Burnham, "Medical Inspection of Prostitutes in America in the Nineteenth Century: St. Louis Experiment and Its Sequel," *Bulletin of the History of Medicine* 45 (May-June 1971): 203–18.

24. Connelly, chap. 6; Pivar, 135–39; Walkowitz, epilogue; Deborah Gorham, "'The Maiden Tribute of Modern Babylon' Re-examined: Child Prostitution and the Idea of Childhood in Late Victorian England," *Victorian Studies* 21 (Spring 1978): 353–79; Mari Jo Buhle, *Women and American Socialism, 1870–1920* (Urbana: University of Illinois Press, 1981), 253–56.

25. Jeanette Young Norton, "Women Builders of Civilization," *Women's Political World,* 1 September 1913, 5.

26. On efforts to raise the age of consent, see Pivar, 139–46; Degler, 288–89; Gorham; Michael Pearson, *The Age of Consent: Victorian Prostitution and Its Enemies* (London: Newton Abbot, David and Charles, 1972).

27. Steven Schlossman and Stephanie Wallach, "The Crime of Precocious Sexuality: Female Juvenile Delinquency in the Progressive Era," *Harvard Educational Review* 48 (February 1978): 65–94; Steven Schlossman, *Love and the American Delinquent* (Chicago: University of Chicago Press, 1977); William I. Thomas, *The Unadjusted Girl, with Cases and Standpoint for Behavior Analysis* (Boston: Little, Brown, 1923).

28. Leslie Fishbein, "Harlot or Heroine? Changing Views of Prostitution, 1870–1920," *Historian* 43 (December 1980): 23–35.

29. Quoted in Pivar, 157.

30. This is one of the themes in *The Maimie Papers*. Wrote sometime prostitute Maimie Pinzer, "I would like to have women friends—but I can't have . . . I dreaded [they] would find out, perhaps inadvertently, something about me, and perhaps cut me, and I couldn't stand that" (10).

31. On the free love movement in general, see Taylor Stoehr, *Free Love in America: A Documentary History* (New York: AMS Press, 1979); Hal D. Sears, *The Sex Radicals: Free Love in High Victorian America* (Lawrence, Kans.: Regents Press of Kansas, 1977); Gordon, chaps. 5 and 6; Mary S. Marsh, *Anarchist Women, 1870–1920* (Philadelphia: Temple University Press, 1981), chap. 4; William Leach, *True Love and Perfect Union: Feminist Reform of Sex and Society* (New York: Basic Books, 1981), 82–83 and *passim*. We use the term "pro-sex" provisionally, in lieu of a more precise term which is yet to emerge.

32. Victoria C. Woodhull, *Tried as by Fire: Or, the True and the False Socially: An Oration* (New York: Woodhull & Claflin, 1874).

33. *Elizabeth Cady Stanton, Susan B. Anthony*, 94–98 and 185–87.

34. Alice Stockham, *Karezza: Ethics of Marriage* (Chicago: Alice B. Stockham, 1897), 22.

35. William L. O'Neill, *Divorce in the Progressive Era* (New York: Franklin Watts, 1973); *Elizabeth Cady Stanton, Susan B. Anthony, passim*; Leach, *passim*.

36. Gordon, chap. 5; James Reed, *From Private Vice to Public Virtue: The Birth Control Movement and American Society since 1830* (New York: Basic Books, 1978).

37. Caroline Ware, *Greenwich Village, 1920–1930* (Boston: Houghton Mifflin, 1935); Floyd Dell, *Love in Greenwich Village* (New York: George H. Doran, 1926); Rheta Childe Dorr, *A Woman of Fifty* (New York: Funk & Wagnalls, 1924); Judith Schwarz, *Radical Feminists of Heterodoxy, Greenwich Village, 1912–1940* (Lebanon, N.H.: New Victoria Publishers, 1982); Buhle, 257–68; Gordon, 189–99.

38. For lesbianism among the Greenwich Village feminists, see Schwarz, 30–31 and 67–72. Also see Marion K. Sanders, *Dorothy Thompson: A Legend in*

Her Time (Boston: Houghton Mifflin, 1973). Emma Goldman's relationship with Almeda Sperry is discussed in Katz, 523–29. Elizabeth Gurley Flynn's long relationship with the pioneering lesbian, Marie Equi, is traced in Rosalyn F. Baxandall, *Words on Fire: The Life and Writings of Elizabeth Gurley Flynn* (New Brunswick: Rutgers University Press, 1987), 1–72; there is also some suggestion that Flynn gave lesbianism a positive treatment in her original draft of *The Alderson Story: My Life as a Political Prisoner* (New York: International Publishers, 1972), but that Communist party officials insisted that she rewrite the material and make her portrait more judgmental and negative (Baxandall, private communication to authors, 1982). The larger issue of repression of evidence of lesbianism is considered in Blanche Wiesen Cook, "The Historical Denial of Lesbianism," *Radical History Review* 5 (Spring/Summer 1979): 55–60.

39. Gordon, 359–80; note the new insistence on the importance of the vagina, replacing an older recognition of the role of the clitoris in women's experience of orgasm.

40. Faderman, pts. 2 and 3; Christina Simmons, "Compassionate Marriage and the Lesbian Threat," Special Issue on Lesbian History, *Frontiers* 4 (Fall 1979): 54–59; Nancy Sahli, "Smashing: Women's Friendships before the Fall," *Chrysalis* 8 (Summer 1979): 17–27.

41. For a major modern feminist study of rape, extremely important to our movement but marred by its ahistorical assumptions, see Susan Brownmiller, *Against Our Will: Men, Women, and Rape* (New York: Simon & Schuster, 1975).

9

The Limitations of Sisterhood
Elizabeth Cady Stanton and Division in the American Suffrage Movement, 1875–1902

In the 1850s and 1860s, divisive political conflict character-ized most efforts of American feminists, but by the mid-1870s and on through the end of the century, these conflicts had lessened. During the Gilded Age, politically active women made a strong commitment to consolidation. Ideologically, women emphasized their similarities rather than their differences; organizationally, they emphasized unity over di-vision. Women of the period tended to create multi-issue, all-inclusive, and nonideological organizations that, at least theoretically, embraced all women and united them in a sisterhood dedicated to the elevation of their sex. The consolidation of women's reform efforts might be said to have begun with Frances Willard's assumption of the presidency of the Woman's Christian Temperance Union (WCTU) in 1879 and to have reached maturity with the formation of the National Council of Women and the General Federation of Women's Clubs, both in the late 1880s.[1] By this time, suffragists participated enthusiastically in the move to unite women politically, consolidate them organizationally, and harmonize them ideologically. In 1890 the suffrage movement, which had divided in 1869, reunified into a single organization that foreswore all political distinctions among proponents of woman suffrage and welcomed all women, whatever their differences, to work for "the Cause."[2] Even Susan

Originally published in *Women and the Structure of Society*, edited by Barbara J. Harris and JoAnn K. McNamara. Durham: Duke University Press, 1984.

B. Anthony, who had always gloried in a good factional fight, embraced this strategy. She displayed an excessive reverence for harmony in fighting for the suffrage and avoided any issue that would split the unity she was intent on building around the demand for the vote.[3]

How real in fact was the harmony and consensus that seemed to predominate in late nineteenth-century feminism? Under the calm surface feminists presented to the world, there is evidence of a considerable amount of conflict, which their belief in the overriding importance of unity and dedication to the principle of sisterhood led them to obscure in the historical record. Here I wish to examine the ideas and experiences of the leading feminist dissident of the late nineteenth century, Elizabeth Cady Stanton. The quality of Stanton's thought is so extraordinary, so original and thought-provoking, that it is always profitable to examine her ideas closely. Moreover, in a situation in which she had to fight against a stifling ideological consensus to get a hearing, her insights and criticism were considerably sharpened. The issues that divided the late nineteenth-century women's movement—religion, sex, and family, and the role of the state in women's liberation—are critical for an understanding of the development of feminism. We can gain a perspective on our own situation by considering how feminists differed over these matters and how the relation of these issues to women's liberation has changed over the last eighty years.

Central to the conflict between Stanton and other leaders of the late nineteenth-century feminist movement were differences over the role of religion, especially Christianity, in the oppression of women.[4] Stanton had been a militant anticleric since she was a teenager, when exposure to secular and rationalist ideas helped her to recover her emotional balance after an evangelical revival.[5] Politically, she was much more influenced by secular than by evangelical radicalism. Encouraged by Lucretia Mott, she read Frances Wright, Mary Wollstonecraft, and Tom Paine.[6] In the 1840s she knew of and was influenced by the two leading secular feminists in the United States, Robert Dale Owen and Ernestine Rose.[7] In the early phases of her career, she advocated reforms for women that these two had championed and that were generally associated with secular radicalism—the liberalization of divorce law and property rights for married women.[8] Even Stanton's role in developing the demand for the vote, and the emphasis she placed on politics, is most comprehensible when we recognize the militantly secular and anti-evangelical character of her approach to change, and her preference, throughout her career as a leader of American feminism, for political as opposed to moral reform.

In the 1860s and early 1870s, Stanton's interest in religion temporarily abated—perhaps because she concerned herself more with other reforms, perhaps because the clergy were less uniform in their opposition to women's rights, perhaps because women of orthodox religious belief were drawing closer to feminism. In 1878 Stanton's friend and political comrade, Isabella Beecher Hooker, held a prayer meeting in connection with the National Woman Suffrage Association convention and introduced pro-Christian resolutions at its proceedings. "I did not attend," Stanton wrote to Anthony, " . . . as Jehovah has never taken a very active part in the suffrage movement, I thought I would stay at home and get ready to implore the [congressional] committee, having more faith in their power to render us the desired aid."[9]

In the early 1880s, however, she became convinced once again that religion held the key to women's oppression. What led to this reawakening of her interest in religion, and how did it differ from her pre–Civil War anticlericalism? Social developments in the United States, particularly the revival of crusading Protestantism, helped to alert her to the continuing hold religion had on women's consciousness. Postwar Christianity spoke less of hellfire than of divine love and, in part because of the growth of the women's rights movement itself, women were especially active in its spread. Indeed, one of the major avenues for the growth both of revivalism and feminism in the late nineteenth century was the Woman's Christian Temperance Union.

Stanton was also affected by political developments in England, where she went in 1882 to be with her daughter and lived, on and off, for the next decade. In England Stanton was involved with and influenced by many political movements—Fabian socialism, the movement to repeal the Contagious Diseases Act, the suffrage movement, and above all, British secularism. The continued existence in England of an established church meant that the secularist demand for separation of church and state remained a powerful political issue. Non-Christians still could not sit in Parliament, and blasphemy, which included antigov-

ernment remarks, remained a civil crime.[10] Stanton's diary in this period
is filled with remarks about religion. Soon after she arrived in London,
she gave a speech on the religious dimension of women's subordination
to the progressive congregation of her old friend, Moncure Conway. "I
never enjoyed speaking more than on that occasion," she wrote in her
autobiography, "for I had been so long oppressed with the degradation
of woman under canon law and church discipline, that I had a sense of
relief in pouring out my indignation."[11]

Stanton was especially impressed with Annie Besant, one of the foremost leaders of British secularism. Besant was a feminist and a sexual
radical as well as a militant secularist. In 1878 she was arrested, along
with Charles Bradlaugh, for distribution of a pamphlet advocating birth
control. While the more moderate wing of the secularist movement held
to ideas about gender and sexuality that were too genteel for Stanton's
taste, Besant combined militant secularism with sexual radicalism and
the kind of uncompromising individualism that had always been so important to Stanton's feminism.[12] Stanton wrote of Besant, "I consider
her the greatest woman in England."[13] As a result of Stanton's experiences in England, as well as the impact on her of the American Protestant revival, her approach to religion in the 1880s was closely linked to
her ideas about sexuality and to new questions she began to form about
social coercion and state interference with individual development and
personal freedom.

Stanton contributed to late nineteenth-century secularism by examining the impact religion had on women. She believed that all organized
religions degraded women and that women's religious sentiments had
been used to keep them in bondage. However, she concentrated her fire
on Christianity, and on refuting the assertion, made in its defense, that
Christianity had elevated woman's status by purifying marriage, spreading social justice, and insisting on the spiritual equality of men and
women.[14] On the basis of considerable historical scholarship, she
demonstrated that the status of women in pre-Christian societies had
been high, and conversely, that the impact of Christianity had been to
debase and degrade the position of women. She also argued that historically the church had tolerated prostitution, polygamy, and other practices associated with the slavery of women. Christianity, she charged, ex-

cluded women from the priesthood and identified the deity solely with the male element. Finally, she argued that, with the Reformation, Christianity had abandoned what little respect it had retained for women, in particular the cult of the Virgin Mary and the existence of the religious sisterhoods. Given the confidence with which late nineteenth-century Protestants believed their faith represented the absolute height of human civilization, we can imagine that they found Stanton's assertion that Catholicism treated women with more respect than Protestantism especially infuriating.

Stanton's criticisms of Christianity's spiritual claims were closely related to her challenge to its sexual morality. She suspected that part of the explanation for Christianity's hold over women was the fact that it denied the power of female sexuality, while at the same time drawing on it in the form of religious passion. To her daughter she suggested that "the love of Jesus, among women in general, all grows out of sexual attraction."[15] Stanton was particularly critical of the doctrine of original sin, which identified sex with evil and both with the carnal nature of women.[16] This fear of female sexuality permeated Pauline doctrine, which treated marriage primarily as an institution to permit men to satisfy their sexual cravings without having to resort to sin.[17] Stanton dissented from the idea, at the center of late nineteenth-century Christian morality, that the "civilized" approach to human sexuality was the establishment of a single, absolute standard of sexual behavior, a morality to which all individuals should be held. Stanton had always been suspicious of official standards of sexual conduct, but the debates of the 1880s and 1890s clarified her position and made her profoundly skeptical of the idea that a universal standard of sexual morality could be ascertained. Of one thing she was sure: sexual purity did not prevail under nineteenth-century Christianity. "There never has been any true standard of social morality and none exists today," she insisted. "The true relation of the sexes is still an unsolved problem that has differed in all latitudes and in all periods from the savage to the civilized man. What constitutes chastity changes with time and latitude; its definition would be as varied as is public opinion on other subjects."[18]

On the basis of her interest in Christianity and its role in the oppression of women, Stanton began as early as 1886 to plan an ambitious feminist analysis of the Bible. She wanted to avoid treating the book as a "fetish," but to assess what it had to say about women's position "as one would any book of human origin."[19] General developments in Biblical criticism, the publication in 1881 of a new revised version of the Bible, and the growing tendency of Biblical scholars to treat the Bible historically rather than metaphysically no doubt inspired her. Stanton's own opinion was that the Bible taught "the subjection and degradation of women."[20] She realized, however, that other feminists interpreted its teachings more positively, and she genuinely sought to stir debate on the nature of the Bible's ethical teachings about women.[21] Years before she had read Voltaire's *Commentary* on the Bible, which was organized in the form of selected Biblical passages at the head of the page, followed by Voltaire's own "arch skeptical" analyses.[22] Stanton adopted this form, but proposed that the commentaries be written by several women of different opinions. The editors would then "add a few sentences, making some criticisms of our inconsistencies." "Our differences would make our readers think," Stanton wrote enthusiastically, "and teach them to respect the right of individual opinion."[23]

Stanton was genuinely surprised when most of the feminists to whom she wrote refused to join the *Woman's Bible* project. She had invited women with a wide range of opinions, including those "belonging to orthodox churches," and at first some of them showed interest in the idea.[24] Ultimately, almost all refused to participate. The reasons they gave varied. Harriot Hanson Robinson and her daughter Harriet Shattuck, close political allies of Stanton for several years, claimed that they did not see why the project was important and doubted their ability to make any contribution of significance.[25] Frances Willard and her friend Lady Henry Somerset withdrew their support because the project did not include enough "women of conservative opinion" and therefore could not "find acceptance with the women for whom we work."[26] Even Anthony refused to cooperate on the grounds that a battle over religion would divert attention from the fight for suffrage. "I don't want my name on that Bible Committee," she wrote Stanton. "I get my share of criticism. . . . Read and burn this letter."[27] Mary Livermore, who shared Stanton's goal of bringing the masses of women to more liberal religious ideas, also feared that any effort to which "the mad dog cry of atheist, infidel, and reviler of holy things" could be attached would do more harm than good.[28] In part, what was at work here were different ideas about how to build and develop a social movement. Livermore thought that leaders should move their followers' ideas gradually, carefully, by persuasion and reassurance, always seeking to preserve ideological consensus. Stanton believed in the value of debate and conflict, in sharpening differences rather than muting them.

This leaves us with the question of why religion should be the source of such deep differences among late nineteenth-century feminists. What did Christianity signify, especially for those who revered the Bible and found Stanton's ideas objectionable? In the context of late nineteenth-century capitalism, surrounded by intensely competitive individualism, many reformers were drawn to Christian values as an alternative to the ideology of laissez-faire. Christianity represented to them a set of beliefs about loving and selfless conduct toward others that, if universally followed, would eliminate tyranny and injustice. "Wherever we find an institution for the care and comfort of the dependent and defective classes," Frances Willard explained, "there the spirit of Christianity is at work."[29] Even to feminists, women were among the dependent classes, placed there by their maternity and the economic relation it put them in with respect to men. "That woman is handicapped by peculiarities of physical structure seems evident," wrote Ednah Dow Cheney, another feminist who objected to the *Woman's Bible*, "but it is only by making her limitations her powers"—her motherhood her glory—"that the balance can be restored."[30] Thus, the most important Christian institution for the care of dependent classes was the family, and women were at its center—dedicated to the care of dependent children, while themselves relying on the protection and goodwill of men. Women's inescapable dependence is what made Christian morality so important to feminists: a common belief in Christian ethics was the only thing that would ensure that men treated women with respect and that the family functioned to protect women and children rather than permit their abuse. "The gospel of Christ has mellowed the hearts of men until they become willing to do women justice," wrote Frances Willard, the most impassioned preacher of feminist Christianity. "To me the Bible is the dear and sacred home book which makes a hallowed motherhood possible because it raises woman up."[31]

While Stanton agreed with some of the elements of this argument— for instance, the practice of appealing to woman's position as mother of the race—at the most basic level she disagreed with this approach to women's emancipation. She believed that the task of the women's movement was not to assume women's vulnerability and to protect them from its consequences, but to so transform women and the condition in which they lived that they would no longer need protection, but would be fully independent. Even while recognizing that the structures of inequality were very strong, she held to the classical feminist goal of equality and continued to emphasize the necessity of achieving it with respect to the sexes. Her most powerful assertion of these ideas can be found in "The Solitude of Self," her 1892 meditation on the relative importance to women's liberation of protection versus freedom, differences between the sexes versus similarities, and community morality and Christian ethics versus individual autonomy and self-determination. Christianity's message was "to bear ye one another's burdens," and Stanton granted that humanity would be better off if we did, but the point of her speech was "how few the burdens that one soul can bear for another." "No matter how much women prefer to lean, to be protected and supported, nor how much men desire them to do so," she explained, "they must make the voyage of life alone, and for safety's sake . . . should know something of the laws of navigation." Stanton believed that the idea of safe dependence was an illusion for women for several reasons: because no matter how secure one's home life, how kindly the husband, emergencies arose and women had to be prepared to care for themselves; because each life was different, each woman had her "individual necessities" with which no one else could grapple but herself; above all, because the philosophical truth of human existence was the same for women as for men, "that in the tragedies and triumphs of human experience, each mortal stands alone." "The talk of sheltering woman from the fierce storms of life is the sheerest mockery," Stanton argued, "for they beat on her just as they do on man, and with more fatal results, for he has been trained to protect himself." Faced with these truths, the only security for women, as for men, was in full self-development. As a positive vision of women's liberation, Stanton stressed women's emancipation into the "infinite diversity in human character," the human condition that simultaneously distinguishes each of us from the other, and is common to all of us, men and women alike.[32]

These philosophical differences became political differences, and debates over religion became debates over government, as Christian reformers worked to introduce religious values into law and religious feminists sought to marshal the power of the government behind their idea of the family. By the end of the century, the idea that government should enforce Christian morality was becoming popular with reformers, as were proposals for Bible education in the public schools, legal enforcement of Sunday closings, a wide variety of sexual morals legislation, and—most hauntingly—a constitutional amendment recognizing the Christian basis of the American political system.[33] The 1888 platform of the Prohibition party, for instance, called for Sunday closing laws and restrictive divorce legislation, as well as for antimonopoly and prolabor measures. Feminists played an important role in this Christian political movement. Their special concern was sexual morality legislation: social purity laws to raise the age of consent, strengthen the bonds of marriage, limit the number of divorces, censor obscene literature, and eliminate prostitution. Feminists involved in social purity politics included Mary Livermore, Julia Ward Howe, Anna Garlin Spencer, Frances Harper, and all of the Blackwells.[34] The WCTU was especially active in social purity politics. Under the leadership of Frances Willard, it allied with Anthony Comstock, formed its own department for repressing impure literature, endorsed a constitutional amendment recognizing Christianity, and formed a department of "Christian citizenship."[35]

Although Christian morality and social purity ideology dominated the late nineteenth-century feminist movement, these ideas did not go unchallenged. A minority of feminists—Matilda Gage, Josephine Henry, Clara Colby, and Olympia Brown, to name a few—tried to halt the interpenetration of feminism and Christian reform in the 1890s.[36] Stanton provided secular feminists with leadership. Despite Anthony's urgings to keep conflict out of the women's movement, Stanton insisted on raising the level of debate and bringing feminists' differences into the open. At the 1890 suffrage unity convention, where pressure to present a united face to the world was great, Stanton's keynote speech challenged feminists' efforts to introduce Christian morality into civil law. "As women are taking an active part in pressing on the consideration of Congress many narrow sectarian measures," she declared, ". . . I hope this convention will declare that the Woman Suffrage Association is opposed to all Union of Church and State and pledges itself . . . to maintain the secular nature of our government."[37] She was particularly incensed over efforts to suppress all nonreligious activities on Sunday, especially the upcoming Chicago World's Fair.[38] She also opposed Christian reformers' attempts to make divorce laws more conservative and divorces harder to get.[39] She criticized both measures on the grounds that they were destructive of individual liberty, especially for women. She particularly objected to the suppression of individual choice when it came to divorce, because women as yet enjoyed so little self-determination in matters of marriage and sexuality. In contrast to her social purity opponents, she argued that liberal divorce laws were in women's interests, that more and more women were initiating divorce, and that the obligation of the women's movement was to encourage this development, not to repress it. "The rapidly increasing number of divorces, far from showing a lower state of morals, proves exactly the reverse," she contended. "Woman is in a transition period from slavery to freedom, and she will not accept the conditions in married life that she has heretofore meekly endured."[40]

Underlying Stanton's objections to the coercive character of social purity legislation was a growing concern over the uses of state power in general. Most late nineteenth-century reformers, including most feminists, relied on a unified community faith, backed by the power of the government, for the creation of a just social order. One has only to think of Edward Bellamy's *Looking Backward,* with its vision of a state-run utopia, where national government organized all aspects of social life and met—one might say anticipated—all one's personal needs.[41] While many reformers embraced this vision, there were those who saw problems with it. "The spring of the [Bellamy nationalist] movement is the very best cooperation in the place of the deadly competition of our so-called Christian civilization," William F. Channing wrote Stanton. "But the spring is made to drive the wheels of a state socialism more arbitrary than the government of the czar or the Emperor William."[42] Stanton was of the same opinion. "All this special legislation about faith, Sabbath, drinking, etc. is the entering wedge of a general government interference," she wrote in 1888, "which would eventually subject us to espionage, which would become tyrannical in the extreme."[43] Stanton's concerns about the impact of Christian ideology on American reform politics are worth considering. The explicitly religious dimension of this approach to reform soon faded, but its coercive and paternalistic aspects remained and formed the basis of the most disturbing, undemocratic elements of twentieth-century Progressivism.[44]

Stanton's ideas about religion and sex were not very popular in the late nineteenth-century women's movement. In 1890 she was narrowly elected president of the National American Woman Suffrage Association (NAWSA), and two years later she resigned, frustrated at the opposition she consistently encountered.[45] In 1895 she finally published the *Woman's Bible,* which only heightened the opposition to her leadership. At the 1896 suffrage convention, Rachel Foster Avery, corresponding secretary of NAWSA and one of Anthony's protégés, criticized the *Woman's Bible* as "a volume with a pretentious title . . . without either scholarship or literary merit, set forth in a spirit which is neither that of reverence or inquiry."[46] Avery recommended that the suffrage association "take some action to show that it was not responsible for the individual actions of its officers"—Stanton was no longer an officer—and moved that NAWSA disavow any connection with the *Woman's Bible.* There was considerable debate: Charlotte Perkins Gilman, at her first suffrage convention, defended Stanton eloquently, but the resolution of censure passed, 53 to 41. The censorship left Stanton bitter. "Much as I desire the suffrage," she wrote in 1896, "I would rather never vote than to see the policy of our government at the mercy of the religious bigotry of such women. My heart's desire is to lift women out of all these dangerous and degrading superstitions and to this end will I labor my remaining days on earth."[47] The low regard in which suffrage leaders held Stanton at the end of her life was carried after her death in 1902 into the historical record of the movement, through organizational histories and autobiographies, so that her historical contribution and her conception of the emancipation of women continued to be undervalued in the feminist tradition. There was not even a full-length biography of Stanton until 1940, in contrast to several written about Anthony within years of her death.

As a modern feminist, I find myself a good deal closer to Stanton's ideas about women's liberation, her focus on independence and egalitarianism, her emphasis on freedom rather than protection, than I feel to her social purity opponents. When I read "Solitude of Self" and ask myself what I think of it, I truly believe that Stanton's description of the dangerous, unpredictable, necessarily "solitary" nature of life describes what it means for women to leave the sheltered world of home and sexually stereotyped social role, each individual to find a way of life and a sense of self appropriate to her. It is interesting that the arguments of Stanton's feminist opponents—that religious values, a strengthened family, and a more uniform social morality offer women the best protection—are no longer put forward primarily by feminists. Although we can hear echoes of such ideals in some aspects of cultural feminism, Christian reform arguments are now primarily the province of the antifeminist movement—the Moral Majority, the right-to-lifers, Phyllis Schlafly, and STOP-ERA. What are we to make of this curious development? On the one hand, the similarities between feminist arguments of the past and antifeminist arguments of the present should give feminists pause and make us think more carefully about just how precisely feminists represent all women's aspirations. Profamily politicians, for all their conservatism, are addressing aspects of women's discontent and offering visions of family and social reform that are attractive, at least to some women.[48] There is no one solution to women's oppression; there may not even be one "women's oppression," and the history of women's efforts to reform their social position, to give voice to their discontent, is as complex a phenomenon as American reform in general, and as contradictory in its development.

At the same time, the appropriation of protectionist arguments by modern antifeminists is also a reason for optimism, a development on which feminists can pin historical faith. Nineteenth-century Christian feminists focused on women's weaknesses and vulnerability, and on the creation of safe environments and external power to protect them from exploitation and abuse. Given the position of the masses of women in the nineteenth century—economically dependent, unable to support themselves or their children, absolutely deprived of personal freedom, either sexual or reproductive—even the feminist movement could aspire to little more than this defensive and protectionist program on women's behalf. This no longer need be the case. Women's lives are no longer so completely circumscribed, at least no longer circumscribed in precisely the same ways. Modern feminist programs are much less protectionist as a result, women's goals much more libertarian and egalitarian. Once we understand that as the conditions of women's lives change, so do their visions of freedom, our approach to the history of feminism changes. We must study feminism's byways as well as its mainstreams, its dissidents as well as its representative voices; we must understand that our heritage is complex, so that we uncover the whole range of precedents on which we can draw.

NOTES

1. Karen J. Blair, *Clubwoman as Feminist: True Womanhood Redefined, 1868–1914* (New York: Holmes and Meier, 1980); Barbara Leslie Epstein, *Politics of Domesticity: Women, Evangelism, and Temperance in Nineteenth-Century America* (Middletown, Conn.: Wesleyan University Press, 1981).

2. Ellen C. DuBois, ed., *Elizabeth Cady Stanton, Susan B. Anthony: Correspondence, Writings, Speeches* (New York: Schocken, 1981), 179–81, 222–27.

3. "Our intention . . . is simply to make every one . . . believe in the great principles of equality of rights and chances for woman. . . . Neither you nor I have the right to complicate the question." Anthony to Stanton, 1884, in *The Life and Work of Susan B. Anthony,* ed. Ida H. Harper (Indianapolis: Bowen and Merrill, 1898), 2: 586. The issue that Anthony feared would complicate the suffrage movement was racism.

4. My emphasis on feminists' conflicts over religion contrasts with that of William R. Leach, in *True Love and Perfect Union: Feminist Reform of Sex and Society* (New York: Basic Books, 1981); Leach stresses the common commitment to religious liberalism, which he believes was shared by virtually all nineteenth-century feminists.

5. Elizabeth Cady Stanton, *Eighty Years and More: Reminiscences, 1815–1897* (New York: T. Fischer Unwin, 1898), 43–44.

6. Lucretia Mott to Richard Webb, 5 Sept. 1855, in *James and Lucretia*

Mott, Life and Letters, ed. Anna D. Hallowell (Boston: Houghton Mifflin and Co., 1884), 357; Stanton to Elizabeth Smith Miller, 20 Sept. 1855, in *Elizabeth Cady Stanton as Revealed in Her Letters, Diary, and Reminiscences,* ed. Theodore Stanton and Harriot Stanton (New York: Harper & Bros., 1922), 60–61.

7. Stanton, *Eighty Years and More,* 150.

8. Owen advocated divorce reform and property rights for married women in Indiana in the 1830s; the two issues were also linked in Massachusetts by Mary Upton Ferin. Rose and Judge Hertell, also a freethinker, led the drive for women's property rights in New York in the 1840s. Stanton helped to circulate petitions for property rights in 1845. She first advocated liberal divorce laws in 1852, in connection with the New York women's temperance movement.

9. Elizabeth Stanton to Susan B. Anthony, 14 Jan. 1878, Stanton Papers, Manuscript Division, Library of Congress (hereafter cited as Stanton Papers, LC).

10. Susan Budd, *Varieties of Unbelief: Atheists and Agnostics in English Society, 1850–1960* (London: Heinemann, 1977).

11. Stanton, *Eighty Years and More,* 356.

12. "Spent the afternoon with some Positivists whom I was invited to meet at Mr. William Hertz's. Though clear on religious questions, I found many of them narrow in their ideas as to the sphere of woman." Diary, 26 Nov. 1882, in *Stanton as Revealed in Her Letters,* 198. For Stanton's first meeting with Besant, see ibid., 25 Nov. 1882, 198. In her first months in England, Stanton also met with Victoria Woodhull and Ernestine Rose, both important figures in the individual rights tradition of feminism at an earlier period.

13. Diary, 18 July 1891, in *Stanton as Revealed in Her Letters,* 274–75.

14. Stanton presented a series of resolutions to the 1885 National Woman Suffrage Association convention indicting "Christian theology" for the oppression of women. The convention altered the resolutions to focus on "religious creeds derived from Judaism." See Stanton, *Eighty Years and More,* 381–82. Stanton developed her ideas on religion fully in "Has Christianity Benefitted Woman?" *North American Review* 342 (May 1885): 389–99.

15. Elizabeth Stanton to Harriot Stanton, 17 Apr. 1880, Stanton Papers, LC.

16. Stanton, "Has Christianity Benefitted Woman?" 395.

17. Ibid.

18. Stanton, "Patriotism and Chastity," *Westminster Review* 135 (Jan. 1891): 1–5.

19. Stanton to Elizabeth Boynton Harbert, 15 Sept. no yr., Harbert Papers, Huntington Library, San Marino, California.

20. Stanton, *Eighty Years and More*, 396.

21. Stanton to May Wright Sewall, 10 Oct. 1886, Harbert Collection, Huntington Library, San Marino, California.

22. Diary, 13 Aug. 1882, in *Stanton as Revealed in Her Letters*, 193.

23. Stanton to Harbert, 15 Sept. no yr., Harbert Collection, Huntington Library, San Marino, California.

24. Stanton, *Eighty Years and More*, 452.

25. Stanton to Harriot Hanson Robinson, 30 Sept. 1886, Robinson Papers, Schlesinger Library, Cambridge, Massachusetts.

26. Lady Henry Somerset to Stanton, 5 June 1895, Stanton Papers, LC.

27. Susan B. Anthony to Stanton, 24 July 1895, Harbert Collection, Huntington Library, San Marino, California.

28. Mary Livermore to Stanton, 1 Sept. 1886, Stanton Papers, LC.

29. Frances Willard to Elizabeth Stanton, n.d., in *The Woman's Bible*, Part II (New York: European Publishing Co., 1898), 200.

30. Ednah Dow Cheney to Stanton, n.d., in ibid., 190.

31. Willard to Stanton, n.d., in ibid., 200–201.

32. Stanton, "The Solitude of Self," in DuBois, *Elizabeth Cady Stanton, Susan B. Anthony*, 246–54.

33. David Pivar, *Purity Crusade: Sexual Morality and Social Control, 1868–1900* (Westport, Conn.: Greenwood Press, 1973). Also see Judith R. Walkowitz, *Prostitution and Victorian Society* (Cambridge: Cambridge University Press, 1980), for similar developments in England.

34. Pivar, *Purity Crusade*, 250; "Purity Conference," *Woman's Journal*, 7 Dec. 1895: 388.

35. Parker Pillsbury to Lillie Devereux Blake, 11 Apr. 1890, Blake Papers, Missouri Historical Society, St. Louis, Missouri. See also Epstein, *Politics of Domesticity*.

36. *Women's National Liberal Union: A Report of the Convention for Organization* (Syracuse: Masters and Stone Printers, 1890); also see Margaret Marsh, *Anarchist Women* (Philadelphia: Temple University Press, 1980).

37. Elizabeth Cady Stanton, "Address to the Founding Convention of the National American Woman Suffrage Association," in DuBois, *Elizabeth Cady Stanton, Susan B. Anthony*, 222–27.

38. Elizabeth Cady Stanton, "Sunday at the World's Fair," *North American Review* 154 (1892): 254–56.

39. Stanton, "Address to the Founding Convention of the National American Woman Suffrage Association," 225; Elizabeth Cady Stanton, "Divorce versus Domestic Warfare," *Arena* 1 (1890): 560–69.

40. Stanton, "Divorce versus Domestic Warfare," 568.

41. Dolores Hayden, *The Grand Domestic Revolution: History of Feminist Designs for American Homes, Neighborhoods, and Cities* (Cambridge, Mass.: MIT Press, 1981), chap. 7; William R. Leach, "Looking Forward Together: Feminists and Edward Bellamy," *Democracy* (Winter 1982).

42. William F. Channing to Stanton, 7 May 1890, Stanton Papers, LC.

43. Diary, 8 Feb. 1888, in *Stanton as Revealed in Her Letters,* 247.

44. Robert M. Crunden, *Ministers of Reform: The Progressive Achievement in American Civilization, 1889–1920* (New York: Basic Books, 1982), stresses the religious aspects of Progressivism.

45. *Life and Work of Susan B. Anthony,* 2, 631–32.

46. *Washington Post,* 27 Jan. 1896 and 29 Jan. 1896, clippings in the Anthony Papers, Manuscript Division, Library of Congress; also, "The Washington Convention," *Woman's Journal,* 1 Feb. 1896: 1.

47. Stanton to Elizabeth Boynton Harbert, 7 June 1900, Harbert Papers, Huntington Library, San Marino, California.

48. Susan Harding, "Family Reform Movements: Recent Feminism and Its Opposition," *Feminist Studies* 7, no. 1 (Spring 1981): 57–75; Barbara Ehrenreich, "The Women's Movements: Feminist and Antifeminist," *Radical America* 15, 1–2 (Spring 1981): 93–104.

10

Working Women, Class Relations, and Suffrage Militance

Harriot Stanton Blatch and the New York Woman Suffrage Movement, 1894–1909

More than any other period in American reform history, the Progressive Era eludes interpretation. It seems marked by widespread concern for social justice and by extraordinary elitism, by democratization and by increasing social control. The challenge posed to historians is to understand how Progressivism could simultaneously represent gains for the masses and more power for the classes. The traditional way to approach the period has been to study the discrete social programs reformers so energetically pushed in those years, from the abolition of child labor to the Americanization of the immigrants. Recently, historians' emphasis has shifted to politics, where it will probably remain for a time. Historians have begun to recognize that the rules of political life, the nature of American "democracy," were fundamentally reformulated beginning in the Progressive Era, and that such political change shaped the ultimate impact of particular social reforms.

Where were women in all this? The new focus on politics requires a reinterpretation of women's role in Progressivism. As the field of women's history has grown, the importance of women in the Progressive Era has gained notice, but there remains a tendency to concentrate on their roles with respect to social reform. Modern scholarship on the Progressive Era thus retains a separate spheres flavor; women are concerned

Originally published in *Journal of American History* 74 (1987).

with social and moral issues, but the world of politics is male. Nowhere is this clearer than in the tendency to minimize, even to omit, the woman suffrage movement from the general literature on the Progressive Era.[1]

Scholarship on woman suffrage is beginning to grow in detail and analytic sophistication, but it has yet to be fully integrated into overviews of the period.[2] Histories that include woman suffrage usually do so in passing, listing it with other constitutional alterations in the electoral process such as the popular election of senators, the initiative, and the referendum. But woman suffrage was a mass movement, and that fact is rarely noticed. Precisely because it was a mass political movement—perhaps the first modern one—woman suffrage may well illuminate Progressive-Era politics, especially the class dynamics underlying their reformulation. When the woman suffrage movement is given its due, we may begin to understand the process by which democratic hope turned into mass political alienation, which is the history of modern American politics.

To illuminate the origin and nature of the woman suffrage movement in the Progressive Era I will examine the politics of Harriot Stanton Blatch. Blatch was the daughter of Elizabeth Cady Stanton, the founding mother of political feminism. Beginning in the early twentieth century, she was a leader in her own right, initially in New York, later nationally. As early as 1903, when politics was still considered something that disreputable men did, like smoking tobacco, Blatch proclaimed: "There are born politicians just as there are born artists, writers, painters. I confess that I should be a politician, that I am not interested in machine politics, but that the devotion to the public cause . . . rather than the individual, appeals to me."[3]

Just as her zest for politics marked Blatch as a new kind of suffragist, so did her efforts to fuse women of different classes into a revitalized suffrage movement. Blatch's emphasis on class was by no means unique; she shared it with other women reformers of her generation. Many historians have treated the theme of class by labeling the organized women's reform movement in the early twentieth century "middle-class." By contrast, I have tried to keep open the question of the class character of women's reform in the Progressive Era by rigorously avoiding the term.

Characterizing the early twentieth-century suffrage movement as "middle-class" obscures its most striking element, the new interest in the vote among women at both ends of the class structure. Furthermore, it tends to homogenize the movement. The very term "middle-class" is contradictory, alternatively characterized as people who are not poor, and people who work for a living. By contrast, I have emphasized distinctions between classes and organized my analysis around the relations between them.

No doubt there is some distortion in this framework, particularly for suffragists who worked in occupations like teaching. But there is far greater distortion in using the term "middle-class" to describe women like Blatch or Carrie Chapman Catt or Jane Addams. For example, it makes more sense to characterize an unmarried woman with an independent income who was not under financial compulsion to work for her living as "elite," rather than "middle-class." The question is not just one of social stratification, but of the place of women in a whole system of class relations. For these new style suffragists, as for contemporary feminists who write about them, the complex relationship between paid labor, marital status, and women's place in the class structure was a fundamental puzzle. The concept of "middle-class" emerged among early twentieth-century reformers, but may ultimately prove more useful in describing a set of relations *between* classes that was coming into being in those years, than in designating a segment of the social structure.

Blatch, examined as a political strategist and a critic of class relations, is important less as a unique figure than as a representative leader, through whose career the historical forces transforming twentieth-century suffragism can be traced. The scope of her leadership offers clues to the larger movement: She was one of the first to open up suffrage campaigns to working-class women, even as she worked closely with wealthy and influential upper-class women; she pioneered militant street tactics and backroom political lobbying at the same time. Blatch's political evolution reveals close ties between other stirrings among American women in the Progressive Era and the rejuvenated suffrage movement. Many of her ideas paralleled Charlotte Perkins Gilman's influential reformulation of women's emancipation in economic terms. Many of Blatch's innovations as a suffragist drew on her prior experience in the Women's Trade

Union League. Overall, Blatch's activities suggest that early twentieth-century changes in the American suffrage movement, often traced to the example of militant British suffragettes, had deep, indigenous roots. Among them were the growth of trade unionism among working-class women and professionalism among the elite, changing relations between these classes, and the growing involvement of women of all sorts in political reform.

The suffrage revival began in New York in 1893–1894, as part of a general political reform movement. In the 1890s New York's political reformers were largely upper-class men concerned about political "corruption," which they blamed partly on city Democratic machines and the bosses who ran them, partly on the masses of voting men, ignorant, immigrant, and ripe for political manipulation. Their concern about political corruption and about the consequences of uncontrolled political democracy became the focus of New York's 1894 constitutional convention, which addressed itself largely to "governmental procedures: the rules for filling offices, locating authority and organizing the different branches."[4]

The New York woman suffrage movement, led by Susan B. Anthony, recognized a great opportunity in the constitutional convention of 1894. Focusing on political corruption, Anthony and her allies argued that women were the political reformers' best allies. For while men were already voters and vulnerable to the ethic of partisan loyalty—indeed a man without a party affiliation in the 1890s was damned close to unsexed—everyone knew that women were naturally nonpartisan. Enfranchising women was therefore the solution to the power of party bosses. Suffragists began by trying to get women elected to the constitutional convention itself. Failing this, they worked to convince the convention delegates to include woman suffrage among the proposed amendments.[5]

Anthony planned a house-to-house canvass to collect signatures on a mammoth woman suffrage petition. For the $50,000 she wanted to fund this effort, she approached wealthy women in New York City, including physician Mary Putnam Jacobi, society leader Catherine Palmer (Mrs. Robert) Abbe, social reformer Josephine Shaw Lowell, and philanthropist Olivia (Mrs. Russell) Sage. Several of them were already associated with efforts for the amelioration of working-class women, notably in the recently formed Consumers' League, and Anthony had reason to think they might be ready to advocate woman suffrage.[6]

The elite women were interested in woman suffrage, but they had their own ideas about how to work for it. Instead of funding Anthony's campaign, they formed their own organization. At parlor meetings in the homes of wealthy women, they tried to strike a genteel note, emphasizing that enfranchisement would *not* take women out of their proper sphere and would *not* increase the political power of the lower classes. Eighty-year-old Elizabeth Stanton, observing the campaign from her armchair, thought that "men and women of the conservative stamp of the Sages can aid us greatly at this stage of our movement."[7]

Why did wealthy women first take an active and prominent part in the suffrage movement in the 1890s? In part they shared the perspective of men of their class that the influence of the wealthy in government had to be strengthened; they believed that with the vote they could increase the political power of their class. In a representative argument before the constitutional convention, Jacobi proposed woman suffrage as a response to "the shifting of political power from privileged classes to the masses of men." The disfranchisement of women contributed to this shift because it made all women, "no matter how well born, how well educated, how intelligent, how rich, how serviceable to the State," the political inferiors of all men, "no matter how base-born, how poverty stricken, how ignorant, how vicious, how brutal." Olivia Sage presented woman suffrage as an antidote to the growing and dangerous "idleness" of elite women, who had forgotten their responsibility to set the moral tone for society.[8]

Yet, the new elite converts also supported woman suffrage on the grounds of changes taking place in women's status, especially within their own class. Jacobi argued that the educational advancement of elite women "and the new activities into which they have been led by it—in the work of charities, in the professions, and in the direction of public education—naturally and logically tend toward the same result, their political equality." She argued that elite women, who had aided the community through organized charity and benevolent activities, should have the same "opportunity to serve the State nobly." Sage was willing to advocate woman suffrage because of women's recent "strides . . . in the acquirement of business methods, in the management of their affairs, in the effective interest they have evinced in civic affairs."[9]

Suffragists like Jacobi and Sage characteristically conflated their class perspective with the role they saw for themselves as women, contending for political leadership not so much on the grounds of their wealth, as of their womanliness. Women, they argued, had the characteristics needed in politics—benevolence, morality, selflessness, and industry; conveniently, they believed that elite women most fully embodied these virtues. Indeed, they liked to believe that women like themselves were elite *because* they were virtuous, not because they were wealthy. The confusion of class and gender coincided with a more general elite ideology that identified the fundamental division in American society not between rich and poor, but between industrious and idle, virtuous and vicious, community-minded and selfish. On these grounds Sage found the purposeless leisure of wealthy women dangerous to the body politic. She believed firmly that the elite, women included, should provide moral—and ultimately political—leadership, but it was important to her that they earn the right to lead.[10]

The problem for elite suffragists was that woman suffrage meant the enfranchisement of working-class, as well as elite, women. Jacobi described a prominent woman who "had interested herself nobly and effectively in public affairs, . . . but preferred not to claim the right [of suffrage] for herself, lest its concession entail the enfranchisement of ignorant and irresponsible women." An elite antisuffrage organization committed to such views was active in the 1894 campaign as well, led by women of the same class, with many of the same beliefs, as the prosuffrage movement. As Stanton wrote, "The fashionable women are about equally divided between two camps." The antis included prominent society figures Abby Hamlin (Mrs. Lyman) Abbott and Josephine Jewell (Mrs. Arthur) Dodge, as well as Annie Nathan Meyer, founder of Barnard College and member of the Consumers' League. Like the elite suffragists, upper-class antis wanted to insure greater elite influence in politics; but they argued that woman suffrage would decrease elite influence, rather than enhance it.[11]

Elite suffragists' willingness to support woman suffrage rested on their confidence that their class would provide political leadership for all women once they had the vote. Because they expected working-class women to defer to them, they believed that class relations among women would be more cooperative and less antagonistic than among men. Elite women, Jacobi argued before the 1894 convention, would "so guide ignorant women voters that they could be made to counterbalance, when necessary, the votes of ignorant and interested men." Such suffragists assumed that working-class women were too weak, timid, and disorganized to make their own demands. Since early in the nineteenth century, elite women had claimed social and religious authority on the grounds of their responsibility for the women and children of the poor. They had begun to adapt this tradition to the new conditions of an industrial age, notably in the Consumers' League, formed in response to the pleas of women wage earners for improvement in their working conditions. In fact, elite antis also asserted that they spoke for working-class women, but they contended that working-class women neither needed nor wanted to vote.[12]

From an exclusively elite perspective, the antisuffrage argument was more consistent than the prosuffrage one; woman suffrage undoubtedly meant greater political democracy, which the political reform movement of the 1890s most fundamentally feared. Elite suffragists found themselves organizing their own arguments around weak refutations of the antis' objections.[13] The ideological weakness had political implications. Woman suffrage got no serious hearing in the constitutional convention, and the 1894 constitutional revisions designed to "clean up government" ignored women's plea for political equality.

The episode revealed dilemmas, especially with respect to class relations among women, that a successful suffrage movement would have to address. Elite women had begun to aspire to political roles that led them to support woman suffrage, and the resources they commanded would be crucial to the future success of suffrage efforts. But their attraction to woman suffrage rested on a portrait of working-class women and a system of class relations that had become problematic to a modern industrial society. Could elite women sponsor the entrance of working-class women into politics without risking their influence over them, and perhaps their position of leadership? Might not working-class women assume a newly active, politically autonomous role? The tradition of class relations among women had to be transformed before a thriving and modern woman suffrage movement could be built. Harriot Stanton Blatch had the combination of suffrage convictions and class awareness to lead New York suffragists through that transition.

The 1894 campaign, which confronted suffragists with the issue of class, also drew Blatch actively into the American woman suffrage movement. She had come back from England, where she had lived for many years, to receive a master's degree from Vassar College for her study of the English rural poor. A powerful orator, she was "immediately pressed into service . . . speaking every day," at parlor suffrage meetings, often to replace her aged mother.[14] Like her mother, Blatch was comfortable in upper-class circles; she had married into a wealthy British family. She generally shared the elite perspective of the campaign, assuming that "educated women" would lead their sex. But she disliked the implication that politics could ever become too democratic and, virtually alone among the suffragists, criticized all "those little anti-republican things I hear so often here in America, this talk of the quality of votes." And while other elite suffragists discussed working-class women as domestic servants and shop clerks, Blatch understood the centrality of industrial workers, although her knowledge of them was still primarily academic.[15]

Blatch's disagreements with the elite suffrage framework were highlighted a few months after the constitutional convention in an extraordinary public debate with her mother. In the *Woman's Journal,* Stanton urged that the suffrage movement incorporate an educational restriction into its demand, to respond to "the greatest block in the way of woman's enfranchisement . . . the fear of the 'ignorant vote' being doubled." Her justification for this position, so at odds with the principles of a lifetime, was that the enfranchisement of "educated women" best supplied "the imperative need at the time . . . woman's influence in public life." From England, Blatch wrote a powerful dissent. Challenging the authority of her venerated mother was a dramatic act that—perhaps deliberately—marked the end of her political daughterhood. She defended both the need and the capacity of the working class to engage in democratic politics. On important questions, "for example . . . the housing of the poor," their opinion was more informed than that of the elite. She also argued that since "the conditions of the poor are so much harder . . . every working man needs the suffrage more than I do." And finally, she insisted on the claims of a group her mother had ignored, working women.[16]

The debate between mother and daughter elegantly symbolizes the degree to which class threatened the continued vitality of the republican tradition of suffragism. Partly because of her participation in the British Fabian movement, Blatch was able to adapt the republican faith to modern class relations, while Stanton was not. As a Fabian, Blatch had gained an appreciation for the political intelligence and power of the working class very rare among elite reformers in the U.S. When she insisted that the spirit of democracy was more alive in England than in the U.S., she was undoubtedly thinking of the development of a working-class political movement there.[17]

Over the next few years, Blatch explored basic assumptions of the woman suffrage faith she had inherited, in the context of modern class relations. In the process, like other women reformers of her era, such as Charlotte Perkins Gilman, Florence Kelley, Jane Addams, and numerous settlement house residents and supporters of organized labor, she focused on the relation of women and work. She emphasized the productive labor that women performed, both as it contributed to the larger social good and as it created the conditions of freedom and equality for women themselves. Women had always worked, she insisted. The new factor was the shift of women's work from the home to the factory and the office, and from the status of unpaid to paid labor. Sometimes she stressed that women's unpaid domestic labor made an important contribution to society; at other times she stressed that such unpaid work was not valued, but always she emphasized the historical development that was taking women's labor out of the home and into the commercial economy. The question for modern society was not whether women should work, but under what conditions, and with what consequences for their own lives.[18]

Although Blatch was troubled by the wages and working conditions of the laboring poor, her emphasis on work as a means to emancipation led her to regard wage-earning women less as victims to be succored, than as exemplars to their sex. She vigorously denied that women ideally hovered somewhere above the world of work. She had no respect for the "handful of rich women who have no employment other than organizing servants, social functions and charities." Upper-class women, she believed, should also "work," should make an individualized contribution to the public good, and where possible should have the value of their labor recognized by being paid for it.[19] As a member of the first generation of college-educated women, she believed that education and professional achievement, rather than wealth and refinement, fitted a woman for social leadership.

Turning away from nineteenth-century definitions of the unity of women that emphasized their place in the home, their motherhood, and their exclusion from the economy, and emphasizing instead the unity that productive work provided for all women, Blatch rewrote feminism in its essentially modern form, around work. She tended to see women's work, including homemaking and child rearing, as a mammoth portion of the world's productive labor, which women collectively accomplished. Thus she retained the concept of "women's work" for the sex as a whole, while vigorously discarding it on the individual level, explicitly challenging the notion that all women had the same tastes and talents.[20]

Her approach to "women's work" led Blatch to believe that the interconnection of women's labor fundamentally shaped relations among them. Here were the most critical aspects of her thought. Much as she admired professional women, she insisted that they recognize the degree to which their success rested on the labor of other women, who cared for their homes and their children. "Whatever merit [their homes] possess," Blatch wrote, "is largely due to the fact that the actress when on the stage, the doctor when by her patient's side, the writer when at her desk, has a Bridget to do the homebuilding for her." The problem was that the professional woman's labor brought her so much more freedom than the housemaid's labor brought her. "Side by side with the marked improvement in the condition of the well-to-do or educated woman," Blatch observed, "our century shows little or no progress in the condition of the woman of the people." Like her friend Gilman, Blatch urged that professional standards of work—good pay, an emphasis on expertise, the assumption of a lifelong career—be extended to the nurserymaid and the dressmaker, as well as to the lawyer and the journalist. Until such time, the "movement for the emancipation of women [would] remain . . . a well-dressed movement."[21]

But professional training and better wages alone would not give labor an emancipatory power in the lives of working-class women. Blatch recognized the core of the problem of women's work, especially for working-class women: "How can the duties of mother and wage earner be reconciled?" She believed that wage-earning women had the same desire as professional women to continue to enjoy careers and independence after marriage. "It may be perverse in lowly wage earners to show individuality as if they were rich," Blatch wrote, "but apparently we shall have to accept the fact that all women do not prefer domestic work to all other kinds." But the problem of balancing a career and a homelife was "insoluble—under present conditions—for the women of the people." "The pivotal question for women," she wrote, "is how to organize their work as home-builders and race-builders, how to get that work paid for not in so called protection, but in the currency of the state."[22]

As the female labor force grew in the late nineteenth century, so did the number of married women workers and demands that they be driven from the labor force. The suffrage movement had traditionally avoided the conflict between work and motherhood by pinning the demand for economic equality on the existence of unmarried women, who had no men to support them.[23] Blatch confronted the problem of work and motherhood more directly. In a 1905 article, she drew from the utopian ideas of William Morris to recommend that married women work in small, worker-owned manufacturing shops where they could have more control over their hours and could bring their children with them. Elsewhere, she argued that the workplace should be reorganized around women's needs, rather than assume the male worker's standards, but she did not specify what that would mean. She never solved the riddle of work and children for women—nor have we—but she knew that the solution could not be to force women to choose between the two nor to banish mothers from the labor force.[24]

Blatch's vision of women in industrial society was democratic—all must work and all must be recognized and rewarded for their work—but it was not an egalitarian approach nor one that recognized most working women's material concerns. According to Blatch, women worked for psychological and ethical reasons, as much as for monetary ones. "As human beings we must have work," she wrote; "we rust out if we have not an opportunity to function on something." She emphasized the common promises and problems work raised in women's lives, not the differences in how they worked, how much individual choice they had, and especially in how much they were paid. She was relatively unconcerned with the way work enabled women to earn their livings. No doubt, her own experience partially explains this. As a young woman fresh out of college in the 1870s, she had dared to imagine that her desire for meaningful work and a role in the world need not deprive her of marriage and motherhood, and it did not. Despite her marriage, the birth of two children, and the death of one, she never interrupted her political and intellectual labors. But she also never earned her own living, depending instead on the income from her husband's family's business. In later years, she joked about the fact that she was the only "parasite" in the organization of self-supporting women she headed.[25]

But the contradictions in her analysis of the problem of work and women reflected more than her personal situation. There were two problems of work and women: the long-standing exploitation of laboring women of the working classes and the newly expanding place of paid labor in the lives of all women in bourgeois society. While the two processes were not the same, they were related, and women thinkers and activists of the Progressive period struggled to understand how. As more women worked for pay and outside of the home, how would the meaning of "womanhood" change? What would be the difference between "woman" and "man" when as many women as men were paid workers? And what would be the class differences between women if all of them worked? Indeed, would there be any difference between the classes at all, once the woman of leisure no longer existed? Virtually all the efforts to link the gender and class problems of work for woman were incomplete. If Blatch's analysis of work, like Gilman's, shorted the role of class, others' analyses, for instance Florence Kelley's, underplayed what work meant for women as a sex.

Blatch rethought the principles of political equality in the light of her emphasis on women's work. At an 1898 congressional hearing, Blatch hailed "the most convincing argument upon which our future claims must rest—the growing recognition of the economic value of the work of women."[26] Whereas her mother had based her suffragism on the nineteenth-century argument for natural rights and on the individual, Blatch based hers on women's economic contribution and their significance as a group.

The contradictions in Blatch's approach to women and work also emerged in her attempts to link work and the vote. On the one hand, she approached women's political rights as she did their economic emancipation, democratically: Just as all sorts of women must work, all needed the vote. Wealthy women needed the vote because they were taxpayers and had the right to see that their money was not squandered; women industrial workers needed it because their jobs and factories were subject to laws, which they had the right to shape. On the other hand, she recognized the strategic centrality of the enormous class of industrial workers, whose economic role was so important and whose political power was potentially so great. "It is the women of the industrial class," she explained, "the wage-earners, reckoned by the hundreds of thousands, . . . the women whose work has been submitted to a money test, who have been the means of bringing about the altered attitude of public opinion toward woman's work in every sphere of life."[27]

Blatch returned to New York for several extended visits after 1894, and she moved back for good in 1902. She had two purposes. Elizabeth Stanton was dying, and Blatch had come to be with her. Blatch also intended to take a leading role in the New York City suffrage movement. On her deathbed in 1902, Stanton asked Anthony to aid Blatch. However, hampered by Anthony's determination to keep control of the movement, Blatch was not able to make her bid for suffrage leadership until Anthony died, four years later.[28]

Meanwhile, Blatch was excited by other reform efforts, which were beginning to provide the resources for a new kind of suffrage movement. During the first years of the twentieth century two movements contributed to Blatch's political education—a broadened, less socially exclusive campaign against political corruption and a democratized movement for the welfare of working women. By 1907, her combined experience in these two movements enabled her to put her ideas about women and work into practice within the suffrage movement itself.

Women had become more active in the campaign against political corruption after 1894. In New York City, Josephine Shaw Lowell and Mary Putnam Jacobi formed the Woman's Municipal League, which concentrated on educating the public about corruption, in particular the links between the police and organized prostitution. Women were conspicuous in the reform campaigns of Seth Low, who was elected mayor in 1901.[29]

By the early 1900s, moreover, the spirit of political reform in New York City had spread beyond the elite. A left wing of the political reform movement had developed that charged that "Wall Street" was more responsible for political corruption than "the Bowery." Women were active in this wing, and there were women's political organizations with links to the Democratic party and the labor movement, a Women's Henry George Society, and a female wing of William Randolph Hearst's Independence League. The nonelite women in these groups were as politically enthusiastic as the members of the Woman's Municipal League, and considerably less ambivalent about enlarging the electorate. Many of them strongly supported woman suffrage. Beginning in 1905, a group of them organized an Equal Rights League to sponsor mock polling places for women to register their political opinions on election day.[30]

Through the 1900s Blatch dutifully attended suffrage meetings, and without much excitement advocated the municipal suffrage for propertied women favored by the New York movement's leaders after their 1894 defeat. Like many other politically minded women, however, she found her enthusiasm caught by the movement for municipal political reform. She supported Low for mayor in 1901 and believed that his victory demonstrated "how strong woman's power really was when it was aroused." By 1903 she suggested to the National American Woman Suffrage Association (NAWSA) that it set aside agitation for the vote, so that "the women of the organization should use it for one year, nationally and locally, to pursue and punish corruption in politics." She supported the increasing attention given to "the laboring man" in reform political coalitions, but she pointedly observed that "the working woman was never considered."[31]

However, working-class women were emerging as active factors in other women's reform organizations. The crucial arena for this development was the Women's Trade Union League (WTUL), formed in 1903 by a coalition of working-class and elite women to draw wage-earning women into trade unions. The New York chapter was formed in 1905, and Blatch was one of the first elite women to join. The WTUL represented a significant move away from the tradition of elite, ameliorative sisterhood at work in the 1894 campaign for woman suffrage. Like the Consumers' League, it had been formed in response to the request of women wage earners for aid from elite women, but it was an organization of both classes working together. Blatch had never been attracted to the strictly ameliorative tradition of women's reform, and the shift toward a partnership of upper-class and working-class women paralleled her own thinking about the relation between the classes and the role of work in women's lives. She and other elite women in the WTUL found themselves laboring not for working-class women, but with them, and toward a goal of forming unions that did not merely "uplift" working-class women, but empowered them. Instead of being working-class women's protectors, they were their "allies." Instead of speaking on behalf of poor women, they began to hear them speak for themselves. Within the organization wage earners were frequently in conflict with allies. Nonetheless, the league provided them an arena to articulate a working-class feminism related to, but distinct from, that of elite women.[32]

Although prominent as a suffragist, Blatch participated in the WTUL on its own terms, rather than as a colonizer for suffrage. She and two other members assigned to the millinery trade conducted investigations into conditions and organized mass meetings to interest women workers in unions. She sat on the Executive Council from 1906 through 1909 and was often called on to stand in for President Mary Dreier. Her academic knowledge of "the industrial woman" was replaced by direct knowledge of wage-earning women and their working conditions. She was impressed with what she saw of trade unionism, especially its unrelenting "militance." Perhaps most important, she developed working relations with politically sophisticated working-class women, notably Leonora O'Reilly and Rose Schneiderman. Increasingly she believed that the organized power of labor and the enfranchisement of women were closely allied.[33]

Working-class feminists in the league were drawn to ideas like Blatch's—to conceptions of dignity and equality for women in the workplace and to the ethic of self-support and lifelong independence; they wanted to upgrade the condition of wage-earning women so that they, too, could enjoy personal independence on the basis of their labor. On the one hand, they understood why most working-class women would want to leave their hateful jobs upon marriage; on the other, they knew that women as a group, if not the individual worker, were a permanent factor in the modern labor force. Mary Kenney O'Sullivan of Boston, one of the league's founders, believed that "self support" was a goal for working-class women, but that only trade unions would give the masses of working women the "courage, independence, and self respect" they needed to improve their conditions. She expected "women of opportunity" to help in organizing women workers, because they "owed much to workers who give them a large part of what they have and enjoy," and because "the time has passed when women of opportunity can be self respecting and work *for* others."[34]

Initially, the demand for the vote was less important to such working-class feminists than to the allies. Still, as they began to participate in the organized women's movement on a more equal basis, wage-earning women began to receive serious attention within the woman suffrage movement as well. Beginning about 1905, advocates of trade unionism and the vote for women linked the demands. At the 1906 suffrage convention WTUL member Gertrude Barnum pointed out that "our hope as suffragists lies with these strong working women." Kelley and Addams wrote about the working woman's need for the vote to improve her own conditions. In New York, Blatch called on the established suffrage societies to recognize the importance of the vote to wage-earning women and the importance of wage-earning women to winning the vote. When she realized that existing groups could not adapt to the new challenges, she moved to form her own society.[35]

In January 1907, Blatch declared the formation of a new suffrage organization, the Equality League of Self-Supporting Women. The *New York Times* reported that the two hundred women present at the first meeting included "doctors, lawyers, milliners and shirtmakers."[36] Blatch's decision to establish a suffrage organization that emphasized female "self-support"—lifelong economic independence—grew out of her ideas about work as the basis of women's claim on the state, the leadership role she envisioned for educated professionals, and her discovery of the power and political capacity of trade-union women. The Equality League provided the medium for introducing a new and aggressive style of activism into the suffrage movement—a version of the "militance" Blatch admired among trade unionists.

Initially, Blatch envisioned the Equality League of Self-Supporting Women as the political wing of the Women's Trade Union League. All the industrial workers she recruited were WTUL activists, including O'Reilly, the Equality League's first vice-president, and Schneiderman, its most popular speaker. To welcome working-class women, the Equality League virtually abolished membership fees; the policy had the added advantage of allowing Blatch to claim every woman who ever attended a league meeting in her estimate of its membership. She also claimed the members of the several trade unions affiliated with the Equality League, such as the bookbinders, overall makers, and cap makers, so that when she went before the New York legislature to demand the vote, she could say that the Equality League represented thousands of wage-earning women.[37]

Blatch wanted the Equality League to connect industrial workers, not with "club women" (her phrase), but with educated, professional workers, who should, she thought, replace benevolent ladies as the leaders of their sex. Such professionals—college educated and often women pioneers in their professions—formed the bulk of the Equality League's active membership. Many were lawyers, for instance Ida Rauh, Helen Hoy, Madeleine Doty, Jessie Ashley, Adelma Burd, and Bertha Rembaugh. Others were social welfare workers, for instance the Equality League's treasurer, Kate Claghorn, a tenement housing inspector and the highest paid female employee of the New York City government. Blatch's own daughter, Nora, the first woman graduate civil engineer in the United States, worked in the New York City Department of Public Works. Many of these women had inherited incomes and did not work out of economic need, but out of a desire to give serious, public substance to their lives and to make an impact on society. Many of them expressed the determination to maintain economic independence after they married.[38]

Although Blatch brought together trade-union women and college-educated professionals in the Equality League, there were tensions between the classes. The first correspondence between O'Reilly and Barnard graduate Caroline Lexow was full of class suspicion and mutual recrimination. More generally, there were real differences in how and why the two classes of working women demanded the vote. Trade-union feminists wanted the vote so that women industrial workers would have power over the labor laws that directly affected their working lives. Many of the college-educated self-supporters were the designers and administrators of this labor legislation. Several of them were, or aspired to be, government employees, and political power affected their jobs through party patronage. The occupation that might have bridged the differences was teaching. As in other cities, women teachers in New York organized for greater power and equal pay. The Equality League frequently offered aid, but the New York teachers' leaders were relatively conservative and kept their distance from the suffrage movement.[39]

Blatch's special contribution was her understanding of the bonds and common interests uniting industrial and professional women workers. The industrial women admired the professional ethic, if not the striving careerism, of the educated working women, and the professionals admired the matter-of-fact way wage-earning women went out to work. The fate of the professional woman was closely tied to that of the industrial worker; the cultural regard in which all working women were held affected both. Blatch dramatized that tie when she was refused service at a restaurant because she was unescorted by a man (that is, because she was eating with a woman). The management claimed that its policy aimed to protect "respectable" women, like Blatch, from "objectionable" women, like the common woman worker who went about on her own, whose morals were therefore questionable. Blatch rejected the division between respectable women and working women, pointing out that "there are five million women earning their livelihood in this country, and it seems strange that feudal customs should still exist here."[40]

The dilemma of economically dependent married women was crucial to the future of both classes of working women. Blatch believed that if work was to free women, they could not leave it for dependence on men in marriage. The professional and working-class members of the Equality League shared this belief, one of the distinguishing convictions of their new approach to suffragism. In 1908 Blatch and Mary Dreier chaired a debate about the housewife, sponsored by the WTUL and attended by many Equality League members. Charlotte Perkins Gilman took the Equality League position, that the unemployed wife was a "parasite" on her husband, and that all women, married as well as unmarried, should work, "like every other self-respecting being." Anna Howard Shaw argued that women's domestic labor was valuable, even if unpaid, and that the husband was dependent on his wife. A large audience attended, and although they "warmly applauded" Gilman, they preferred Shaw's sentimental construction of the economics of marriage.[41]

A month after the Equality League was formed, Blatch arranged for trade-union women to testify before the New York legislature on behalf of woman suffrage, the first working-class women ever to do so. The New York Woman Suffrage Association was still concentrating on the limited, property-based form of municipal suffrage; in lethargic testimony its leaders admitted that they had "no new arguments to present." Everyone at the hearing agreed that the antis had the better of the argument. The Equality League testimony the next day was in sharp contrast. Clara Silver and Mary Duffy, WTUL activists and organizers in the garment industry, supported full suffrage for all New York women. The very presence of these women before the legislature, and their dignity and intelligence, countered the antis' dire predictions about enfranchising the unfit. Both linked suffrage to their trade-union efforts: While they struggled for equality in unions and in industry, "the state" undermined them, by teaching the lesson of female inferiority to male unionists and bosses. "To be left out by the State just sets up a prejudice against us," Silver explained. "Bosses think and women come to think themselves that they don't count for so much as men."[42]

The formation of the Equality League and its appearance before the New York legislature awakened enthusiasm. Lillie Devereux Blake, whose own suffrage group had tried "one whole Winter . . . to [interest] the working women" but found that they were "so overworked and so poor that they can do little for us," congratulated Blatch on her apparent success. Helen Marot, organizing secretary for the New York WTUL, praised the Equality League for "realizing the increasing necessity of including working women in the suffrage movement." Blatch, O'Reilly, and Schneiderman were the star speakers at the 1907 New York suffrage convention. "We realize that probably it will not be the educated workers, the college women, the men's association for equal suffrage, but the people who are fighting for industrial freedom who will be our vital force at the finish," proclaimed the newsletter of the NAWSA.[43]

The unique class character of the Equality League encouraged the development of a new style of agitation, more radical than anything practiced in the suffrage movement since Elizabeth Stanton's prime. The immediate source of the change was the Women's Social and Political Union of England (WSPU), led by Blatch's comrade from her Fabian days, Emmeline Pankhurst. Members of the WSPU were just beginning to be arrested for their suffrage protests. At the end of the Equality League's first year, Blatch invited one of the first WSPU prisoners, Anne Cobden-Sanderson, daughter of Richard Cobden, to the United States to tell about her experiences, scoring a coup for the Equality League. By emphasizing Cobden-Sanderson's connection with the British Labour Party and distributing free platform tickets to trade-union leaders, Blatch was able to get an overflow crowd at Cooper Union, Manhattan's labor temple, two-thirds of them men, many of them trade unionists.[44]

The Equality League's meeting for Cobden-Sanderson offered American audiences their first account of the new radicalism of English suffragists, or as they were beginning to be called, suffragettes. Cobden-Sanderson emphasized the suffragettes' working-class origins. She attributed the revival of the British suffrage movement to Lancashire factory workers; the heroic figure in her account was the working-class suffragette Annie Kenney, while Christabel Pankhurst, later canonized as the Joan of Arc of British militance, went unnamed. After women factory workers were arrested for trying to see the prime minister, Cobden-Sanderson and other privileged women, who felt they "had not so much to lose as [the workers] had," decided to join them and get arrested. She spent almost two months in jail, living the life of a common prisoner and coming to a new awareness of the poor and suffering women she saw there. Her simple but moving account conveyed the transcendent impact of the experience.[45]

Cobden-Sanderson's visit to New York catalyzed a great outburst of suffrage energy; in its wake, Blatch and a handful of other new leaders introduced the WSPU tactics into the American movement, and the word "suffragette" became as common in New York as in London. The "militants" became an increasingly distinct wing of the movement in New York and other American cities. But it would be too simple to say that the British example caused the new, more militant phase in the American movement. The developments that were broadening the class basis and the outlook of American suffragism had prepared American women to respond to the heroism of the British militants.[46]

The development of militance in the American suffrage movement was marked by new aggressive tactics practiced by the WSPU, especially open-air meetings and outdoor parades. At this stage in the development of British militance, American suffragists generally admired the heroism of the WSPU martyrs. Therefore, although the press emphasized dissent within the suffrage movement—it always organized its coverage of suffrage around female rivalries of some sort—the new militant activities were well received throughout the movement. And, conversely, even the most daring American suffragettes believed in an American exceptionalism that made it unnecessary to contemplate going to prison, to suffer as did the British militants.[47]

Despite Blatch's later claims, she did not actually introduce the new tactics in New York City. The first open-air meetings were organized immediately after the Cobden-Sanderson visit by a group called the American Suffragettes. Initiated by Bettina Borrman Wells, a visiting member of the WSPU, most of the American Suffragettes' membership came from the Equal Rights League, the left-wing municipal reform group that had organized mock polling places in New York since 1905. Feminist egalitarians with radical cultural leanings, its members were actresses, artists, writers, teachers, and social welfare workers—less wealthy versions of the professional self-supporters in the Equality League. Their local leader was a librarian, Maud Malone, whose role in encouraging new suffrage tactics was almost as important as, although less recognized than, Blatch's own.[48]

The American Suffragettes held their first open-air meeting in Madison Square on New Year's Eve, 1907. After that they met in the open at least once a week. Six weeks later, they announced they would hold New York's first all-woman parade. Denied a police permit, they determined to march anyway. The twenty-three women in the "parade" were many times outnumbered by the onlookers, mostly working-class men. In a public school to which they adjourned to make speeches, the American Suffragettes told a sympathetic audience that "the woman who works is the underdog of the world"; thus she needed the vote to defend herself. Socialists and working women rose from the floor to support them. Two years later the Equality League organized a much more successful suffrage parade in New York. Several hundred suffragettes, organized by occupation, marched from Fifty-ninth Street to Union Square. O'Reilly, the featured speaker, made "a tearful plea on behalf of the working girl that drew the first big demonstration of applause from the street crowd."[49]

Perhaps because the American Suffragettes were so active in New York City, Blatch held the Equality League's first open-air meetings in May 1908 upstate. Accompanied by Maud Malone, she organized an inventive "trolley car campaign" between Syracuse and Albany, using the interurban trolleys to go from town to town. The audiences expressed the complex class character of the suffrage movement at that moment. In Syracuse Blatch had her wealthy friend Dora Hazard arrange a meeting among the workers at her husband's factory. She also held a successful outdoor meeting in Troy, home of the Laundry Workers' Union, one of the oldest and most militant independent women's trade unions in the country. Albany was an antisuffrage stronghold, and its mayor tried to prevent the meeting, but Blatch outwitted him. The highlight of the tour was in Poughkeepsie, where Blatch and Inez Milholland, then a student at Vassar College, organized a legendary meeting. Since Vassar's male president forbade any woman suffrage activities on college grounds, Blatch and Milholland defiantly announced they would meet students in a cemetery. Gilman, who was extremely popular among college women, spoke, but it was the passionate trade-union feminist Schneiderman who was the star.[50]

Blatch believed that the first function of militant tactics was to gain much-needed publicity for the movement. The mainstream press had long ignored suffrage activities. If an occasional meeting was reported, it was usually buried in a small back-page article, focusing on the absurdity and incompetence of women's efforts to organize a political campaign. Gilded Age suffragists themselves accepted the Victorian convention that respectable women did not court public attention. The Equality League's emphasis on the importance of paid labor for women of all classes struck at the heart of that convention. Blatch understood "the value of publicity or rather the harm of the lack of it." She encouraged open-air meetings and trolley car campaigns because they generated much publicity, which no longer held the conventional horror for her followers.[51]

Militant tactics broke through the "press boycott" by violating standards of respectable femininity, making the cause newsworthy, and embracing the subsequent ridicule and attention. "We . . . believe in standing on street corners and fighting our way to recognition, forcing the men to think about us," an American Suffragette manifesto proclaimed. "We glory . . . that we are theatrical." The militant pursuit of publicity was an instant success: Newspaper coverage increased immediately; by 1908 even the sneering *New York Times* reported regularly on suffrage. The more outrageous or controversial the event, the more prominent the coverage. Blatch was often pictured and quoted.[52]

The new methods had a second function: they intensified women's commitment to the movement. Militants expected that overstepping the boundary of respectability would etch suffrage beliefs on women's souls, beyond retraction or modification. Blatch caught the psychology of this process. "Society has taught women self sacrifice and now this force is to be drawn upon in the arduous campaign for their own emancipation," she wrote. "The new methods of agitation, in that they are difficult and disagreeable, lay hold of the imagination and devotion of women, wherein lies the strength of the new appeal, the certainty of victory." Borrman Wells spoke of the "divine spirit of self-sacrifice," which underlay the suffragette's transgressions against respectability and was the source of the "true inwardness of the movement."[53]

If suffrage militants had a general goal beyond getting the vote, it was to challenge existing standards of femininity. "We must eliminate that abominable word ladylike from our vocabularies," Borrman Wells proclaimed. "We must get out and fight." The new definition of femininity the militants were evolving drew, on the one hand, on traditionally male behaviors, like aggression, fighting, provocation, and rebelliousness. Blatch was particularly drawn to the "virile" world of politics, which she characterized as a male "sport" she was sure she could master. On the other hand, they undertook a spirited defense of female sexuality, denying that it need be forfeited by women who participated vigorously in public life. "Women are no longer to be considered little tootsey wootseys who have nothing to do but look pretty," suffragette Lydia Commander declared. "They are determined to take an active part in the community and look pretty too." A member of a slightly older generation, Blatch never adopted the modern sexual ethic of the new woman, but she constantly emphasized the fact that women had distinct concerns that had to be accommodated in politics and industry. These two notes—the difference of the sexes and the repressed ability of women for manly activities—existed side by side in the thought of all the suffrage insurgents.[54]

The militant methods, taking suffrage out of the parlors and into the streets, indicated the new significance of working-class women in several ways. Blatch pointed out that the new methods—open-air meetings, newspaper publicity—suited a movement whose members had little money and therefore could not afford to rent halls or publish a newspaper. As a style of protest, "militance" was an import from the labor movement; WTUL organizers had been speaking from street corners for several years. And disrespect for the standards of ladylike respectability showed at least an impatience with rigid standards of class distinction, at most the influence of class-conscious wage-earning women.[55]

Working-class feminists were eager to speak from the militants' platform, as were many Socialists. A Socialist cadre, Dr. Anna Mercy, organized a branch of the American Suffragettes on the Lower East Side, which issued the first suffrage leaflets ever published in Yiddish. Militants also prepared propaganda in German and Italian and, in general, pursued working-class audiences. "Our relation to the State will be determined by the vote of the average man," Blatch asserted. "None but the converted . . . will come to us. We must seek on the highways the unconverted."[56]

However, it would be a mistake to confuse the suffragettes' radicalism with the radicalism of a working-class movement. The ultimate goal of the suffragettes was not a single-class movement, but a universal one, "the union of women of all shades of political thought and of all ranks of society on the single issue of their political enfranchisement." While the Equality League's 1907 hearing before the state legislature highlighted trade-union suffragists, at the 1908 hearing the league also featured elite speakers, in effect deemphasizing the working-class perspective.[57] Militants could neither repudiate the Socialist support they were attracting, and alienate working-class women, nor associate too closely with Socialists, and lose access to the wealthy. Blatch—who actually became a Socialist after the suffrage was won—would not arrange for the Socialist party leader Morris Hillquit to join other prosuffrage speakers at the 1908 legislative hearing. Similarly, the American Suffragettes allowed individual Socialists on their platform but barred Socialist propaganda. Speaking for Socialist women who found the "idea of a 'radical' suffrage movement . . . very alluring," Josephine Conger Kaneko admitted that the suffragettes left her confused.[58]

Moreover, the militant challenge to femininity and the emphasis on publicity introduced a distinctly elite bias; a society matron on an open-air platform made page one while a working girl did not, because society women were obliged by conventions and could outrage by flouting them. In their very desire to redefine femininity, the militants were anxious to stake their claim to it, and it was upper-class women who determined femininity. In Elizabeth Robin's drama about the rise of militance in the British suffrage movement, *The Convert*, the heroine of the title was a beautiful aristocratic woman who became radical when she realized the emptiness of her ladylike existence and the contempt for women obscured by gentlemen's chivalrous gestures. The Equality League brought *The Convert* to New York in 1908 as its first large fund-raising effort; working-class women, as well as elite women, made up the audience. Malone was one of the few militants to recognize and to protest against excessive solicitousness for the elite convert. She resigned from the American Suffragettes when she concluded that they had become interested in attracting "a well-dressed crowd, not the rabble."[59]

Blatch's perspective and associations had always been fundamentally elite. The most well connected of the new militant leaders, she played a major role in bringing the new suffrage propaganda to the attention of upper-class women. She presided over street meetings in fashionable neighborhoods, where reporters commented on the "smart" crowds and described the speakers' outfits in society-page detail. Blatch's first important ally from the Four Hundred was Katherine Duer Mackay, wife of the founder of the International Telephone and Telegraph Company and a famous society beauty. Mackay's suffragism was very ladylike, but other members of her set who followed her into the movement were more drawn to militance: Alva Belmont, a veritable mistress of flamboyance, began her suffrage career as Mackay's protégé. The elitist subtext of militance was a minor theme in 1908 and 1909. But by 1910 becoming a suffragette was proving "fashionable," and upper-class women began to identify with the new suffrage style in significant numbers. By the time suffragette militance became a national movement, its working-class origins and trade-union associations had been submerged, and it was in the hands of women of wealth.[60]

From the beginning, though, class was the contradiction at the suffrage movement's heart. In the campaign of 1894, elite women began to pursue more power for themselves by advocating the suffrage in the name of all women. When Cobden-Sanderson spoke for the Equality League at Cooper Union in 1907, she criticized "idle women of wealth" as the enemies of woman suffrage, and she was wildly applauded. But what did her charge mean? Were all rich women under indictment, or only those who stayed aloof from social responsibility and political activism? Were the militants calling for working-class leadership of the suffrage movement or for cultural changes in bourgeois definitions of womanhood? This ambiguity paralleled the mixed meanings in Blatch's emphasis on working women; it coincided with an implicit tension between the older, elite women's reform traditions and the newer, trade-union politics they had helped to usher in; and it was related to a lurking confusion about whether feminism's object was the superfluity of wealthy women or the exploitation of the poor. It would continue to plague suffragism in its final decade, and feminism afterward, into our own time.

NOTES

1. A good overview of political history in the Progressive Era can be found in Arthur S. Link and Richard L. McCormick, *Progressivism* (Arlington Heights, Ill., 1983), 26–66. The "separate spheres" framework of Progressive-Era historiography has been identified and challenged by Paula Baker, "The Domestication of Politics: Women and American Political Society, 1780–1920," *American Historical Review,* 89 (June 1984), esp. 639–47; and by Kathryn Kish Sklar, "Hull House in the 1890s: A Community of Women Reformers," *Signs,* 10 (Summer 1985), 658–77; Kathryn Kish Sklar, "Florence Kelley and the Integration of 'Women's Sphere' into American Politics, 1890–1921," paper delivered at the annual meeting of the Organization of American Historians, New York, April 1986 (in Sklar's possession).

2. Steven M. Buechler, *The Transformation of the Woman Suffrage Movement: The Case of Illinois, 1850–1920* (New Brunswick, 1986); Mari Jo Buhle and Paul Buhle, eds., *The Concise History of Woman Suffrage: Selections from the Classic Work of Stanton, Anthony, Gage and Harper* (Urbana, 1978); Carole Nichols, *Votes and More for Women: Suffrage and After in Connecticut* (New York, 1983); Anne F. Scott and Andrew Scott, eds., *One Half the People* (Philadelphia, 1975); and Sharon Strom, "Leadership and Tactics in the American Woman Suffrage Movement: A New Perspective from Massachusetts," *Journal of American History,* 52 (Sept. 1975), 296–315.

3. "Mrs. Blatch's Address," clipping, 1903, Women's Club of Orange, N.J., Scrapbooks, IV (New Jersey Historical Society, Trenton). Thanks to Gail Malmgreen for this citation.

4. Richard L. McCormick, *From Realignment to Reform: Political Change in New York State, 1893–1910* (Ithaca, 1979), 53. An excellent account of the political reform movement in the 1890s in New York City can be found in David C. Hammack, *Power and Society: Greater New York at the Turn of the Century* (New York, 1982).

5. Susan B. Anthony and Ida Husted Harper, eds., *The History of Woman*

Suffrage, vol. IV: *1883–1900* (Rochester, 1902), 847–52; New York State Woman Suffrage Party, *Record of the New York Campaign of 1894* (New York, 1895); Ida Husted Harper, ed., *The Life and Work of Susan B.* Anthony (3 vols., Indianapolis, 1898–1908), II, 758–76, esp. 759.

6. Mary Putnam Jacobi, "Report of the 'Volunteer Committee' in New York City," in *Record of the New York Campaign,* 217–20; Maud Nathan, *The Story of an Epoch-making Movement* (Garden City, 1926); William Rhinelander Stewart, ed., *The Philanthropic Work of Josephine Shaw Lowell* (New York, 1926), 334–56.

7. *New York Times,* April 14, 1894, 2; ibid., April 15, 1894, 5. Mrs. Robert (Catherine) Abbe's suffrage scrapbooks provide extensive documentation of the New York suffrage movement, beginning with this campaign. Mrs. Robert Abbe Collection (Manuscript Division, New York Public Library). Theodore Stanton and Harriot Stanton Blatch, eds., *Elizabeth Cady Stanton as Revealed in Her Letters, Diary, and Reminiscences* (2 vols., New York, 1922), II, 299.

8. Mary Putnam Jacobi, "Address Delivered at the New York City Hearing," in *Record of the New York Campaign,* 17–26; Olivia Slocum Sage, "Opportunities and Responsibilities of Leisured Women," *North American Review,* 181 (Nov. 1905), 712–21.

9. Ibid.

10. Ibid

11. Jacobi, "Report of the 'Volunteer Committee,'" 217; Stanton and Blatch, eds., *Elizabeth Cady Stanton,* II, 305; *New York Times,* May 3, 1894, 9. Abby Hamlin Abbott and Josephine Jewell Dodge were both Brooklyn residents; the division between suffragists and antis reflected a conflict between the elites of Manhattan and Brooklyn over the 1894 referendum to consolidate the two cities into Greater New York. See Hammack, *Power and Society,* 209.

12. Jacobi, "Address Delivered at the New York City Hearing," 22; *New York Times,* April 12, 1894, 5. "The woman in charge of the [anti] protest . . . told a reporter . . . that her own dressmaker has secured about forty signatories to the protest among working women." Ibid., May 8, 1894, 1.

13. *Woman's Journal,* May 12, 1894, 147.

14. Ibid., May 19, 1894. The study, patterned after Charles Booth and Mary Booth's investigation of the London poor, on which Blatch worked, was published as Harriot Stanton Blatch, "Another View of Village Life," *Westminster Review,* 140 (Sept. 1893), 318–24.

15. Stanton and Blatch, eds., *Elizabeth Cady Stanton,* II, 304; unidentified clipping, April 25, 1894, Scrapbook XX, Susan B. Anthony Collection (Manu-

script Division, Library of Congress); *New York Times,* April 25, 1894, 5; ibid., May 3, 1894, 9; *New York Sun,* April 15, 1894, n.p.

16. *Woman's Journal,* Nov. 3, 1894, 348–49; ibid., Dec. 22, 1894, 402; ibid., Jan. 5, 1895, 1. Blatch wrote that her mother's position "pained" her but there is no evidence of any personal conflict between them at this time. Ibid., Dec. 22, 1894, 402.

17. Harriot Stanton Blatch and Alma Lutz, *Challenging Years: The Memoirs of Harriot Stanton Blatch* (New York 1940), 77. *Woman's Journal,* Jan. 18, 1896, 18.

18. *Woman's Journal,* May 12, 1900, 146–47. Along with Blatch and Charlotte Perkins Gilman, Florence Kelley and Jane Addams were the most important figures to focus on women and class. See Charlotte Perkins Gilman, *Women and Economics: A Study of the Economic Relation between Men and Women as a Factor in Social Evolution* (Boston, 1898); Florence Kelley, *Woman Suffrage: Its Relation to Working Women and Children* (Warren, Ohio, 1906); Florence Kelley, "Women and Social Legislation in the United States," *Annals of the American Academy of Political and Social Science,* 56 (Nov. 1914), 62–71; Jane Addams, *Newer Ideals of Peace* (New York, 1907); and Jane Addams, *Twenty Years at Hull House* (New York, 1910). Some of the other women reformers who wrote on women and work early in the century were Rheta Childe Dorr, *What Eight Million Women Want* (Boston, 1910); Lillian Wald, "Organization among Working Women," *Annals of the American Academy of Political and Social Science,* 27 (May 1906), 638–45; and Anna Garlin Spencer, *Woman's Share in Social Culture* (New York, 1913).

19. Harriot Stanton Blatch, "Specialization of Function in Women," *Gunton's Magazine,* 10 (May 1896), 349–56, esp. 350.

20. Ibid.

21. Ibid., 354–55; see also Blatch's comments at a 1904 suffrage meeting in New York, *Woman's Journal,* Dec. 31, 1904, 423.

22. Blatch, "Specialization of Function in Women," 350, 353.

23. See, for example, the response of the New York City Woman Suffrage League to a proposal before the American Federation of Labor to ban women from all nondomestic employment. *New York Times,* Dec. 23, 1898, 7.

24. Harriot Stanton Blatch, "Weaving in a Westchester Farmhouse," *International Studio,* 26 (Oct. 1905), 102–5; *Woman's Journal,* Jan. 21, 1905; ibid., Dec. 31, 1904, 423.

25. Blatch, "Weaving in a Westchester Farmhouse," 104; Blatch and Lutz, *Challenging Years,* 70–86; Rhoda Barney Jenkins interview by Ellen Carol DuBois, June 10, 1982 (in Ellen Carol DuBois's possession); Ellen DuBois,

"'Spanning Two Centuries': The Autobiography of Nora Stanton Barney," *History Workshop*, no. 22 (Fall 1986), 131–52. esp. 149.

26. Anthony and Harper, eds., *History of Woman Suffrage*, IV, 311.

27. "Mrs. Blatch's Address," Women's Club of Orange, N.J., Scrapbooks; Anthony and Harper, eds., *History of Woman Suffrage*, IV, 311.

28. Harriot Stanton Blatch to Susan B. Anthony, Sept. 26, 1902, in *Epistolary Autobiography*, Theodore Stanton Collection (Douglass College Library, Rutgers University, New Brunswick, N.J.).

29. Oswald Garrison Villard, "Women in New York Municipal Campaign," *Woman's Journal*, March 8, 1902, 78–79.

30. *New York Times*, Jan. 14, 1901, 7. The Gertrude Colles Collection (New York State Library, Albany) is particularly rich in evidence of the less elite, more radical side of female political reform in these years. On the mock voting organized by the Equal Rights League, see *Woman's Journal*, Dec. 28, 1905, and *New York Times*, Nov. 7, 1906, 9.

31. Anthony and Harper, eds., *History of Woman Suffrage*, IV, 861; Ida Husted Harper, ed., *History of Woman Suffrage*, vol. VI: *1900–1920* (New York, 1922), 454; *New York Times*, March 2, 1902, 8; *Woman's Tribune*, April 25, 1903, 49. After Blatch had become an acknowledged leader of the New York suffrage movement, the coworker who, she felt, most shared her political perspective was Caroline Lexow, daughter of the man who had conducted the original investigation of police corruption in New York in 1894. See Blatch and Lutz, *Challenging Years*, 120–21; and Isabelle K. Savelle, *Ladies' Lib: How Rockland Women Got the Vote* (Nyack, N.Y., 1979).

32. Minutes, March 29, 1906, reel 1, New York Women's Trade Union League Papers (New York State Labor Library, New York). On the WTUL, see Nancy Schrom Dye, *As Equals and as Sisters: Feminism, the Labor Movement, and the Women's Trade Union League of New York* (Columbia, 1980); and Meredith Tax, *The Rising of the Women: Feminist Solidarity and Class Conflict, 1880–1917* (New York, 1980), 95–124.

33. Dye, *As Equals and as Sisters*, 63; Minutes, April 26, Aug. 23, 1906, New York Women's Trade Union League Papers; *New York Times*, April 11, 1907, 8.

34. Mary Kenney O'Sullivan, "The Need of Organization among Working Women (1905)," Margaret Dreier Robins Papers (University of Florida Library, Gainesville); Sarah Eisenstein, *Give Us Bread but Give Us Roses: Working Women's Consciousness in the United States, 1890 to the First World War* (London, 1983), 146–50.

35. *Woman's Journal*, March 17, 1906, 43; Kelley, *Woman Suffrage*; Jane Addams, "Utilization of Women in Government," in *Jane Addams: A Centennial*

Reader (New York, 1960), 116–18; *Woman's Journal,* Dec. 31, 1904, 423; "Mrs. Blatch's Address," Women's Club of Orange, N.J., Scrapbooks. There was a lengthy discussion of working women's need for the vote, including a speech by Rose Schneiderman, at the 1907 New York State Woman Suffrage Association convention. See Minute Book, 1907–10, New York State Woman Suffrage Association (Butler Library, Columbia University, New York). The WTUL identified woman suffrage as one of its goals by 1907. Dye, *As Equals and as Sisters,* 123.

36. *New York Times,* Jan. 3, 1907, 6; *Woman's Journal,* Jan. 12, 1907, 8.

37. *Progress,* June 1907. Carrie Chapman Catt to Millicent Garrett Fawcett, Oct. 19, 1909, container 5, Papers of Carrie Chapman Catt (Manuscript Division, Library of Congress).

38. *Woman's Journal,* Aug. 17, 1907, 129. On Nora Blatch (who later called herself Nora Stanton Barney), see DuBois, "'Spanning Two Centuries,'" 131–52. Those self-supporters who, I believe, had independent incomes include Nora Blatch, Caroline Lexow, Lavinia Dock, Ida Rauh, Gertrude Barnum, Elizabeth Finnegan, and Alice Clark. See, for example, on Nora Blatch, ibid., and on Dock, see *Notable American Women: The Modern Period,* ed. Sicherman et al. (Cambridge, 1980), 195–98.

39. Caroline Lexow to Leonora O'Reilly, Jan. 3, 1908, reel 4, Leonora O'Reilly Papers (Schlesinger Library, Radcliffe College, Cambridge, Mass.); O'Reilly to Lexow, Jan. 5, 1908, ibid.; Robert Doherty, "Tempest on the Hudson: The Struggle for Equal Pay for Equal Work in the New York City Public Schools, 1907–1911," *Harvard Educational Quarterly,* 19 (Winter 1979), 413–39. The role of teachers in the twentieth-century suffrage movement is a promising area for research. For information on teachers' organizations in the Buffalo, New York, suffrage movement, I am indebted to Eve S. Faber, Swarthmore College, "Suffrage in Buffalo, 1898–1913" (unpublished paper in DuBois's possession).

40. *New York Times,* June 6, 1907, 1.

41. On self-support for women after marriage, see *New York World,* July 26, 1908, 3; and Lydia Kingsmill Commander, "The Self Supporting Woman and the Family," *American Journal of Sociology,* 14 (March 1909), 752–57. On the debate, see *New York Times,* Jan. 7, 1909, 9.

42. *New York Times,* Feb. 6, 1907, 6. Harriot Stanton Blatch, ed., *Two Speeches by Industrial Women* (New York, 1907), 8. The Equality League's bill authorized a voters' referendum on an amendment to the New York constitution, to remove the word "male" from the state's suffrage provisions, thus enfranchis-

ing New York women. Since the U.S. Constitution vests power to determine the electorate with the states, the aim was to win full suffrage in federal, as well as state, elections for New York women. With minor alterations, the measure finally passed, but in 1915 New York voters refused to enfranchise the women of their state; a second referendum in 1917 was successful. See Blatch and Lutz, *Challenging Years*, 156–238.

43. *Woman's Tribune*, Feb. 9, 1907, 12; Minutes, April 27, 1909, New York Women's Trade Union League Papers; *Progress*, Nov. 1908.

44. Blatch and Lutz, *Challenging* Years, 100–101; *Progress*, Jan. 1908, p. 1.

45. *Woman's Journal*, Dec. 28, 1907, 205, 206–7.

46. By 1908, there was a racehorse named "suffragette." *New York Evening Telegram*, Sept. 16, 1908. Blatch noted that once she left England in the late 1890s, she and Emmeline Pankhurst did not communicate until 1907, after they had both taken their respective countries' suffrage movements in newly militant directions. Blatch to Christabel Pankhurst, in Christabel Pankhurst, *Unshackled: How We Won the Vote* (London, 1959), 30.

47. The first American arrests were not until 1917. For American suffragists' early response to the WSPU, see the *Woman's Journal*, May 30, 1908, 87. Even Carrie Chapman Catt praised the British militants at first. *Woman's Journal*, Dec. 12, 1908, 199. For an example of divisive coverage by the mainstream press, see "Suffragist or Suffragette," *New York Times*, Feb. 29, 1908, 6.

48. On Bettina Borrman Wells, see A. J. R., ed., *Suffrage Annual and Women's Who's Who* (London, 1913), 390. Thanks to David Doughan of the Fawcett Library for this reference. The best sources on the Equal Rights League are the Gertrude Colles Collection and *The American Suffragette*, which the group published from 1909 through 1911. See also Winifred Harper Cooley, "Suffragists and 'Suffragettes,'" *World To-Day*, 15 (Oct. 1908), 1066–71; and Elinor Lerner, "Jewish Involvement in the New York City Woman Suffrage Movement," *American Jewish History*, 70 (June 1981), 444–45. The American Suffragettes found a predecessor and benefactor in seventy-five-year-old Lady Cook, formerly Tennessee Claflin, in 1909 the wife of a titled Englishman. "Our Cook Day," *American Suffragette*, 1 (Nov. 1909), 1.

49. On the first open-air meeting, see *New York Times*, Jan. 1, 1908, 16. On the parade, see ibid., Feb. 17, 1908, 7; there is also an account in Dorr, *What Eighty Million Women Want*, 298–99; *New York Evening Journal*, May 21, 1910.

50. Equality League of Self-Supporting Women, *Report for Year 1908–1909* (New York, 1909), 2; Blatch and Lutz, *Challenging Years*, 107–9. On Vassar, see also *New York American*, June 10, 1908.

51. Harriot Stanton Blatch, "Radical Move in Two Years," clipping, Nov. 8, 1908, suffrage scrapbooks, Abbe Collection. Blatch "starred" in a prosuffrage movie, *What Eighty Million Women Want,* produced in 1912. Kay Sloan, "Sexual Warfare in the Silent Cinema: Comedies and Melodramas of Woman Suffragism," *American Quarterly,* 33 (Fall 1981), 412–36. She was also very interested in the propaganda possibilities of commercial radio, according to Lee de Forest, a pioneer of the industry, who was briefly married to her daughter. Lee de Forest, *Father of Radio: The Autobiography of Lee de Forest* (Chicago, 1950), 248–49.

52. Mary Tyng, "Self Denial Week," *American Suffragette,* 1 (Aug. 1909); *New York Herald,* Dec. 19, 1908.

53. Blatch, "Radical Move in Two Years"; Mrs. B. Borrman Wells, "The Militant Movement for Woman Suffrage," *Independent,* April 23, 1908, 901–3.

54. "Suffragettes Bar Word 'Ladylike,'" clipping, Jan. 13, 1909, suffrage scrapbooks, Abbe Collection; Blatch and Lutz, *Challenging Years,* 91–242; *New York Herald,* March 8, 1908. On militants' views of femininity and sexuality, see also "National Suffrage Convention," *American Suffragette,* 2 (March 1910), 3.

55. Blatch and Lutz, *Challenging Years,* 107; Dye, *As Equals and as Sisters,* 47.

56. *Woman's Journal,* May 30, 1908, 87; Blatch, "Radical Move in Two Years."

57. Borrman Wells, "Militant Movement for Woman Suffrage," 901; *Woman's Journal,* Feb. 29, 1908, 34.

58. *New York Times,* Feb. 11, 1908, 6; [Josephine C. Kaneko], "To Join, or Not to Join," *Socialist Woman,* 1 (May 1908), 6.

59. On *The Convert,* see Equality League, *Report for 1908–1909,* 4; Jane Marcus, "Introduction," in *The Convert* (London, 1980), v–xvi; *New York Call,* Dec. 9, 1908, 6; and Minutes, Dec. 22, 1908, New York Women's Trade Union League Papers. Maud Malone also charged the American Suffragettes with discrimination against Socialists and Bettina Borrman Wells with personal ambition. For her letter of resignation, see *New York Times,* March 27, 1908, 4.

60. *New York Times,* May 14, 1909, 5. On Mackay and her Equal Franchise Society, see *New York Times,* Feb. 21, 1909, part 5, 2. On Blatch's relation to Mackay, see Blatch and Lutz, *Challenging Years,* 118. "As for the suffrage movement, it is actually fashionable now," wrote militant Inez Haynes, who very much approved of the development. "All kinds of society people are taking it

up." Inez Haynes to Maud Wood Park, Dec. 2, 1910, reel 11, National American Woman Suffrage Association Papers (Manuscript Division, Library of Congress). Gertrude Foster Brown, another wealthy woman recruited by Blatch, wrote her own history of the New York suffrage movement in which she virtually ignored the role of working-class women. Gertrude Foster Brown, "On Account of Sex," Gertrude Foster Brown Papers, Sophia Smith Collection (Smith College, Northampton, Mass.).

11

Making Women's History

Historian-Activists of Women's Rights, 1880–1940

> The impression conveyed by our text books is that this world has been made by men and for men and the ideals they are putting forth are colored by masculine thought. . . . Our text books on Civics do not show the slightest appreciation of the significance of the "woman's movement." —Pauline Steinem, 1909[1]

The subject of this paper is the history of women's history in the years following the passage of the Nineteenth Amendment, giving women the right to vote, and the waning of the public face of organized feminism.

This subject is important for several reasons. Most of the people involved in writing and promoting the history of women's rights in those formative years were veterans of the suffrage movement, who thought the preservation of history would contribute to "the cause." They were not academically trained, but popular, even amateur, historians. The enthusiasm and sense of political mission with which they pursued the preservation and writing of the past in the 1920s and 1930s characterizes an important phase in the missing history of the feminist movement between the decline of suffragism and the rise of women's liberation.

Originally published in *Radical History Review* 49 (1991).

Furthermore, the activities of these historian-activists proceed and underlie the current surge in women's history. The archives they created, the books they wrote in the 1920s, 1930s, and early 1940s, awaited— even enticed—feminists of the 1960s and 1970s to become historians of women. In a basic way, the emergence of a field of women's history over the last two decades was the belated realization of the mission they had begun years before. There is precious little historiography of women's history before 1970 but the few articles there are have focused exclusively on female academic historians, as if these were the significant predecessors of today's women's historians.[2]

But there were only a handful of women in the profession until recently, and they—for obvious reasons—stayed away from the subject that would have drawn attention to their difference. Mary Beard, of course, has been the object of much interest, but even she has been examined in isolation, rather than as part of a larger group of former activists who were making women's history in the same years.[3]

Finally, this episode sheds light on larger problems: why and how political insurgence is related to the historical impulse; why a group pushing its way into civil society and political recognition becomes hungry for a history of itself and for a recognized place in the larger past. Extrapolating from this particular episode suggests a way to formulate the link between politics and history, between the past and the future. Feminist, labor, black liberation and similar movements all rest on two somewhat contradictory postulates which only a theory about the movement of history can resolve. On the one hand, such movements declare a past of oppression, subordination and injustice; on the other, they assert the possibility of a future of an entirely different order—a future of emancipation or liberation. Activists committed to social change need to create for themselves a historical interpretation which can take them from one kind of past to a different kind of future. Moreover, this need for history takes on different forms during different stages in a movement's development: sometimes the purpose of history is to inspire, sometimes to sustain, sometimes to recall.

Examining the link between politics and history can help us to understand not only the history of social movements, but history in general. "Memory is the thread of personal identity," writes Richard Hofstadter in the opening sentence of *The Progressive Historians*, "History of Public Identity."[4] The current attacks of official, right-wing critics of "history from the bottom up" have been particularly effective in insisting that passion and scholarship are enemies, that history cannot be "true" and argue a case at the same time. As practicing historians, we are so busy defending against these onslaughts that we have no time to investigate the relationship between partisanship and scholarship in other, less defensive ways. But impulses other than academic are important—perhaps fundamental—in the recording, writing and interpreting of history.

This paper focuses on contributions to the history of women's rights between 1920 and 1940. Needless to say, the women's rights movement does not constitute the entirety of women's past. There are other strains of women's historiography that are not dealt with here. While the historians examined here have virtually nothing to say about the history of women in the wage-labor force, there are important books on this subject, dating at least as far back as the federally sponsored *History of Women in Industry* published in 1911, which have helped to shape subsequent work on this subject.[5] Similarly, there is a historiography of African-American women reaching back to the group biographies of women worthies of color published in conjunction with the black women's club movement at the turn of the century.[6] These and other aspects of women's historical action need to be situated in their own politically informed historiography.

The Evolution of a Master Narrative of Women's History

The links between women's rights activism and women's history begin even before woman suffrage was secured. Elizabeth Stanton had wanted to write a book on the history of women's aspirations for emancipation as a way to develop the argument for sexual equality as early as the 1840s.[7] After a series of political defeats in the mid 1870s, her partner Susan B. Anthony revived the idea, and along with Matilda Joslyn Gage they undertook what they imagined would be a one volume "history of woman suffrage." To those who contended even then that "the actors themselves cannot write impartial history," Elizabeth Stanton responded that "a history written by its actors get[s] nearer the soul of the subject."[8] By the time Stanton gave up the project, more than a decade later, the *History of Woman Suffrage* had reached three volumes and more than 3,000 pages; in 1922, long after all three of the original editors had died, the sixth and final volume was finished. There is nothing in the annals of American reform quite like the *History of Woman Suffrage,* a prolonged, deliberate effort on the part of activists to ensure their place in the historical record.

All the volumes situate women's demands for political equality in a larger context, not only of women's legal rights, but of the long elevation and emancipation of the sex. The initial volumes are very broadly conceived, a combination of Stanton's broad philosophical range, Anthony's organizational energies and Gage's historical sensibilities. Although the editors were not shy about their own historical interpretations (Stanton, for instance, saw women's rights in terms of the long history of individualism), they included an enormous amount of primary material so that readers could reach their own conclusions. Personal reminiscences, conference proceedings, newspaper articles and stump speeches are linked together by a loose narrative, a lovely, long string of separate historical jewels. Anthony also insisted on expensive steel-plate portraits of important women's rights figures, so that future generations would have counter-evidence to the charge that all strong-minded women were desexed.[9]

Stanton wrote a great deal of the text and her interpretation of the rise of the movement pervades the volumes. Gage supplied important supplementary essays, on the history of women in the American Revolution, on the rise of newspaper publishing and most notably on the long history of Christian misogyny and attacks on witchcraft, which extended the project's historical range. Anthony, for whom the project came to take on great personal meaning, was the business manager. For volume three, she solicited state by state essays, written by local activists, with enormously detailed information about the growth of a movement at the rank and file level. "Put a request . . . asking any person who knows of any fact or any person that you have not mentioned to send it to you at once," she advised the author of the Illinois chapter. "That way you'll get everything."[10] She hired the indexer from the *New York Tribune* to prepare a very detailed index to all three volumes, to increase their accessibility.[11] She then sold and gave away thousands of volumes—largely at her own expense. "Every normal, high school, college, and public library ought to have the books," she insisted. "It is the only place that the facts about the work done by and for women can be found."[12]

Anthony's name also appeared on volume four, but by this time most of the work was being done by her biographer and protégé, Ida H. Harper, who finished the last two volumes in 1922.[13] The last three volumes of the *History* are quite different from the first three. They are less a history of a social movement than of an organization—the National American Woman Suffrage Association. Chapters are organized around annual conventions, lists of officers and accounts of speeches and committee reports, which makes for a much less exciting narrative of historical transformation. Intra- and inter-organizational conflicts were read out of the account, even as they shaped what was included and what was excluded.[14] The exclusion of all evidence of conflict or alternatives—historical, strategic or even interpretive—made for a sense of historical inevitability rather than social struggle. Women's enfranchisement was depicted as part of the inevitable unfolding of American democracy, of women being drawn along with men into the national destiny. Oddly enough, this Whiggish tale of the steady climb of women toward collective advancement was combined with an anti-democratic suspicion of and hostility to the political impulses of the (male) masses. (By contrast, the earlier volumes had tended to situate women's rights as part of the long march of oppressed humanity against unjust authority.)[15]

The last three volumes of the *History of Woman Suffrage* also engaged the problem of leadership—and more deeply, of the relation of individuals to the movement—in a different way than had the earlier volumes. The early volumes were lavish in their appreciation of individual achievement: numerous individuals, each the "first" woman to do something, were named and included in the *History's* account of the progress of women.[16] In the final volumes, the individual achievements of fewer women are given more weight. The complex history of the movement is merged into the person of a handful of leaders, who in turn are rendered as saints, selfless embodiments of a larger cause.

Chief of these was Susan B. Anthony, who was universally recognized as the summit of the women's rights pantheon. Not only did the focus on Anthony tend to shut out recognition of many other leaders, but it set a pattern for the treatment of the relationship between private life and public achievement that was eminently Victorian. Leaders either lacked distinct private lives (this was the case with Anthony, whose ultimate contribution to the movement was to live her life in total devotion to it), or, as the official version of Stanton's life would have it, they were perfect in their expression of motherly devotion and home-maker excellence.

Thus, by the last phase of the woman suffrage movement, and the final volumes of the *History of Woman Suffrage,* the historical account within which the women's rights movement was situated had narrowed considerably. By 1910 or so, there was considerable consensus around a single, controlling version of women's rights history: that in the early nineteenth century, American women had begun to "awaken," to follow the road that lay waiting to lead them to "advancement" through higher education and the opening up of the professions, past temperance societies and women's clubs, ultimately to arrive at the temple of political equality.[17] This frozen account of the past, a history characterized by celebration, inevitability and canonization, as well as by a rigid separation between public achievement and personal life, constituted what might be called a "master narrative" (the patriarchal reference is intended) of women's rights.

In the years immediately before and after the ratification of the Nineteenth Amendment, the two wings into which suffragism had split waged an intense intra-movement war over, among other things, the history of the women's rights movement. Each version stressed different political virtues: the size and efficiency of the National American Woman Suffrage Association versus the National Woman's Party's militancy.[18] They disagreed intensely over which wing was ultimately responsible for passage of the Nineteenth Amendment, so much so that they read each other out of their factional versions of history. These historical skirmishes were conducted with great vehemence—in 1921, for instance, the two factions fought over who would dedicate a statue to women's rights pioneers in the Capitol rotunda.[19]

Ultimately, however, neither account diverged from the "master narrative." They shared the same basic framework for their history. Both wings, for instance, apotheosized Anthony, disagreeing only on which faction was her rightful heir. Both embraced the notion that the ultimate victory of woman suffrage was a result of its being a "single issue" movement, one which regarded all other causes as competitive with women's advancement, and all "politics" as male manifestations, equally hostile to the cause of women.[20] The dispute between factions was not over the basic content of the history of women's rights, but only over who controlled its telling and which side would reap the glory of past triumphs.

While the "master narrative" continued to be reproduced for many decades, from 1920 on processes worked to complicate this historical account and widen the resources with which American women's history could be written.[21] The meaning of the past began to change, against a background of general transformation in organized women's politics— especially the challenge and threat posed by the successful end to the long struggle for the vote and the replacement of Victorian norms of selfless service with modern standards of individualism and self-realization. At the deepest level, the ratification of the Nineteenth Amendment undermined the consensus about what women's path through history signified. The achievement of woman suffrage ironically threatened to bring to a close the long told history of women's steady ascent into public life. That it called into question the future organization and purpose of the organized women's movement is increasingly well understood; but it also called into question the meaning of the past. The winning of woman suffrage stimulated a reaction against the dominant account of women's past and started the search for themes in women's history not fully satisfied by enfranchisement.

Feminist Women's History

A new, more modernist approach can be detected in women's history writing beginning in the 1920s. This might best be characterized as "feminist" women's history, using the term as Nancy Cott develops it in *The Grounding of Modern Feminism*.[22] She uses "feminism," not to describe the long movement for women's rights, but to describe a particular ideology of female emancipation and sexual justice, first appearing in the 1910s, which both superceded and repudiated the prior, Victorian woman movement. Whereas the woman movement stood for selflessness in service to the cause, feminism stood for self-development as the route to women's emancipation. Whereas the woman movement rested on the principle of social purity, feminism went in search of female sexuality. Whereas the woman movement looked to the elevation of women collectively, feminism aspired to the liberation of individual women from social constraints, including those imposed by other women. Feminists reacted against the history associated with this movement. They replaced the "master narrative" of women's collective advancement with the search for individual women in conflict with social norms, a history which concentrated less on the inevitability of social reform than on the triumph of the individual over narrow social restrictions.

Feminist women's history in the 1920s paralleled larger currents in the practice of history. As Peter Novick observes, the post-war period was one in which academic historians in general were frequently eclipsed by historians who believed in and wrote to a popular audience.[23] Feminist historians were not academically trained and employed historians but rather professional writers and journalists. Like male progressive historians, they rejected the Whiggish tales of inevitable progress and national destiny. Instead, these feminists wanted to get under the surface, to push past appearances, to discover "the inside story." In their case, the inside story, the hidden reality, was more likely to be psychological and sexual than economic. Like male progressive historians, the feminist historians saw no conflict between the "scientific" pursuit of "reality" and their own convictions. They believed it was possible to look at the past with both an impartial eye and "the warmth of the advocate."[24]

An interesting and early example of this new feminist approach to women's history is Katherine Anthony's 1920 biography of Margaret Fuller.[25] Anthony, a University of Chicago graduate, Greenwich Village "new woman" and pioneering psycho-biographer, had already written an important study of the German and Scandinavian women's rights movements, in which she had praised them for going beyond legal equality to address the sexual and maternal particularities of women's lives.[26] Now "that suffrage is out of the way," Anthony was looking for a representative of a "broader kind of feminism" in the American tradition as well; she found it in Margaret Fuller.[27] While earlier biographers had justified or excused Fuller's eccentricities of personality in order to defend her literary stature, her personal extravagances were precisely what fascinated Anthony. Unlike a prior generation of women's historians who preferred their heroines to have harmonious domestic situations and to live in service to a larger cause, these feminist revisionists found chaotic personal lives a source of both interest and inspiration. Although Anthony praised Fuller's writings for the degree to which they anticipated twentieth-century feminism, she admired Fuller's life, its turbulence and its passions, even more. As a favorable review in the *Nation* noted, Fuller was so interesting precisely because her life "was dissociated from any movement except in the broadest sense of the word."[28]

Similar in conception to Anthony's *Margaret Fuller* is a 1927 biography of George Sand, by Marie Jenney Howe.[29] Howe was a close friend of Katherine Anthony and the founder of the important feminist literary and social club Heterodoxy, to which several other feminist historians belonged.[30] Howe admired Sand as "a modern woman born one hundred years too soon." Sand's modernism lay in the way she had lived her personal life ("she regarded laws and customs as ephemeral"), in her combination of masculinity and femininity into a character that was "inclusively human" and in her "generous self-revelations"—her willingness to make the complexity of her life accessible to others. "She ruined her life several times," Howe wrote admiringly, "but always crawled out from the debris and built up a new existence, until in the end she learned to adjust herself to life as it is and people as they are."[31]

In all the feminist histories of this period, sexual expression, not enfranchisement, was the redeeming goal of women's history. Women's past appeared different in light of Freudian ideas and the "scientific eroticism" of the 1920s. But whereas male modernists tended to blame women as the agents of Victorian sexual repression, feminist historians used pro-sex ideas to retrieve rather than condemn the women's rights tradition. In the case of Margaret Fuller, Anthony used Freudian tools to explore and defend Fuller's intimate bonds with other women, the implicit eroticism of which she regarded as healthy and vital. Anthony also regarded Fuller as a predecessor of the modern movement for sexual emancipation. "She was one of those who stood as sign posts along the road which was to lead in time to a scientific view of the nature of love."[32] In Howe's biography of Sand, subtitled *The Search for Love,* she retold Sand's life as a series of turbulent affairs and conflicts between her "desire for freedom and the need for human ties."[33] Even Sand's intense advocacy of the revolution of 1848, which Howe regarded as the climax of Sand's life, is presented in terms of her conflicting desires for transcendent love and a separate self. Howe's treatment of Sand's sex life, while deeply romantic, is nonetheless thoroughly feminist: Howe's heroine is in lifelong revolt against men's aspirations to possess and dominate women.

The publication, in 1927, of Paxton Hibben's anti-Victorian biography *Henry Ward Beecher: An American Portrait* made an important contribution to the feminist rereading of women's history.[34] Hibben, a war correspondent whose only previous book was a biography of King Constantine I, decided to take on Beecher, the leading Protestant minister of the 1860s and 1870s, to expose the sordid "reality" beyond his shining reputation for moral rectitude. In particular, Hibben rediscovered a half-century-old festering scandal in which Beecher had been accused of seducing Elizabeth Tilton, wife of his close friend Theodore Tilton. Hibben demonstrated conclusively that Henry Ward Beecher had been an adulterer. Hibben's research involved probing the secrets, not only of Henry Ward Beecher and Elizabeth and Theodore Tilton, but also of women's rights. Hibben discovered that Susan B. Anthony and Elizabeth Cady Stanton were the ones who had spilled the beans, albeit inadvertently, about the Beecher/Tilton affair. Moreover, the person they had told, who told the world, was the notorious "free lover" Victoria Woodhull, whom sexually conservative women's rights leaders had long been trying to suppress.

Within a year, two books appeared which explored the implications for women's history of Hibben's research. The more original of the two was " *The Terrible Siren,*" Emanie Sachs' biography of Victoria Woodhull (who had died the year before at the age of 89).[35]

Sachs, a "new woman" and successful novelist, found in Woodhull the perfect counter-heroine for a feminist rereading of women's rights history. Using Hibben's research for a start, Sachs unearthed the entirety of Woodhull's extraordinary life. Coming from an impoverished, unlettered background, Woodhull had risen to national prominence in the early 1870s as a radical leader. She was a stockbroker and a communist, a woman suffragist and a free lover. In short, she violated all of the oppositions on which Gilded Age culture was premised. Sachs celebrated Woodhull's "healthy eroticism," and her resistance to the enforcers of Victorian morality, not only Henry Ward Beecher but also other women—including his sisters—who monitored the boundaries of "true womanhood." Above all, Sachs appreciated Woodhull, as Katherine Anthony had Margaret Fuller, for her irrepressible individuality. Upon reading Sachs' book, Inez Haines Irwin, another feminist historian of the time, confessed to an embarrassed glee. Woodhull and her sister, Tennessee Claflin, "made me blush," Irwin wrote in 1928. "At the same time I could not help taking a rich and wicked joy in the way they walked rough shod, spike heeled and copper toed over the entire male sex."[36]

In 1928, Rheta Childe Dorr's life of Susan B. Anthony, *The Woman Who Changed the Mind of a Nation,* was published, the first to appear since the authorized life that Anthony herself had supervised in 1898.[37] With the help of Paxton Hibben, Dorr had tried to get a hold of Anthony's diaries, but Anthony's literary executors resisted, wondering whether destroying the sources might be preferable to letting them fall into the wrong hands.[38] Without fresh sources, Dorr primarily drew on Hibben's version of the Beecher/Tilton scandal to reexamine Anthony's life. In an interpretation which has carried over into much subsequent history, Dorr linked the Beecher/Tilton scandal up with the political split within the woman suffrage movement that lasted from 1869 to 1890. Like Victoria Woodhull herself, this split had become an embarrassment to later woman suffrage leaders, and discussions of it had virtually disappeared from official movement histories. Dorr revived the history of this nineteenth-century split, in part to anticipate the twentieth-century split of the suffrage movement, in which she was vitally involved. As a feminist historian, she also gave the nineteenth-century split an essentially sexual, rather than personal or political, interpretation. On the one side stood Lucy Stone and the American Woman Suffrage Association, like Henry Ward Beecher himself, "as puritanically conservative as Plymouth Rock."[39] The other wing, Dorr argued, consisted of social radicals. They supported divorce, defended daring women like Woodhull, and challenged middle-class convention. Anthony, in particular, she characterized as a crusader for "sex freedom."[40] Because she had broken through the control that the guardians of Anthony's memory exercised over the meaning of her life, her book caused a great stir. Ida Harper, Anthony's official biographer, publicly criticized Dorr for doing in Anthony's name what Anthony herself would not do: disclose what she knew about the Beecher/Tilton affair.[41]

In this genre of feminist history, the issue of secrets and the notion that it is the historian's job to expose them loomed quite large. In fact, the woman suffrage movement itself had been suppressing things for a long time. From the 1890s on, its leaders had become set in the habit of denying any sexual unconventionality in or around their movement. Partly, they had made a strategic decision to fit in with, rather than challenge, the moral convictions of American women; and partly, as the years progressed, Victorian morality became more coercive and they became more implicated in it. Nor was sexual unconventionality the only secret in the woman suffrage movement. The existence of political conflict among suffragists was as strenuously denied as sexual unconventionality, perhaps because it was as much at odds with Victorian notions of womanhood. Indeed, sexual and political secrets became inextricably linked, if only by the common process of suppression. As a young suffragist in the 1890s, right after the twenty-year factionalization of the movement was ended, Carrie Chapman Catt recalled there was much buzzing about the other side's sexual infractions among veterans of the split.[42]

Over the years, keeping these secrets became part of the general obligation that suffrage leaders felt to control the history of their movement in order to best serve its larger purposes. This habit of suppression contributed to the rigid quality of the "master narrative." The iconoclasm of the feminist historians of the 1920s broke through the control that suffrage leaders had long exercised over the history of their movement. Even among ex-suffragists who had always subscribed to the Victorian conviction that facts which upset people were best ignored, the impact of Jazz Age women's history was to encourage curiosity and weaken the taboo against independent inquiry and interpretation. Anthony's literary executors made discrete inquiries about her part in the Beecher/Tilton scandal to satisfy themselves that Hibben had been wrong, only to discover that he was right.[43]

Carrie Chapman Catt is a good example of this process. When the feminist histories of the late 1920s first appeared, she objected to the exposing of old conflicts and intra-movement "gossip" which, she thought, harmed the historical reputation of the suffrage movement. Gradually, however, she began to change her sense of obligation to the past from control to exposure. She admitted that she had always wondered about certain "mysteries" of the suffrage movement, confessed to old friends what her real feelings about nineteenth-century leaders had been and even entertained the possibility that Anthony had been motivated by personal passions and not merely selfless dedication.[44]

As with other aging ex-suffragists, Catt's changing relation to the past reflected a larger change in the historical consciousness about women's rights. In general, the efforts of ex-suffragists and feminists to record and re-examine women's rights history in the late 1920s coincided with— and was a reaction against—a growing amnesia about their movement in the larger society. Throughout the early 1920s, when the passage of the Nineteenth Amendment was still a living memory to many, general audience periodicals regularly told the history of woman suffrage. But by 1930, knowledge of and interest in the women's rights past was fading, a casualty of the general disinterest in the cause of women's equality, as well as the deaths of many movement participants. Even among younger activists in the organized women's movement, ignorance about the women's rights past was a problem. At a 1933 meeting of the National Council of Women, Catt suggested that the American women attending knew as little of the history of their own movement as did their foreign guests.[45] Within the women's movement the long habit of control exercised over its own written history, and the excessive concern with politically correct meanings, contributed to the erosion of memory. Old narratives of selfless service, the only accounts in circulation, didn't have much meaning for younger generations. For the history of women's rights to stay alive, new generations had to be able to find their own meanings in the past. As interpretations of the past became less rigidly patrolled, this history took on more of the flexibility and organic quality that it needed to stay vital.

History's Daughters

Between the exposing of suppressed secrets, the breaking of the taboo against conflicting interpretations of the past and the creation of new interpretations that had meaning for younger women, these feminist histories of women's rights succeeded in stimulating even greater curiosity about the past. Among those particularly affected by this deepening interest in women's history were Lucy Stone's daughter, Alice Stone Blackwell, and Elizabeth Cady Stanton's daughter, Harriot Stanton Blatch, both of them activists in their own right.[46] By 1930, to anyone who knew anything about her, Lucy Stone was remembered simply as the woman who refused to take her husband's name upon marriage. Likewise, knowledge about Stanton had faded until she was known as Anthony's sidekick, her white curls the most familiar thing about her.[47] As they neared the end of their own lives, both Blackwell and Blatch seemed to have been seized with a deep sense of devotion to their mothers' memories and the desire to come to their defense. The opening up of the historical arena made it possible for them to act on these feelings as well as record for the future aspects of the past about which they had direct knowledge. As historians, their contributions were simultaneously personalistic and substantive.

Alice Stone Blackwell's 1930 biography of her mother, Lucy Stone, was stimulated by the Hibben, Sachs and especially Dorr books. Blackwell found it difficult to believe that Beecher, whom her parents had defended, had really been an adulterer. She disapproved of Sachs' fascination with Victoria Woodhull, whom she had been raised to believe had damaged the cause. And she was incensed by Dorr's dismissal of Lucy Stone as someone who had made no significant contribution to women's history after her marriage in 1854.[48]

In response, Blackwell wrote the first full biography of Stone. The reviewer for the National Woman's Party weekly, who had been ignorant of the magnitude of Stone's historic significance, praised the book for demonstrating the "potency and courage" of her equal rights activism.[49] Blackwell especially contributed an elaborate account, from her mother's perspective, of the 1869-1890 split among suffragists. Compared to Dorr, she gave a genuinely political version of the rift. She demonstrated that the movement had split primarily because of deep differences over "the race question and the sex question."[50] In particular, she countered Dorr's racist treatment of the post–Civil War reconstruction period and recalled what a tragedy the splitting apart of black and woman suffrage was for Stone's generation.[51] At the same time, when it came to the next twenty years of intra-movement conflict, Blackwell gave as nasty as she got, answering Dorr's insults to her mother with all the vile things her parents had ever said about Stanton and Anthony.[52] This part of the book had the character of a family quarrel that had stewed for a half century. Even her friend Carrie Chapman Catt urged her to tone it down. "You must remember that a whole series of unjust whacks have been given to the American side," Blackwell responded petulantly. "Could it reasonably be expected that I would not state [my mother's] side of the case in a matter where her motives had been so much misrepresented?"[53]

Blackwell's biography of Stone in turn led Harriot Stanton Blatch to act on behalf of her own mother's fading reputation. Blatch had made an initial stab at documenting her mother's contribution, decades before, at the time of Stanton's death. But the project fell by the wayside as more pressing matters, namely the still unmet demand for woman suffrage, took her energies. In 1922, Blatch and her brother reissued Stanton's autobiography and a collection of her letters and diary entries. Both volumes were heavily edited, and conformed to the standards of the "master narrative" inasmuch as they stressed Stanton's exemplary domestic life and traditional female virtues. Stanton and Blatch were also concerned that the overarching sanctification of Anthony was obscuring their mother's role in history and they downplayed Anthony's presence in the documents accordingly, by judicious cutting.[54]

Stanton's place in history was further "disturbed"—that is, both highlighted and slighted—by the women's rights histories of the late 1920s. As Hibben and Sachs made clear, Stanton had played a central role in the Beecher/Tilton scandal, the Victoria Woodhull episode and the split within the woman suffrage movement. Meanwhile, Rheta Childe Dorr essentially dismissed her as a rotund and witty foil to the steely Anthony. Even Alice Stone Blackwell, in her eagerness to rehabilitate her own mother's reputation, charged Stanton with the impulsive and destructive course that the Stanton/Anthony wing of the movement had taken. There was something unavoidably competitive in the rewriting of women's history in this period: elevating one woman seems to have involved denigrating another. Thus one reader who believed she had found in Stone a modern heroine, combining devotion to the equal rights cause and an admirable marital life, contrasted her with Stanton, who could not really speak her mind because she was "considerably submerged by her marriage."[55] In the same spirit, Blatch wrote an angry review of Blackwell's book, calling Stone a "desiccated saint" and her mother one of the "juicy radicals" that history would ultimately vindicate.[56] Stanton as a "juicy radical" was a far cry from the perfect Victorian homemaker and mother of the 1922 edition of the autobiography, and suggests the impact of new feminist standards even on Blatch's and Blackwell's portraits of their mothers.

Above all, Blatch deeply resented that her mother's memory was increasingly being crowded out by what she called "the advertising" of Susan B. Anthony. Blatch was particularly incensed that the National Woman's Party was crediting the woman suffrage amendment, which her mother had introduced in 1878, to Anthony, for whom it had been posthumously named. "You may admire above all women Mary Queen of Scots & I Queen Elizabeth," she wrote about the elevation of Anthony at her mother's expense. "But . . . when you take off the belongings of my queen and dress your queen up in them it is a high offense."[57]

When and why Blatch became so enraged at Anthony remains to be determined by scholarship which untangles these complex and ever-changing relations between the present and the past. At the time of her mother's death, Blatch was still quite close to Anthony, but sometime after Anthony's death, certainly by 1920, her feelings about Anthony had changed radically. As angry as she was, Blatch's resentment was concentrated less on what Anthony had been than on what she had become. She asked questions about interpretation and meaning: why had Anthony been elevated, her mother denigrated, and by whom? She came up with two answers. One was that, unlike Anthony, her mother had linked woman suffrage to various "heresies," notably free love and free thought, and that starting in the 1890s, rival leaders who wanted "a pure suffrage movement" began to "bury her alive," and remove her from history.[58] Blatch's other hypothesis was that as a "single woman," Anthony had an advantage in memory over Stanton, the wife and mother. Like the cutting remark about the "desiccated" Lucy Stone, Blatch was using modern standards for sexual activity to recoup her mother at the expense of allegedly more Victorian and less sexual women's rights leaders, notably the unmarried Anthony. But in addition, she suspected that Stanton, who had her own family, was not available for general historical appropriation, while Anthony, whose life was the cause, functioned as a *symbolic* mother for feminists, with all the sentiment invested in such figures. Thus Gertrude Stein titled her modernist yet reverent opera about Anthony *The Mother of Us All.*[59] And Dorr, in her own effort to appropriate Anthony's historical cachet, referred to the campaign for a woman suffrage amendment as "Susan's child," which subsequent NAWSA leaders had "abandoned."[60]

Stimulated by her criticisms of the Dorr and Blackwell books, Blatch came to feel that she must do even more to preserve her mother's memory. She especially wanted a "very aggressive biography . . . a stirring, fighting volume" of her mother, but was unable or unwilling to write it herself and critical of "the untrained persons" who were "making up history if not making it."[61]

So, when Alma Lutz, a young member of the National Woman's Party who had previously written a biography of Emma Willard, began to correspond with her about her mother, Blatch knew she had found Stanton's biographer. By 1931 or 1932, they had embarked together on a life of Stanton. Blatch made sure to include in it whatever hints of sexual adventurousness she could find in her mother's life: Stanton's unrequited love for her sister's husband is prominently featured. Separate chapters are also devoted to "that dangerous subject, divorce," and to Stanton's role in the Beecher/Tilton scandal. Blatch also began work on her own memoirs of the final phases of the suffrage movement. Both books were published by Alma Lutz, after Blatch's death, in 1940.[62]

Archiving Women's History: Entrusting the Past to the Future

In the late 1920s, at about the same time she began to imagine a biography of her mother, Blatch arranged for Stanton's papers to be deposited at the Library of Congress.[63] "How beautifully you prepared her papers for the Congressional Library and for posterity," Mary Beard wrote when she saw them some time later. "All your penned notations, all your ties, and folders touch me to the core."[64] In contrast to her earlier, intrusive editing of her mother's autobiography, Blatch's decision to give the raw materials of her mother's life to the public domain was a democratic archival act.[65] Anthony had much earlier donated her own book collection and several scrapbooks of newspaper clippings—though not her personal papers—to the Library of Congress; the Librarian agreed to her request that the books be kept separately and prominently featured, but his successor allowed Anthony's collection to be merged into the general holdings.[66] Until Blatch deposited Stanton's papers, the only significant manuscript collection concerned with the history of women's rights to be found in a public depository were papers donated by Carrie Chapman Catt to the New York Public Library in 1923. Catt was sufficiently dissatisfied with how her papers were managed that in 1938 she sent the remainder to the Library of Congress.[67]

The lack of interest, slow pace and outright mismanagement which beset the archiving of the materials of women's history eventually drew the attention of Mary Beard, so often regarded as the only woman active in the development of women's history in this period. It is with Beard, and with the systematic archiving of women's history sources that she assiduously promoted through the 1930s, that this stage in the development of women's history culminated. Beard was a suffrage activist before she was a historian. In 1933, in the midst of the all the new activity and excitement in recording women's past, Beard's anthology on women's history in the United States, *America through Women's Eyes,* appeared.[68] The book included selections from many of the new feminist histories of women's rights: Sachs' biography of Woodhull and Blackwell's life of Stone were excerpted; many selections were included from the *History of Woman Suffrage* as well. Blatch was also featured in the anthology. This book signifies the beginning of Beard's passionate project of reinterpreting women's history.

Beard's goal was to use the materials of women's history to criticize the politics of "equality." Whether or not she fully understood what she was doing, she was beginning to develop a feminist critique of the history of feminism. Inasmuch as the complexities and contradictions of Beard's work continue to permeate the field of women's history, the historical context in which she labored is important to establish. Her opposition to a version of women's past which focused too exclusively on woman's subordination is related to other challenges to the "master narrative" of suffrage history. Without meaning to ignore the originality of Beard's approach to women's history, her work as a historian was not *sui generis,* but an enterprise she shared with others, who, like her, were concerned with women's past as part of their commitment to women's future.[69]

Beard's greatest contribution to the development of women's history was her leadership in the archiving of the materials of women's past. Until original documents were collected by concerned participants, deposited with sympathetic archivists and made available in public depositories, even the past of the women's rights movement could not become "history"; it lacked a public dimension and the capacity to outlive the individuals who had participated in it. In the 1930s, as important figures and then their children died, a few collections of papers were deposited—California suffragist Alice Park arranged for her papers to go to the Huntington Library in San Marino, California, and Swarthmore College bought Jane Addams' papers. But these were a drop in the barrel compared to what was out there in attics and basements, being ignored, destroyed and/or lost.

The demoralization of women's rights leaders combined with external disinterest in the cause to create a situation in which depositories neither sought out nor were offered primary source collections in women's history. The importance of public archives as an antidote for the fragility of the past and the rapidity with which memory fades can be seen in an extraordinary incident concerning Blatch, Beard and Stanton. When *America through Women's Eyes* was published, even though Blatch's own writings were liberally included, she was enraged because her mother

was barely mentioned. She chided Beard for omitting her mother's historical contribution and the rich history of women's rights to which she
was a key. But Beard, it seems, knew little about the nature and scope of
Stanton's social thought, or of the political tradition within women's
rights which she represented. However, Stanton's papers were now available at the Library of Congress, so Blatch was able to have Beard read
them. Beard found them a revelation. "I have longed to rush in upon
you with my excitement over your mother!" she wrote Blatch. "I consider your mother a basic thinker and it is [a] genuine delight to get
closer to her in the way you have made possible. . . .I was so ignorant
that I feared I should not find the fundamental economic thought [in
her papers]. Thank God, it is there!"[70] Exposure to the range of Stanton's
thought had a positive impact on Beard's assessment of the feminist tradition. Soon after reading Stanton's writings, she wrote an article on
"feminism as a social phenomenon," in which she gave an appreciative
account of the early phases of women's rights.[71]

In other words, the deliberate collection and preservation of source
materials was necessary to establish even the contribution to public life
of a figure as well known as Stanton. Women of equivalent historical significance—Frances Willard and Charlotte Perkins Gilman—were not as
lucky as Stanton; inasmuch as their papers were held back until the
1960s (by organizational and familial protectors respectively) their role
in history became even more invisible. Perhaps if Beard had known even
more of the rich history of the women's rights movement, she might
have condemned it less.

Beard organized a feminist movement for the preservation and pro-
motion of women's history beginning in the mid 1930s. The idea for a
World Center for Women's Archives originally came from the Hungarian feminist and pacifist Rosika Schwimmer. Schwimmer's concerns
were both scholarly and political. A European, anti-Fascist, and Jew, she
was deeply pessimistic about what the future held for women. Archives
were a way to preserve what was most inspiring about the past until such
time as the women of the future would be in a position to remember it.
"It is at this period of retrogression in women's rights and pacifist activities," Schwimmer wrote in 1935, "that it becomes of utmost importance to assemble the facts of women's struggle and achievements during

the last century at least, so that historians of the future will find it possible to establish the truth about today."[72] Blatch suggested that Schwimmer present her idea to Mary Beard, who dedicated herself to the project from 1935 until the eve of the Second World War.

Beard was joined by many other American feminists and ex-suffragists, who needed little to convince them of the importance of collecting and preserving the sources of women's history. Blatch and Blackwell both served as trustees to the project. As Schwimmer had sensed earlier from a European perspective, preserving women's history was a way, perhaps the only way, to serve the cause of women's equality in these years. Eventually Beard's World Center for Women's Archives fell victim to the global tragedies of the 1940s (as well as to lingering factional battles among former suffragists). However, the two major depositories of women's history sources in the United States, the Sophia Smith Collection at Smith College and the Schlesinger Library at Radcliffe, begun in 1942 and 1943 respectively, were spin-offs of the World Center project. As war settled on women and men alike, Carrie Chapman Catt gloomily predicted that "the women's movement will be forgotten and *almost* buried in the great tragedies that have succeeded it. So I think it is very important to put all the memorial collections available into museums and libraries while we are still alive. There may be some persons who desire to investigate in the direction of the woman movement and there should be source materials to aid them."[73]

Afterword

It was more than two decades before Catt's hesitant prophecy was fulfilled. With few exceptions in the intervening decades, the women's history project begun by ex-suffragists and feminists of the 1920s and 1930s was not resumed until the late 1960s and early 1970s. Since then, women's history has grown into a large, thriving and remarkably popular enterprise. Unlike our predecessors, most of us who write and teach it are academics. This has had an enormous—and not entirely positive—impact on the expansiveness with which we pose our questions, the boldness with which we answer them and our willingness and ability to recognize the contemporary concerns that underlie our reconsideration of the past. On the other hand, while it is increasingly fashionable to condemn the taming of radical intellectual life within institutions of higher learning, the admission of women (and women's concerns) into the academy actually represents a tremendous advance. For the first time, someone other than white gentlemen have the freedom (and the income) to develop, teach and write their own understandings of the past.

But since the immediate context of most women's historians is the university, we tend to be more conscious of academic and disciplinary influences on our work than social and political ones. The "Sears case" a few years ago was a good sign: when faced with an overt political conflict over the contemporary implications of women's history, most women in the field took a side and almost none hid behind the facade of scholarly neutrality or indifference to controversial issues.[74] But much of the time, the contemporary political meanings of our work remain subtextual, even to ourselves. Hopefully this exercise in historiography will further quicken our political sensibilities as women's historians. From our predecessors we may learn not to patrol our own interpretive borders or insist on politically correct history, but to become more politically conscious about the history that we are crafting. The more we learn about the historiography, not only of previous generations of women's history, but of our own as well, the more aware we will be of the larger context in which we work.

NOTES

1. Ida H. Harper, ed., *History of Woman Suffrage*, vol. 4 (New York: National American Woman Suffrage Association, 1922), 263.

2. Kathryn Sklar, "American Female Historians in Context, 1770–1930," *Feminist Studies*, vol. 3 (1975), 71–84; Joan W. Scott, "History and Difference," *Daedalus*, Vol. 116 (1987), 93–118.

3. On Beard, see Ann D. Gordon, Mari Jo Buhle, Nancy Schrom, *Women in American Society: An Historical Contribution* (Madison, Wis.: Radical America, 1972), 2–3; Ann J. Lane, ed., *Mary Ritter Beard: A Sourcebook* (New York: Schocken, 1977); Berenice Carroll, "Mary Beard's *Woman as Force in History:* A

Critique," in *Liberating Women's History,* ed. Carroll (Urbana: University of Illinois Press, 1976), 26–41; Bonnie G. Smith, "Seeing Mary Beard," *Feminist Studies,* vol. 10 (Fall, 1984), 399–416; Suzanne Lebsock, "Reading Mary Beard," *Reviews in American History,* vol. 17 (June, 1989), 324–39; Nancy Cott, "Two Beards: Coauthorship and the Concept of Civilization," *American Quarterly,* vol. 42 (1990), 274–300; and Cott, ed., *A Woman Making History: Mary Ritter Beard Through Her Letters* (New Haven: Yale University Press, 1991).

    4. Richard Hofstadter, *The Progressive Historians: Turner, Beard, Parrington* (New York: Knopf, 1968), 3.

    5. Helen L. Sumner, *History of Women in Industry in the U.S.,* vol. 9 of *Report of the Condition of Woman and Child Wage-Earners in the U.S.,* U.S. Senate Document 645, 61st Congress, 2nd Session (Washington, D.C., 1911); similarly, Alice Henry, *The Trade Union Movement* (New York, D. Appleton and Co., 1915).

    6. Lawson Andrew Scruggs, *Women of Distinction: Remarkable of Words and Invincible in Character* (Raleigh, N.C.: L. A. Scruggs, 1893); N. R Moselke, *The Work of the Afro-American Woman* (Philadelphia: S. Ferguson Co., 1908); Sadie Daniels, *Women Builders* (Washington, D.C.: Associated Publishers, 1931); Elizabeth Davis, *Lifting as They Climb: The National Association of Colored Women* (Washington, D. C.: NACW, 1933). Thanks to Ann D. Gordon for this suggestion.

    7. Elisabeth Griffith, *In Her Own Right: The Life of Elizabeth Cady Stanton* (New York: Oxford University Press, 1984), 87.

    8. Elizabeth Stanton, Susan B. Anthony and Matilda Joslyn Gage, eds., *History of Woman Suffrage,* vol. 1 (2nd ed., Rochester: Susan B. Anthony, 1889), 7.

    9. On these and other matters concerning the production and publication of the first three volumes, see Anthony's correspondence with Elizabeth Boynton Harbert, 1878–1882, Harbert Papers, Huntington Library, San Marino, California.

    10. Anthony to Harbert, Ibid., May 11, 1882.

    11. Anthony to Harbert, Ibid., April 2, 1882.

    12. Anthony to Harbert, Ibid., June 6, 1903.

    13. Susan B. Anthony and Ida Husted Harper, eds., *History of Woman Suffrage,* vol. 4 (Rochester: Susan B. Anthony, 1902); Harper, ed., *History of Woman Suffrage,* vols. 5 and 6 (New York: National American Woman Suffrage Association, 1922).

    14. See, for instance, an exchange between Carrie Chapman Catt and Harper about whether "the truth" should be told about Harriet Taylor Upton's

resignation from NAWSA office (Catt to Harper, October 14, 1921, Carrie Chapman Catt Papers, Library of Congress Manuscript Division). Similarly, Harriot Stanton Blatch complained that volume six included an account of a 1910 meeting at which open-air agitation was discussed when in fact Anna Howard Shaw had forced her to call off the session. "So much for the accuracy of that Harper book." (Blatch to Caroline Lexow Babcock, September 18, 1925, Babcock-Hurlburt Papers, Schlesinger Library, Cambridge, Mass.).

15. Contrast Harper's comments about the "prejudiced, conservative and in a degree ignorant and vicious electorate" which has "the power to withhold the suffrage from women" in volume four (p. xxiii) with the much more democratic treatment in Matilda J. Gage's essay on "Preceding Causes" in volume one. In Gage's account, conservatism and fear of change is a characteristic of the majority of both men and women; similarly women's rights are part of a larger process of democratic transformation.

16. For instance, the frontispiece of volume one is dedicated to "the memory of Mary Wollstonecraft, Frances Wright, Lucretia Mott, Harriet Martineau, Lydia Maria Child, Margaret Fuller, Sarah and Angelina Grimké, Josephine S. Griffing, Martha C. Wright, Harriet K. Hunt, M.D., Mariana W. Johnson, Alice and Phebe Carey, Ann Preston, M.D., Lydia Mott, Eliza W. Farnham, Lydia E. Fowler, M.D., and Paulina Wright Davis.

17. Here is a version from the introduction to volume five of the *History of Woman Suffrage:*

One step led to another; business opportunities increased; women accumulated property; Legislatures were compelled to revise the laws and the church was obliged to liberate its interpretation of the Scriptures. Women began to organize; their missionary and charity societies prepared the way for clubs for self improvement; these in turn broadened into civic organizations whose public work carried them to city councils and State Legislatures, where they found themselves in the midst of politics and wholly without influence. Thus they were led into the movement for the suffrage. It was only a few of the clear thinkers, the far seeing, who realized at the beginning that the principal cause of women's inferior position and helplessness lay in their disfranchisement and until they could be made to see it they were a dead weight on the movement. Men fully understood the power that the vote would place in the hands of women, with a lessening of their own, and in the mass they did not intend to concede it. (xvi–xvii)

18. For the National Woman's Party version, see Doris Stevens, *Jailed for Freedom* (New York: Liveright Publishing Corp., 1920); Inez Haines Irwin, *The Story of the Woman's Party* (New York: Harcourt, 1921). For the National American Woman Suffrage Association version, see Carrie Chapman Catt and Nettie Rogers Shuler, *Woman Suffrage and Politics* (New York: Charles Scribner's Sons, 1923); Maud Wood Park, *Front Door Lobby* (Boston: Beacon Press, 1960); and, of course, volume six of the *History of Woman Suffrage*. Given the almost total exclusion of the Woman's Party from the final volumes of the *History of Woman Suffrage,* Harriot Stanton Blatch humorously suggested to Doris Stevens that she publish *Jailed for Freedom* in the same format and call it *History of Woman Suffrage, Volume Four* (Alice Paul to Harriot Blatch, September 30, 1920, Alma Lutz Papers, Vassar College, Poughkeepsie, New York). Paul did not get the joke.

19. See my *Harriot Stanton Blatch and the Winning of Woman Suffrage* (New Haven: Yale University Press, 1997), 248.

20. Note the similarities, for instance, among Catt and Shuler, and Irwin.

21. See Chapter 12 in this volume, in which I argue that Flexner's 1959 work was the first original synthesis of the history of women's rights to break through this half-century-old narrative framework.

22. Nancy F. Cott, *The Grounding of Modern Feminism,* (New Haven: Yale University Press, 1987), especially chapter one.

23. Peter Novick, *The Noble Dream: The "Objectivity Question" and the American Historical Profession* (Cambridge: Cambridge University Press, 1988), 193.

24. The phrase is Katherine Anthony's, from *Margaret Fuller: A Psychological Biography* (New York: Harcourt, Brace and Howe, 1920), v.

25. Ibid.

26. Judith Schwartz, *Radical Feminists of Heterodoxy: Greenwich Village, 1912–1940* (Lebanon, New Hampshire: New Victoria Publishers, Inc., 1982). Katherine Anthony, *Feminism in Germany and Scandinavia* (New York: Henry Holt and Company, 1915).

27. Anthony, *Fuller,* v.

28. *Nation,* January 12, 1921.

29. Marie Jenney Howe, *George Sand: The Search for Love* (Garden City, N.Y.: Garden City Publishing Co., Inc., 1927).

30. Schwartz, *Heterodoxy.* Katherine Anthony, Doris Stevens, Inez Haines Irwin and Rheta Childe Dorr were all members.

31. Howe, *Sand,* xii–xiv.

32. Anthony, *Fuller*, 36.

33. Howe, *Sand*, 337.

34. Paxton Hibben, *Henry Ward Beecher: An American Portrait* (New York: George H. Doran Co., 1927).

35. Emanie Sachs, *"The Terrible Siren": Victoria Woodhull (1838–1927)* (New York: Harper & Brothers Publishers, 1928). Sachs also wrote under her married name, Arling. Little seems to be known about Sachs, but how she came to write a book about Woodhull so soon after her death surely invites investigation.

36. Inez Haines Irwin to Maud Wood Park, June 20, 1929, National American Woman Suffrage Association Papers, Library of Congress Manuscript Division, reel 1.

37. Rheta Childe Dorr, *Susan B. Anthony: The Woman Who Changed the Mind of a Nation* (New York: AMS Press, 1928). Ida H. Harper, ed., *The Life and Work of Susan B. Anthony* (Indianapolis: Bowen-Merrill Co., 1898).

38. Ida H. Harper to Maud Wood Park, July 13, 1930, Carrie Chapman Catt Papers, Library of Congress Manuscript Division.

39. Ibid., 220.

40. Ibid., 3.

41. Ida Harper, review of *"The Terrible Siren," Woman's Journal*, January 1929, 35.

42. Carrie Chapman Catt to Alice Stone Blackwell, September 8, 1930, Catt Papers, Library of Congress.

43. Catt asked Harper "if it was true" and Harper told her Anthony herself had told her the story (Catt to Blackwell, September 8, 1930, Catt Papers, Library of Congress). Catt also thought Blatch had told Hibben (Catt to Lucy Anthony, November 8, 1930, Catt Papers, Library of Congress).

44. She wondered if Anthony had so unceasingly promoted Stanton out of "simple affection and devotion" or whether there was more; I believe she was suggesting that Anthony had been in love with Stanton (Catt to Alice Stone Blackwell, August 18, 1930, Catt Papers, Library of Congress).

45. Carrie Chapman Catt, "Only Yesterday," in *Our Common Cause, Civilization, Report of the International Congress of Women, July 16-22, 1933, New York, New York* (New York: National Council of Women, 1933), 235.

46. There were other daughters of activists who wrote history or wanted to: Julia Ward Howe's daughters, Maud Howe Elliott and Florence Howe Hall; Katherine Devereux Blake, teacher-feminist and daughter of Lillie Devereux Blake; even Victoria Woodhull's daughter, Zulu Maud, who wanted more than

anything to prove that her mother had never been a free lover, and tried to swim upstream into the feminist historical river to do so. See especially the symposium organized in the *Woman's Journal*, December, 1929, "Glimpses of Three Pioneers, by Two Daughters and One Niece," 22–23. This anti-Dorr symposium featured daughterly reminiscences of Howe, Stanton and Anthony (by Lucy Anthony).

47. Ruby A. Black, "A Soul as Free as the Air," *Equal Rights* (December 20, 1930), 363; Blatch complained about the excessive focus on Stanton's white curls, to the exclusion of her "unusual brain," in an undated letter, ca. 1939, to Alma Lutz (Lutz Papers, Vassar College, Poughkeepsie).

48. Dorr, *Anthony*, 191.

49. Black, "A Soul as Free as the Air," 362–65.

50. Alice Stone Blackwell, *Lucy Stone: Pioneer of Women's Rights* (Boston: Little, Brown and Company, 1930), 206.

51. Dorr considered black suffrage "the most ghastly mistake of reconstruction," and described ex-slaves as "unclean beasts" with "savage instincts" (*Anthony*, 172, 175, 215).

52. For instance, she charged that Stanton advocated ultra-radical issues because it "amused her to watch the fluttering in the dovecotes that followed," and that Anthony had charged her parents with not really being married (Blackwell, 219, 230).

53. Catt to Blackwell, September 13, 1943, Catt Papers, Library of Congress.

54. Theodore Stanton and Harriot Stanton Blatch, eds. *Elizabeth Cady Stanton as Revealed in Her Letters, Diary, and Reminiscences*, 2 vols. (New York: Harper and Brothers Publishers, 1922). On Harriot Stanton Blatch's and Theodore Stanton's "tampering" with their mother's letters, see Amy Dykeman, "'To Pour Forth from My Own Experience': Two Versions of Elizabeth Cady Stanton," *Journal of the Rutgers University Libraries*, Vol. 44 (June 1982), 1–16.

55. Black, "A Soul as Free as the Air."

56. Harriot Stanton Blatch, "Pioneering in the Fight for Women's Rights: A Daughter's Eulogy," an undated and uncited clipping in the Lutz Collection, Vassar College, Poughkeepsie.

57. Harriot Stanton Blatch to Alma Lutz, n.d., Lutz Papers, Vassar College, Poughkeepsie.

58. Blatch to Lutz, undated but probably September 1933, Lutz Papers, Vassar College, Poughkeepsie.

59. Gertrude Stein and Virgil Thomson, *The Mother of Us All* (New York: Music Press, 1947).

60. Dorr, *Anthony*, 355.

61. Blatch to Lutz, September 2, 1934, Lutz Papers, Vassar College; "untrained person" from Blatch to Lutz, n.d., perhaps July 26, 1933, ibid.

62. Alma Lutz, *Created Equal: A Biography of Elizabeth Cady Stanton, 1815–1902* (New York: John Day Company, 1940); Harriot Stanton Blatch and Alma Lutz, *Challenging Years: The Memoirs of Harriot Stanton Blatch* (New York: G. P. Putnam's Sons, 1940).

63. The Library of Congress "Case File" dates the initial deposit as September 1928.

64. Mary Beard to Harriot Stanton Blatch, January 24 [1937], Lutz Papers, Vassar College.

65. The Chief of the Manuscript Division of the Library of Congress wrote to Alice Stone in 1915 for her mother's papers, but she ignored his request and the papers did not arrive at the Library until 1961. "Introduction," *Register of Papers in the Manuscript Division of the Library of Congress: The Blackwell Family, Carrie Chapman Catt and the National American Woman Suffrage Association* (Washington, D. C.: Library of Congress, 1975), iv.

66. Leonard N. Beck, "The Library of Susan B. Anthony," *Quarterly Journal of the Library of Congress,* Vol. 32 (1975), 325–335.

67. Catt to Helen Tufts Bailey, September 29, 1927, and Catt to Alice Stone Blackwell, February 4, 1938, Catt Papers, Library of Congress Manuscript Division. In the 1927 letter, Catt mentions six file cases of four drawers each as the size of her gift to the New York Public Library; the rare book division of the Library's current holdings under Catt's name are much smaller.

68. Mary R. Beard, *America through Women's Eyes* (New York: Macmillan Company, 1933).

69. I owe a debt of gratitude to Nancy Cott for stimulating discussions on many of these points.

70. Beard to Blatch, January 24, 1937, Lutz Papers, Vassar College.

71. Mary R. Beard, "Feminism as a Social Phenomenon," 1940, in Lane, ed., *Mary Ritter Beard.*

72. Rosika Schwimmer, "A World's Center for Women's Archives," *Equal Rights* (October 5, 1935), 245, Maryann Turner, *Biblioteca Femina: A Herstory of Book Collections Concerning Women* (New York: Tower Press, 1978), 35–40.

73. Catt to Blackwell, September 13, 1943, Catt Papers, Library of Congress Manuscript Division.

74. The "Sears Case" involved women's historians testifying on either side of an Equal Employment Opportunity Commission suit against Sears Roebuck for failure to promote significant numbers of women into high commission sales positions. See Ruth Milkman, "Women's History and the Sears Case," *Feminist Studies*, Vol. 12 (1986), 375–400; Alice Kessler-Harris, "EEOC v. Sears Roebuck and Co.: A Personal Account," *Radical History Review*, Vol. 35 (1986), 57–79.

12

Eleanor Flexner and the History of American Feminism

Century of Struggle: The Woman's Rights Movement in the United States by Eleanor Flexner has stood for thirty years as the most comprehensive history of American feminism up to the enfranchisement of women in 1920.[1] In *Century of Struggle,* Flexner did what had never been done before: she used the history of the suffrage movement, not as a way for veterans of the movement to congratulate themselves, but as a window on the larger history of American women. A whole generation of historians of American women who came after her profited immensely both from the large historical analyses and the small scholarly details of *Century of Struggle.* Like *The Feminine Mystique,* which was published five years later, *Century of Struggle* anticipated—and helped generate—the subsequent feminist revival. To understand the significance of her accomplishment, Flexner's work needs to be set in its own historical context.

First of all, the postwar years, during which *Century of Struggle* was conceived and executed, were decidedly inhospitable to the idea and traditions of feminism. To the degree that individual women, such as Eleanor Roosevelt or Helen Keller, were acknowledged for their achievements, they were regarded as exceptions, merely confirming the absence of their sex from the public realm. *Modern Woman: The Lost Sex,* published in 1947, by Ferdinand Lundberg and Marynia Farnham, is an example of the more overt antifeminism of this period. Lundberg and Farnham insisted that modern American women had nothing left to

Originally published in *Gender & History* 3 (1991).

complain about: adored, enfranchised, surrounded by innumerable household goods, whatever grievances women still had could only be a result of their own individual psychological problems. Not only was the modern feminist either a joke or a madwoman, but even in the past, feminist beliefs had been merely a cover for deep psychological problems. Lundberg and Farnham treated the first feminist in the Anglo-American tradition, Mary Wollstonecraft, as a classic neurotic, an unhappy woman displacing her personal failures onto a misguided indictment of "society" for "wronging" her sex.[2] Thus, when *Century of Struggle* appeared, it was virtually unique in its bold reassertion of the importance of feminism to women and across the long sweep of American history.[3]

Despite the hostile environment to feminist activism in post–World War II America, there were resources for the writing of women's history available to those, like Flexner, who were looking for them. She began her research in Washington, D.C., at the National Archives, the Library of Congress and Howard University. She also worked in her home town of New York City, at the New York Public Library. Then, in Northampton, Massachusetts, she found the Sophia Smith Collection, with its rich resources for exploring the history of women's rights. Smith College had begun its extraordinary research collection in the history of women in 1942 and a year later Radcliffe established the Schlesinger Library; both collections were offshoots of Mary Beard's prewar efforts to establish a World Center of Women's Archives.[4] Eventually, Flexner followed her scholarship and moved to Northampton, where she remained for the next three decades.

She had, mind you, no formal relation to any of the colleges in the area, and held, all her life, a very mixed attitude to academic historians, whom she aspired to influence but who caused her considerable bitterness when they ignored her contributions. Even after the field of women's history began to grow within the academy, a development to which her own work was fundamental, she remained an active and important independent scholar, an increasingly rare creature in American intellectual life. After writing *Century of Struggle,* she helped the Harvard-based editors of a new biographical dictionary of women—*Notable American Women*—to identify important historical figures; she also wrote a dozen of the entries, mostly biographies of working class women leaders. Her final project was a major biography of Mary Wollstonecraft, but the book was largely ignored, which grieved her.[5] When, beginning in the early 1970s, the field of women's history began to blossom and grow, she was still in Northampton, where I first met her. About four years ago, her life-companion, Helen Terry, died and her own health failed, and she moved to a retirement community near Boston. In the summer of 1988, I visited her there and interviewed her about her life, her work, and *Century of Struggle.*

Eleanor Flexner comes from an extraordinary family, although, like her subjects in *Century of Struggle,* she considers herself her own woman, and wishes to be known by her individual accomplishments. She is the daughter of Abraham Flexner, internationally renowned educator and policy intellectual, best known as the author of an early twentieth-century report on the state of medical education in the United States. It is to her mother, however, that *Century of Struggle* is dedicated. Anne Crawford Flexner was a successful playwright and a turn of the century New Woman. When she married Abraham, he agreed that the basis of their marriage would be the principle "that her interests and work were as sacred as mine."[6] Indeed her success came before his. She had a play produced on Broadway (and lived in New York City for its run) while her first child was still breast feeding. Her greatest success was "Mrs. Wiggs of the Cabbage Patch," an immensely popular comedy about rural poverty in Kentucky, which she did not write but dramatized, and which ran, first on the stage, and then in radio versions, well into the thirties.[7] The royalties supported Eleanor through crucial stages of her own career as a writer. "She wanted me to be a writer and she helped to make it possible." Eleanor continued her mother's interest in the theater. In the 1930s, after graduating from Swarthmore College, she became active in what was then called "the progressive theater movement." Her first book, *American Playwrights, 1918–1938,* was a survey of American drama from the point of view of social relevance and a call for a politically engaged "people's theatre."[8] This background in the theatre shows through in the fine dramatic sensibility that enlivens *Century of Struggle.* Anne Crawford Flexner died in 1955, when *Cen-*

tury, Eleanor's second book, was already under way. It was published in 1959.

Here is a biographical irony and a historical and political truth worth observing: although Eleanor Flexner was born into an environment rich in feminist tradition, she had to rediscover it on her own to write *Century of Struggle.* In her dedication to her mother, Eleanor observes, "Her life was touched at many points by the movement whose history I have tried to record"(v). When I interviewed her, she recalled, as a child, seeing her mother and her father, both dressed in white, going out to march in the 1913 New York suffrage parade. Her paternal aunt, Helen Thomas Flexner, was a New York suffrage leader of some prominence, and the younger sister of M. Carey Thomas, founder and first dean of Bryn Mawr College.[9] Yet my presumption, fueled by these kinds of provocative details, that Eleanor Flexner carried knowledge of feminism, acquired from her own life, into her scholarship, seems to have been wrong. When I asked her if this personal connection is why she wrote *Century of Struggle,* she simply said no. The feminist past, so very vital only a few years before, was barely known and even less appreciated by the 1940s. Flexner was as affected by this "social amnesia" as the rest of her generation. Though born into the feminist tradition, she seems to have had to rediscover, even to reinvent, it on her own.

I emphasize this point because I had hoped, in the continuity between Eleanor Flexner's personal history and her interests as a writer and scholar, to find the answer to the question of why *Century of Struggle* was written. Like many of her readers, I wondered how, in the deadened atmosphere of the 1950s, Flexner conceived, researched and executed this deeply felt history of a despised women's rights politics. Indeed, this is one of the reasons I went to interview her. She has an answer to this question, but she would not tell me. She has recorded her account of why she wrote *Century of Struggle* in her papers at the Schlesinger Library, and we will have access to it once they are opened and not before.

What I did learn from talking with her was how carefully chosen and personally meaningful was her use of the word "struggle" in the book's title. "The element of struggle in my own life is very real," she explained, and when she repeated the term, it was always verbally underlined. As I understand her usage, "struggle" is a term that comes from the left, and refers to mass based political efforts that challenge American society in a radical fashion rather than merely seek to include women in established power structures. This is how she understood and presented the women's rights tradition in *Century of Struggle.* Flexner also used the term "struggle" to describe her own work in the 1940s as an organizer of office workers in New York City, probably with the left-leaning United Office and Professional Workers of America. She still remembers vividly Susan B. Anthony's description of the actual physical experience of the work of organizing in the 1850s, which she identifies with her own memories of "what it was like to hand out leaflets at 7 a.m. on Wall Street when the temperature was near zero."

In other words, Flexner's perspective on the history of women's rights is what I would call "left feminist." By "left feminist" I mean a perspective which fuses a recognition of the systematic oppression of women with an appreciation of other structures of power underlying American society (what we now most often call "the intersections of race, class and gender"). Therefore, by "left feminism," I also mean an understanding that the attainment of genuine equality for women—all women—requires a radical challenge to American society, the mobilization of masses of people and fundamental social change.

By characterizing the perspective of *Century of Struggle* as "left feminist," I mean to suggest as well how discontinuous it was with feminism as it was understood in the 1940s and 1950s. "Feminism" in this period was a term claimed only by a tiny group of people—a sect, really—the National Woman's Party (NWP), which after 1923 pushed almost exclusively for the Equal Rights Amendment (ERA) under the leadership of Alice Paul. As part of her research Flexner met with the aging Paul, whom she found a "stone wall," dwelling on old grievances which Flexner considered largely irrelevant to the history she was writing. In the first edition Flexner does not use the word "feminism." Instead, she relies on "women's rights," a term which predates not only the term "feminism" (which did not come into usage in the United States until the 1910s) but the woman suffrage movement itself. "Women's rights" as a term links women's claims (or rights) to the rights of other marginalized groups; perhaps this too was why she chose it.

The dominant character of the politics which claimed the term "feminism" in the 1950s was much closer to the right than the left. Alice Paul flirted with anti-Communism and tried to get the NWP on the redbaiting bandwagon in the 1950s; what little party support was enjoyed by the ERA in the 1950s came from Republicans. Meanwhile, among Communist party members, while the term "feminism" was repudiated as "bourgeois," the principle of gender equality constituted a fundamental if schematic political commitment. Within the party were a number of individual women with feminist backgrounds and interests, not only legendary Communists such as Elizabeth Gurley Flynn and Ella Reeve Bloor, but also women with a live commitment to the emancipation of women, such as Mary Inman.[10]

As *Century of Struggle* was taking form in the early 1950s, the Communist party, was, of course, deeply beleaguered, under attack by Senator Joseph McCarthy and a slew of anti-Communists. The first notable figure that Flexner wrote about in *Century* was Anne Hutchinson, of whom Flexner says that "she was subjected to the harassment common to persecution from that day to this; her words were falsified." Was she thinking of McCarthyism and its victims? Was she thinking of accused atomic spies Julius and Ethel Rosenberg?

In addition to the National Woman's Party, another wing of women activists claimed to be the inheritors of the suffrage movement. These "social reformers" were opponents of the Equal Rights Amendment and defenders of protective labor legislation for women. Flexner's emphasis on working women and her respect for the settlement house and Women's Trade Union League traditions shows the influence of this perspective, as does her approach to the Equal Rights Amendment, of which in the first edition (but not in the 1975, second edition) she is openly critical.

Yet the hatred and suspicion of NWP "feminists" that had been a fundamental principle to most women social reformers through the 1930s and 1940s is nowhere to be found in *Century of Struggle*. Whereas most women who identified with this tradition, many of whom were in the Women's Bureau, Democratic Party and League of Women Voters by the forties and fifties, no longer focused on the systematic power that men as a sex wielded over women, *Century of Struggle* is pervaded with an understanding of and a rage against what we would soon be calling "sexism." The sense, so pervasive in the fifties, that women's subordination was a thing of the past, that emancipation was something to celebrate (at best) rather than a goal to strive for, was rejected by Flexner as she wrote her study. What *Century of Struggle* did was to combine what had been separated in the 1920s, when a united women's movement dissolved into warring feminist and social reform wings.[11] That is, Flexner fused a sense of women's systematic oppression with a larger understanding of social inequality.

In her introduction to *Century of Struggle,* Flexner makes clear her fundamental sympathy with the women's rights project. She believed that the expansion of "opportunity for complete human development" to "one half the nation" represented human progress, despite the fact that "such opportunity inevitably brought with it new problems." She believed that women had "the right to take part in the political and social life of their time and to stand on a plane of equal human dignity with men in their personal relationships"(xi). This admission led her male reviewers to charge her with writing "from a thoroughly partisan standpoint" or with being too sympathetic to "feminists' statements on the extent of their oppression."[12] In other words, they claimed that her convictions about women's equality kept her work from being sufficiently scholarly, objective, professional.

Female reviewers, virtually to a woman, had a different response. They were aware that the aging suffrage veterans and their younger recruits had been writing about the history of women's rights all along, and thus they understood what a scholarly and analytical breakthrough *Century of Struggle* was by contrast. They recognized that Flexner's deeper achievement was precisely her *non*-partisanship, her transcendence of "the narrow and self-serving interpretations that warring factions of that movement had been recreating for decades." Janet James, former director of the Women's Archives at Radcliffe, wrote in the *New England Quarterly* that *Century of Struggle* was "the first balanced and scholarly account of the women's rights movement." "Earlier chronicles of the movement, writing before the dust had settled, were intent on celebrating the triumph of a crusade and placing laurels on the heads of the greatest and least of its leaders. Miss Flexner is interested in untangling the facts and searching out the causes of an historical phenomenon, which engages her strong liberal sympathies but in which she herself had no part."[13]

Despite her fundamental sympathy with the "struggle" for women's equality, Flexner's intent was not to write a reverential account of the "gallantry" of suffrage heroines. Instead she was deeply committed to re-establishing the history of women's rights on a solid scholarly basis. In an opinionated bibliographic essay, Flexner wrote that there were voluminous unexplored sources waiting in archives such as the Sophia Smith Collection for the serious student of women's rights to explore. Previous accounts were either too broad and superficial, popular rather than scholarly history, or they were "written by participants" and "suffer[ed] from severe bias." She observed that even the raw sources had been subjected to factional interference. "Differences of opinion" were often edited out of sources because they were considered "unladylike." In our interview, she told me that before Edna Stantial deposited Carrie Chapman Catt's letters at Radcliffe College, she took "out anything that [she thought] might be derogatory to Catt, including some of [Mary Grey] Peck's more passionate letters." (Flexner, anticipating the problem, took copious notes from the letters in their original version, in Stantial's home, before they were edited and deposited.)

As several women reviewers noted at the time of publication, Flexner's transcendence of partisanship is most notable in her treatment of the last phase of the suffrage movement.[14] Confronting the two antagonistic factions into which the woman suffrage movement split after 1920, Flexner threads her way between the competing historical claims about who was most responsible for winning the Nineteenth Amendment. She credits Alice Paul and the militant suffragettes with revitalizing the suffrage movement on a national level and injecting "new life into the federal amendment" after 1913 (262). On the other side was Carrie Chapman Catt, centrist leader during the last stage of the suffrage movement. Flexner credits her with the "realistic" perspective and tactical brilliance that led the movement through to victory after 1916.[15] But the question of "who won suffrage" is not really what preoccupies Flexner in this section of the book. Rather, Flexner is most concerned with the intense politics, the shifting relations within and between political parties, which shaped the options of both mainstream suffragists and militant suffragettes. Flexner still thinks about the political twists and turns that had to be negotiated to get Congressional passage and state ratification; in our final discussion, she suggested that work needed to be done on the significance of the Seventeenth Amendment which established the direct election of Senators, for the successful Senate vote on woman suffrage that finally came in 1919. Thus, while Flexner's appreciation for what it took to start the women's rights movement enlivens *Century of Struggle* in its first chapters, her admiration for the different kinds of political skills required in the final phases animates it at the end.

Anyone who has read *Century of Struggle* knows that the other innovation that Flexner brought to prior traditions of writing women's rights history was her dedicated inclusion of material on white working class and black women in virtually every chapter of *Century of Struggle*. Her interest in class was anticipated by and rested on the political efforts of Progressive Era feminists, but Flexner goes beyond this tradition to individualize particular figures and to illuminate the content of their distinctive working class feminism. During her research she located and interviewed Clara Lemlich, heroine of the 1909–1910 shirtwaist strike of New York City, by then an old lady. And in a research breakthrough that she still remembers with delight, she found the granddaughter of Knights of Labor organizer Leonora Barry, who helped her reconstruct the later phases of Barry's life. After *Century of Struggle* and through her work on *Notable American Women,* Flexner continued her interest in rescuing working class female activists from historical anonymity. She wrote biographies of Barry and Augusta Lewis Troup (first woman member of a male trade union), and tracked down the fate of Mary Kenney O'Sullivan, working class founder of the Women's Trade Union League, in a virtuoso piece of research, to bring yet another working class woman into the women's rights pantheon.

But of course, it is Flexner's work on black women which most distinguishes her perspective from all prior and many subsequent histories of women's rights. With the exception of Flexner's work, black women—with the occasional nod in the direction of Sojourner Truth—had been virtually excluded from all twentieth-century histories of women's rights. Over a century of struggle she traced suffragism's deepening racism, at the same time as she uncovered the separate activist and organizational traditions—the clubs and suffrage societies—among black women. By doing so, her work challenged white suffragists' simple confidence that they spoke for the entire sex, for "woman." And because black women were *de facto* disfranchised after 1920, including them in her history challenged the notion that women's emancipation had been won in that climactic year. The inclusion of black women helps *Century of Struggle* to point beyond the Nineteenth Amendment, rather than to look backward from it, to recognize the needs of the future even while appreciating the achievements of the past. If there is any single element of *Century of Struggle* which still dares us to follow its lead, it is Flexner's tremendous effort to insert black women into a past—and therefore a future—from which they had steadily and energetically been excluded.

"I knew from the beginning I was going to write about Negro women," she said. But the omission of black women from the historical record was almost total. She went to see W. E. B. Du Bois, early in her project, but even he dismissed the possibility of writing a history of women's rights with black women in it. "I never was so disappointed in my life!" she told me. The people who helped her most were archivists at Howard and at the Schomburg branch of the New York Public Library—Dorothy Porter and Jean Blackwell Hudson. Also her brother-in-law, Paul Lewisohn, labor archivist at the National Archives, had a special interest in black history and was the author of *Race, Class and Party* (1932). Prior histories of women's rights—Rheta Childe Dorr's 1928 biography of Susan B. Anthony is a particularly egregious example—made invidious comparisons between black suffrage and woman suffrage.[16] By contrast, Flexner began her story with women's activism in the anti-slavery movement.

Flexner began her research before 1954, that is, before the Supreme Court desegregation decision in *Brown v. Board of Education,* which reinserted racial equality into the national agenda. When she sent an early version of her book to Harpers for possible publication, it was rejected on the grounds that there was too much material in it about black women, and that this would weaken whatever popular audience it might otherwise have. Urged to do so by Arthur Mann, Harvard University

Press finally accepted the manuscript in 1959. In 1975, in the flush of the rebirth of feminism, Harvard published a second edition. The present having caught up with Flexner's sense of the significance of the past, she was now able to make the link between black liberation and women's liberation explicit.[17] Most of the material she added in the 1975 revision was about black women (which by the way not only indicates how important this topic remained to her, but how little of her 1950s work needed to be revised in light of subsequent scholarship.) Flexner's account of the black women's club movement, a phenomenon entirely ignored in all previous understandings of the history of the organized women's movement, is particularly important. Not only does she emphasize the role of these clubs in social welfare and racial uplift work, but she identifies the intertwined issues that later scholars would point to as central—the lynching of black men and the sexual harassment of black women.

Within a decade after *Century of Struggle* appeared, the climate of the fifties gave way to the very different sixties. A mass feminist movement emerged, which called itself "women's liberation" and was hungry for a past. We all read *Century of Struggle*, but so closely did our perspective come to Flexner's that I think, ironically, we simply absorbed her work without fully appreciating how original and innovative it was. Since then, I hope those of us who study women's history have learned to understand feminism as part of a larger history of social movements, particularly those challenging class and racial inequality. And to the degree that this "sex/class/race" framework is a feminist commonplace now, Eleanor Flexner's historical vision deserves some of the credit. At the same time, this "holistic" way of understanding the feminist tradition is being overtaken by a different, more "eighties" kind of feminism, which dresses for success and wants it all. In this atmosphere, it's time to reread *Century of Struggle*, to remember Flexner's vision of the past and to reevaluate our own vision of the future.

NOTES

1. Eleanor Flexner, *Century of Struggle: The Woman's Rights Movement in the United States* (Belknap Press of Harvard University, Cambridge, Massachusetts,

1959); 2nd ed., 1975. All references to the book in the text will be to the first edition unless otherwise indicated and will include page numbers in parentheses. All other quotes from Eleanor Flexner are from an interview, June 1988, at Westboro, Massachusetts.

2. Ferdinand Lundberg and Marynia F. Farnham, M.D., *Modern Woman: The Lost Sex* (Harper & Brothers Publishers, New York, 1947).

3. See Leila J. Rupp and Verta Taylor, *Survival in the Doldrums: The American Women's Rights Movement, 1945 to the 1960s* (Oxford University Press, New York, 1987); and Joanne Meyerowitz, "Beyond the Feminine Mystique: The Discourse on American Women, 1945–1960," paper presented at Berkshires Conference on Women's History, Rutgers University, June 1990.

4. Ellen C. DuBois, "Making Women's History: Historian-Activists of Women's Rights, 1880–1940," *Radical History Review,* 49 (1990); Nancy F. Cott, ed., *A Woman Making History: Mary Ritter Beard through Her Letters* (Yale University Press, New Haven, 1990).

5. Eleanor Flexner, *Mary Wollstonecraft* (Coward, McCann & Geoghegan, Inc., New York, 1972).

6. "Anne Crawford Flexner," *American Women Writers: A Critical Reference Guide from Colonial Times to the Present,* ed. Lina Mainiero, v. 1 (Ungar, New York, 1980), pp. 50–52.

7. James Thomas Flexner, *An American Saga: The Story of Helen Thomas and Simon Flexner* (Little, Brown, Boston, 1984), chap. 44.

8. Eleanor Flexner, *American Playwrights, 1918–1938* (Simon and Schuster, New York, 1938).

9. Flexner, *An American Saga.*

10. Rupp and Taylor, *Survival in the Doldrums,* chapter 7.

11. In *The Grounding of Modern Feminism* (Yale University Press, New Haven, 1987), Nancy Cott seeks to understand this period not so much in terms of the movement's collapse as in its shifting understandings of women's emancipation. In "What's in a Name: The Limits of 'Social Feminism'" (*Journal of American History,* 76 [December 1989]) she builds on this analysis to challenge the tendency of historians to borrow from William O'Neill's 1969 history of women's rights, *Everyone Was Brave,* a typology which splits feminism into "social" and "hardcore" varieties. She objects to this framework both with respect to the 1910s (when, she argues, the opposition does not exist) and with respect to the 1920s (when there is a split but it is over "feminism," to which only one side claims to adhere). I agree with much of her argument, and for this reason use the term "social reform" rather than "social feminism" for the post-1920 anti-ERA faction.

12. The first quote is from a review by Gilman Ostrander in *Ohio History,* 70 (1961), p. 90; the second by Carl Degler in *Mississippi Valley Historical Review,* 46 (1960), p. 733.

13. Mary R. Dearing, *American Historical Review,* 65 (1960), p. 620; Janet James, *New England Quarterly,* 33 (1960), p. 118.

14. For instance, Elizabeth Nottingham, *American Sociological Review,* 75 (1960), p. 302; James, *op. cit.*

15. Alma Lutz, a NWP loyalist and pioneering feminist historian, reviewing *Century* in *Saturday Review,* liked the book but, writing from within a NWP perspective, criticized the credit Flexner gave to Catt for leadership in the final years (v. 42, p. 34, August 15, 1959).

16. DuBois, "Making Women's History"; Rheta Childe Dorr, *Susan B. Anthony: The Woman Who Changed the Mind of a Nation* (Frederick A. Stokes Co., New York, 1928).

17. Second edition, 1975, p. ix.

13

Woman Suffrage and the Left

An International Socialist-Feminist Perspective

It is difficult to imagine a richer subject for a comparative history of democracy than the enfranchisement of women. Despite casual remarks about various governments "granting" women the vote, enfranchisement in the overwhelming number of cases was preceded by a women's movement demanding it. Indeed, extending over more than a century and including most nations of the globe, the cause of woman suffrage has been one of the great democratic forces in human history. Whereas manhood suffrage, for instance, or the breaking of the political color bar, have occurred more erratically, with limited links between national experiences, woman suffrage has been a self-consciously transnational popular political movement. As such, it resembles nothing so much as international socialism.

Notwithstanding the subject's richness, much of its history remains to be explored. This is especially true in Asia, Africa and Latin America, where enfranchisement, measured by numbers of countries in which women vote, has actually been accelerating since the 1920s. One factor however that has discouraged scholarship, especially from a left perspective, is the assumption that the enfranchisement of women has been, on balance, a conservative development. This notion, which predates not only the enfranchisement of women but even the woman suffrage movement itself,[1] is based more on prejudice than serious analysis. In particular, the classic socialist account characterizes the history of woman suf-

A version of this article was originally published in *New Left Review* 186 (1991).

frage as a fundamentally bourgeois demand made by conservative, elite "ladies."[2] This perspective insists on the antagonism of feminism and socialism, especially in the 1890–1920 period, and the necessity for women activists to choose one over the other.

I want to challenge this interpretation from a self-consciously socialist-feminist perspective; by which I mean both that I intend to highlight the centrality of a kind of politics I shall call "socialist-feminism" to the history of woman suffrage, and that I will do so on the basis of a modern perspective which calls itself "socialist-feminism." By contrast to the allegedly irreconcilable antagonisms identified in the classic socialist account, contemporary socialist-feminists struggle to tolerate the tension between socialism and feminism and to make of it a creative and powerful progressive politics. To use the metaphor suggested by Mary Bailey, this politics resides precisely at the point of the hyphen that separates and connects "socialism" and "feminism."[3]

The politics I am calling "socialist-feminism" has long been a self-aware wing of modern feminism, playing a major role in the women's liberation revival of the late 1960s, as well as providing the dominant perspective for much women's history scholarship since then.[4] While modern socialist-feminism is uniquely self-aware and self-defined, I believe that it is possible to trace such politics back at least to the mid-nineteenth century and to argue that it has consistently been a radicalizing force in the larger history of feminism. This article can be read, therefore, as a contribution to the reconstitution of the socialist-feminist tradition, as part of a contest with other kinds of feminism for control over the meaning and political direction of the contemporary women's movement.[5] At the same time, it is addressed to a socialist audience, in the spirit of sisterhood and comradely education. I invite all readers to join me, in other words, in temporary suspension of unnecessary oppositions, at the point of the hyphen.

The course of this political reconstruction is as follows. I begin with a brief consideration of the origins of the woman suffrage demand in conjunction with the revolutions of 1848, and its temporary disappearance in the conservative decades that followed. During these years, socialism itself was marked by hostility to women's rights. My primary focus, however, is on the 1890–1920 period, in which suffragism resurfaced and during which both socialism and feminism flourished as international, multi-tendency movements for social change. Under the category "socialist-feminism," I examine two kinds of politics produced by the complex intersection of those movements: the women's movement within the Second International; and the independent feminists, often called in those years "militants," who were influenced by and sympathetic to socialism but remained independent of party discipline. Both groups led the way to the reinvigoration of the demand for woman suffrage in the early twentieth century. In other words, I argue that in the 1890–1920 period woman suffrage was a "left" or "militant" demand, and that it reflected the existence and vigor of both the socialist and feminist movements.[6]

Woman Suffrage in the Early Years

Although the term "women's rights" reaches back to the 1790s (it can be found in the writings of Mary Wollstonecraft) the specific demand for equal political rights for women dates from 1848. Between these two revolutionary years, the issue of "women's rights" was an aspect of utopian socialism and focused on economic rights, especially for married women.[7] The demand for *political* equality for women surfaced mid-century, connected to the rise of popular movements for universal suffrage for men. In Britain, the initial drive for woman suffrage came from women Chartists (themselves influenced by Owenites) who tried but failed to get woman suffrage included in the People's Charter. American Elizabeth Cady Stanton, visiting London in 1840, took the Chartist innovation back to the United States. In 1848, that year of international revolutions, she organized a convention in Seneca Falls, New York, to demand women's rights, most controversially "the sacred right to the elective franchise." The most forceful demand for woman suffrage came from France, where a small group of socialist women protested against the exclusion of women from the universal suffrage declared by the Provisional Government in March 1848. For their efforts, Pauline Roland and Jeanne Deroine were imprisoned in St. Lazare. From jail they wrote to a women's rights convention in Massachusetts: "Sisters of America!

Your socialist sisters of France are united with you in the vindication of the right of women to civil and political equality. . . . Only by the union of the working-classes of both sexes to organize labor, can be acquired, completely and pacifically, the civil and political equality of women and the social right for all." American feminists proudly acknowledged their sorority with the French martyrs.[8]

Despite adherence to ideologies that supported equality and democracy, most mid-nineteenth-century male socialists and democrats were reluctant (or worse) to support women's demands for political equality. Yet this did not endear the women's rights program to conservatives. On the contrary, they identified women's rights with socialism and fought it on that basis. In the aftermath of 1848 women were a particular target of political repression, and their political activities were criminalized. In Germany's northern states women were barred from membership in political clubs from 1850 until 1908; in France the prohibition against women's political activism stood until the establishment of the Third Republic.[9] This association of women's political activism with threats to bourgeois social order is itself important testimony to the radical quality of woman suffrage. Similar repressions took place in China in 1914 and Argentina in 1945.[10]

The socialist movement and the men who led it were a party to the anti-feminism that followed the defeats of 1848. The next two decades were the heyday of what Claire Moses has called "left-wing patriarchalism."[11] In France, Proudhon rebuilt the working-class movement around nostalgia for the male-dominated artisan family. Lasalle played a similar role in Germany. Indeed, it is this context that helps us understand the reputation that Marx, Engels and Bebel achieved among socialists as relatively strong advocates of sexual equality. As for the principle of equal rights for women, the 1848 era left the shallow imprint of formal support, which was virtually emptied of content in the years that followed. In the 1875 Gotha Program that formed the German Social Democratic Party (SPD), for instance, a plank calling for suffrage for "citizens of both sexes," proposed by Bebel, was defeated in favor of the deliberately vague "general equal and direct suffrage . . . for citizens over 20 years of age."[12] While later male socialist leaders never equaled the misogyny of this period, it left its legacy in the stubborn conviction that women were themselves to blame for socialists' reluctance to support woman suffrage, and that the enfranchisement of women would only strengthen the forces of reaction. Women working within the socialist tradition regularly confronted and challenged this hostile undercurrent.

For the most part, the demand for political equality for women faded between 1848 and 1890. In the United States and Britain there were brief resurgences of woman suffragism in connection with the expansion of manhood suffrage in the late 1860s. In the United States, the constitutional abolition of slavery and enfranchisement of the freedmen inspired woman suffragists to work for the constitutional recognition of woman suffrage as well. In Britain, the Reform Act of 1867 encouraged feminists who had previously concerned themselves with education and employment to shift their attention to political rights, and to prevail on John Stuart Mill to sponsor a bill to include women in its provisions.[13] Woman suffrage activism was once again a casualty of the repression of radicalism in the wake of the Paris Commune and the intensified fear of revolution that followed it. In the United States, for instance, the post-Civil War effort for woman suffrage came to a spectacular halt in the controversy surrounding the socialist-feminist Victoria Woodhull, woman suffrage advocate, free love pioneer, and first publisher of *The Communist Manifesto* in the United States. In Britain, suffragism languished during the Tory ascendancy of the 1870s.

Without a thriving socialist left, feminism in the 1870s and 1880s was pulled to the right, toward campaigns for education and away from political power, toward claims of moral superiority and away from equal rights, toward middle-class women's traditions of charitable benevolence and away from working women's aspirations to self-support. In particular, the demand for political power for women shriveled into various "partial" suffrages that bore little relation to the radical, feminist tradition of absolute equality with men. In Britain, Sweden, parts of Australia and the United States, Finland and elsewhere, property-owning or tax-paying women were granted local suffrages. This was usually a modification of an older tradition whereby women who owned property were granted "proxy" voting rights, to be exercised for them by men of their choosing.[14] In Britain, parliamentary traditions were so strong that the woman suffrage movement did not entirely disappear in these years; it was nonetheless timid and conservative and forfeited the basic demand for full political equality with men. The handful of feminists who worked for political rights in the 1870s and early 1880s asked only for parliamentary suffrage for "spinsters and widows," yielding to the framework of coverture that declared that married (that is, most) women were "represented" in and by their husbands.

Individual women who continued to subscribe to the radical suffragist tradition of full political equality for women on the same terms as men were very much isolated from the feminist mainstream in the 1870s and 1880s. Janus-like, they looked backward to 1848 and forward to the socialist and feminist revivals of the 1890s, but their continued agitation for woman suffrage was a lonely and alienating crusade. In the United States, Elizabeth Stanton played this role; in Britain, it was Elizabeth Wolstoneholme-Elmy. In France, Hubertine Auclert represented the democratic feminist tradition, while in Italy it was Anna Mozzoni.[15]

These activists tended to link the enfranchisement of women with the emancipation of the working class, and began to identify themselves with socialism, which rarely returned the favor.[16] The grand historical transformation which underlay the convergence between their faith in the democratic promise of woman suffrage and a growing interest in socialism was the rise of a female wage-labor force and their recognition that wage-earning women would eventually form the core of a radical feminist revival; for the time being, however, male socialist leaders' older, anti-feminist habits of hostility to women workers continued unabated. "As long as capitalism continues to rule," German Social Democrats insisted in 1873, "we have an obligation to strive to keep women and children out of bourgeois industry altogether, both in the interests of the women and children themselves, and in the interests of the proletariat in general."[17]

If we are to find any feminist strains within socialist movements before 1890, they will not be in the classic centers of socialist politics—in the cities and among waged workers—but in more rural areas and among family-oriented women. In the American West, Scandinavia, Australia and elsewhere, left-leaning, quasi-socialist movements gave women room to voice their support for various "moral reforms," especially in campaigns against alcohol and prostitution. Inasmuch as such protests opposed forms of commerce they considered immoral, their moral demands had a political, state-oriented side as well. In the United States, Australia and New Zealand, for instance, women's moral reform movements called for women to be allowed to vote on special matters of moral significance—to control alcohol, criminalize prostitution, or shape the moral content of public school education.[18] Like propertied and partial suffrages, these partial franchises need to be distinguished from the democratic feminist tradition of full political equality with men. Yet they have contributed to the reputation of woman suffrage as a conservative movement—because they run contrary to traditions of personal liberty, involve an increase of state power over individual behavior and seem so foreign to our modern attitudes to pleasure.

To the degree that these moral reform movements were conservative, however, so were some of the roots of social democracy, with which they frequently converged. For instance, in the United States, Mari Jo Buhle has demonstrated that the moralistic, populist politics of the Midwest helped to build an American socialist movement, and that in the 1880s, the Woman's Christian Temperance Union (WCTU) was virtually a conduit for women into socialism.[19] Ross Evans Paulson argues that similar patterns held for the states of Australia. Indeed, the Victorian, traditionalist perspective of moral reform movements on sex roles and the family was welcomed by socialists as a way to reinforce domestic peace in the working-class family. Bonnie Smith observes that one of the barriers to full support for sexual equality within socialist movements was that it raised "questions concerning the working-class family," and "questioning the working-class home ultimately amounted to questioning the backbone of socialism—the working-class male."[20]

Women in the Second International

Beginning about 1890, an openly and aggressively feminist movement began to develop within international socialism, with political equality one of its most consistent demands. The largest socialist women's movements were in Germany, the United States and Austria, but there was also activity in Italy, France, Russia, all of Scandinavia, the Netherlands,

Australia, Ireland, South Africa, Galicia, Argentina, and undoubtedly elsewhere, constituting what was arguably one of the largest international feminist movements ever.[21]

The figure most identified with this international socialist women's effusion was Clara Zetkin, the leading woman in the leading party of the Second International. Throughout the 1890s, Zetkin forged a socialist women's program and practice within the German Social Democratic Party which became the prototype for women in socialist parties around the world.[22] From 1907 to 1915, the size and vigor of this worldwide socialist women's network made possible a sort of shadow women's International, with annual conferences. The Women's History Month that American feminists now celebrate in March is the direct descendent of the International Proletarian Women's Day first authorized by the 1910 international socialist women's conference.[23]

Most accounts of these turn-of-the-century socialist-feminists emphasize either their struggles with the sexism of male socialists or their challenge to middle-class women's movements, but it was really the balance they struck, always fragile and often upset, between these two political forces that determined their political environment.[24] In several of the leading parties the tension between socialism and feminism led to open conflict between socialist women themselves. Among German socialist women, for instance, Zetkin's loyalty to international socialism was counterposed to (and balanced by) Lily Braun's greater inclination to the independent women's movement. There were similar pairings in the French party—Elizabeth Renaud and Louise Saumoneau (who "came to socialism on the rebound from feminism")—and in Italy between Anna Kulisckoff and Anna Mozzoni.[25] If we can resist the temptation to choose sides in such contests, to designate one position alone as correct, the fierce battles between these sororal antagonists can be read as an expression of the dialectical situation of socialist-feminism, the shifting and unstable but distinct and authentic political territory it occupied.

The issue of woman suffrage was at the very center—was the virtual expression—of the balance socialist women struck between the non-socialist women's movement and the male-dominated left. Had its advocates not forced their perspective forward within their parties, woman suffrage would have languished as a principle tainted by socialism but not really sustained by it. On the other hand, it is not an overstatement to say that had it not been for the degree of autonomy socialist women were able to sustain within their parties from the mid-1890s on, and for the new classes of women to whom they brought the issue, the demand for woman suffrage probably would not have been revived and placed at the center of a militant, mass, modern women's movement.

Zetkin first succeeded in getting the German party to adopt the explicit endorsement of political rights "without distinction of sex" into its platform in 1891, at the Erfurt Conference. To the wearying objection of socialist men that women were too reactionary to risk enfranchising, Zetkin responded that the vote "was a means to assemble the masses, to organize and educate them," and that it was precisely political organizing, including working for the vote, that would "educate" women out of whatever relative "backwardness" they suffered.[26] Within the International, the first pro-suffrage resolution was passed in 1900, but the Belgian party in 1904 and the Austrian party in 1906 continued to set aside demands for woman suffrage in order to concentrate on universal manhood suffrage. The campaign led by Zetkin, to reprimand the Belgians and the Austrians and to strengthen organized socialism's commitment to woman suffrage, coincided with the first all-women international socialist conference, at Stuttgart in 1907. There the International accepted the principle that political equality for women was a non-contingent, fundamental demand that socialist parties must pursue "strenuously."[27]

These socialist suffragists liked to argue that the bourgeois case for woman suffrage was a defense of property and individual privilege, while they demanded the vote as a weapon of working-class power and on the basis of fundamentally different presumptions. The issue of property restrictions on proposals for woman suffrage played a major role, first in socialist men's opposition to woman suffrage and then in socialist women's sense of what distinguished them from bourgeois feminists. However, the situation was more complicated, and easy ideological distinctions did not always hold up. It is particularly important to note that property-holding among women was usually related not only to wealth but to marital and professional status. This was certainly the case in Britain, where the legal concept of coverture was invented, which denied the right to hold property to women on the basis of their status as wives, thus making property-holding (and the suffrages tied to it) a marital category for women as much as a class distinction. The 1884 Reform Act expanded the male franchise from property-holders to householders. Even though suffragists demonstrated that extending the householder vote to women would disproportionately benefit the working class, leaders of the Social Democratic Federation contended that anything less than universal womanhood suffrage was a compromise of socialist principles. (Zetkin supported their view.) Even in Germany, where the distinction between bourgeois and socialist cases for woman suffrage was forged, non-socialist suffragists were deeply divided over the issue of property restrictions.[28]

It was not their objections to enfranchising women on a propertied basis, or the allegedly collectivist case they alone made for the vote, that really distinguished socialist women's suffragism from the bourgeois variant, but the link they made between women workers and political equality. The distinctively socialist argument for woman suffrage, which came to be widely accepted among bourgeois suffragists as well, rested on the recognition that the increasingly public character of women's labor had to be matched with an equally public political role.[29] At the founding conference of the Second International, in Paris in 1889, Zetkin caused a sensation by condemning the antagonism to working women that had prevailed for so long in socialist circles. "If we wish women to be free human beings, to have the same rights as men in our society," she insisted, "women's work must be neither abolished nor limited except in certain quite isolated cases."[30] "The demand for woman suffrage results from the economic and social revolutions provoked by the capitalist mode of production," resolved a socialist women's conference in 1904, "but in particular from the revolutionary change in labor and the status and consciousness of women."[31] Thus, substantive support for woman suffrage within socialism required overcoming the powerful heritage of male hostility to wage-earning women. That this occurred was a tribute to the feminist insurgency within the Second International and meant that, in the future, it would be much more difficult "to dismiss the female proletariat as a force impeding the revolution."[32]

The tradition of "proletarian sexism" left its mark, however, in the policy of special regulation of women workers, offered as protection for the most vulnerable in the labor market but actually functioning to keep women in a separate and unequal sector of the labor force.[33] The operative word here was "protection," a rhetorical device which facilitated a reinterpretation of such laws, from hostile to friendly toward women workers. Through the 1880s, laws to regulate only women workers were advocated in the male-dominated trade unions and socialist movements. Into the 1890s such legislation was opposed by feminists, both by those who objected to all state regulation of the wage relation and by those who accepted the necessity of labor legislation but called for its application to all workers, not just women.[34] In the complex interactions that generated feminism within the Second International, support for sex-based labor legislation seems to have been the price paid for substantive support for woman suffrage. Zetkin, who had attacked special restrictions on working women at Stuttgart in 1889, changed her position in 1893, after which time she faithfully advocated special labor legislation for women. All women who remained within socialist parties accepted the principle of special labor laws for women, and through this route the notion worked its way into the women's movement proper, where it lodged until the mid-twentieth century.

Organizationally, the intermediate position of feminists within socialism led to the twin principles of autonomy for women's organizing in socialist parties and antagonism to collaboration with non-socialist feminists. Of these, hostility to bourgeois feminism was the more intensely expressed, perhaps because the efforts of non-socialist women represented such serious competition. The initial impetus for the international socialist movement to organize women in the 1890s, after decades of inactivity, was the necessity of countering the organizational inroads that non-socialist women were making among female wage earners. In the United States, for instance, middle-class feminists successfully established "working girls' clubs" in major cities in the 1880s. In Germany, a working women's movement was beginning to flourish without middle-class leadership but outside of the Social Democratic Party as well.[35] Barbara Clements argues that the great Russian socialist Aleksandria Kollontai was drawn to the organizing of working women and to feminist issues by the fear that the bourgeois women's movement was becoming too influential among working-class women.[36]

In 1896, Zetkin made hostility to the non-socialist women's movement a fundamental principle of socialist women's organizing in Germany. (Earlier there was little threat—or inspiring competition—from bourgeois women activists: Bebel did not object to "collaboration.") The socialist program for women's emancipation included woman suffrage, equal education, freedom of occupation, equal status in domestic law, equal pay for equal work, abolition of domestic service and protective labor legislation for women workers. The non-socialist women's movement supported all but the last two. Despite the fact that their programs were largely the same, Zetkin argued fiercely against any collaboration between women in the "proletarian" and "bourgeois" movements and struggled constantly (if futilely) to draw the line between the two. In 1907 at Stuttgart, Zetkin overcame strong opposition from the Austrians, British, French and Americans to establish non-cooperation with bourgeois feminists as the official policy for socialist women around the world. Like the concessions that Zetkin and other socialist women made to sex-based labor legislation, anti-collaborationism helped to offset the innovation that strong support for woman suffrage from a socialist platform represented. Anti-collaborationism was more important rhetorically than organizationally, and was honored as frequently in the breach as in the observance. In the United States, socialist women kept their sectarian distance from their "enemy sisters" only in New York City; everywhere else there was considerable cooperation throughout the 1910s, especially around votes for women.[37]

Although Zetkin's rhetorical challenges were directed at bourgeois feminists, she also fought to keep socialist women from being overwhelmed by men's definition of socialism. In structural terms, this commitment to autonomy within socialism was expressed by organizing women separately from men within the party, a corollary to the practice of organizing them separately from the non-socialist women's movement. The most vigorous and powerful of the national movements—in the United States, Austria, Finland—followed the lead of the Germans and organized women separately from men.[38] To be sure, in Germany this strategy was dictated by the Anti-Association Laws which prohibited women from engaging in political activities.[39] (By definition, an all-women's organization could not be political.) But the separate organization of women within socialism served an enormously important positive function as well, making it possible to set up the infrastructure of a semi-autonomous women's movement and to nurture an entire generation of socialist women leaders. In 1908, the repeal of the German Anti-Association Laws led the leaders of the SPD to abolish separate women's organization. Zetkin fought furiously against this action, which she felt would lead to women's eventual disempowerment within German socialism, but she lost, and her own power within the SPD declined.

Charles Sowerwine emphasizes the importance of the separate organization of women to their power within socialist parties, by contrasting the strength of German women socialists with the weakness of women in the French party. The French Groupe Feministe Socialiste (organized in 1899) never undertook the separate organization of women in the party (as a consequence of a sectarian split of the organization which separated the feminist and socialist impulses within it). A similar situation occurred in Italy. Perhaps the absence of semi-autonomous socialist women's movements is one of the reasons why woman suffrage did not come to either country after the First World War. Despite the fact that the socialist parties in both countries formally supported woman suffrage as a parliamentary measure, and that, at least in France, there was a non-socialist woman suffrage movement of some size, the absence of a link between the two—those divided and inconsistent feminists within the socialist parties—may well have been crucial. Finland serves as a fitting counter-example. There the SPD was unusually hospitable to feminists within the party, and a large socialist women's network developed, which played a major role in the first victory for woman suffrage in the western world, in 1906.

Independent Suffrage Militancy

The emergence of a newly militant suffragism, influenced by the upsurge of socialist politics after 1890 but ideologically and organizationally independent of it, is the other source for the great growth of the woman suffrage movement internationally in the early twentieth century. While feminists within socialist parties prepared the way for a wage earners' suffragism that helped make woman suffrage a mass movement, these independent feminists made their contribution to the revival of suffragism by linking it to a fundamental challenge to gender definitions and relations and adding a whole new level of tactical militancy to suffrage agitation. Like socialism, this independent feminist militancy was decidedly internationalist, both in spirit and in substance. In Europe, North America, Australia—but also in China, South America and elsewhere—the balance of forces between these two types of feminist radicals, some within socialist parties and others outside, shaped the existence, strength and outcome of the women's movement for political equality in the years prior to World War I.

This independent militant suffragism—whose advocates came to be known as "suffragettes"—radiated out from Britain, where it flourished in the early twentieth century. The British suffragettes are one of the few aspects of the international woman suffrage movement that have entered general historical consciousness, but study of them has, until recently, been limited largely to the complex and contradictory Pankhurst family. However, a new generation of historians of women is offering a revisionist interpretation of the history of suffrage militancy in Britain which better allows us to appreciate its links with the left. They emphasize that the radicalization of the movement in Britain reached far beyond the Pankhurst family; that its roots lay in the organization of working-class women and the dedication of activists inspired by but independent of organized socialism; and that the mainstream of British suffragism eventually established a political alliance with Labour.[40]

Jill Liddington and Jill Norris have demonstrated that the militant revival of British suffragism predates the involvement of the Pankhursts and can be traced to a working-class-based suffrage movement of Lancashire textile workers in the 1890s. Why were British working women so political? While the British trade unions were as hostile to working women as their French or German equivalents, British working women had their own organizations, including the Women's Trade Union League (formed in 1874), the Women's Cooperative Guild (formed in 1883), and the overwhelmingly female textile workers' unions. Middle-class suffragists with socialist inclinations turned to the working-class women of these organizations to generate a working women's suffrage movement. In Manchester, Esther Roper and her companion, Eva Gore Booth, sister of the Irish nationalist leader Constance Markievicz, took the lead. The tactics of this new kind of suffragism were borrowed from trade unionism and emphasized "open-air campaigning, factory-gate meetings and street corner speaking."[41] Politically, its goal was to pressure the fledgling Labour Party to provide a parliamentary route for woman suffrage.

In 1900, Gore Booth took on, as her protégé, Christabel Pankhurst, daughter of Independent Labour Party (ILP) founders Richard and Emmeline Pankhurst. Following the lead of Roper and Gore Booth, Christabel and her mother formed the Women's Social and Political Union (WSPU) in 1903. The Pankhursts initially emphasized public agitation, working-class organization and Labour Party political links. They were especially close to Keir Hardie, and in 1906 campaigned aggressively for him. By then, in the words of her sister Sylvia, Christabel had "lost all interest" in the women of the Lancashire textile unions, and the WSPU moved its operations from Manchester to London.[42]

As the WSPU moved away from Manchester and from its working-class origins, its strategies shifted from mass to illegal tactics. Under the close leadership of Christabel and Emmeline Pankhurst, it developed its own highly influential form of civil disobedience, as an adaptation from the "political law-breaking" tradition of Irish nationalists.[43] Other militant groups split off into their own societies. These included the Women's Freedom League, every bit as daring tactically as the WSPU, and the East End Federation, organized by Sylvia Pankhurst among working-class women. Meanwhile, other suffrage societies, especially the once conventional National Union of Women's Suffrage Societies, continued the organization of the "monster demonstrations" for suffrage pioneered, then abandoned, by the WSPU. By 1911, militant modern tactics under various organizational labels dominated the British suffrage movement.

The British press effectively dubbed the new feminist militants "suffragettes," a term which came to stand around the world for a fundamentally modern and mass approach to building a woman suffrage movement. The term "suffragette" conjured up radical challenges to dominant definitions of womanhood. Whereas bourgeois femininity—in Europe, North America and their cultural outlands—was marked by a devotion to the separation of the domestic and private world of women from the public and political world of men, suffragette militancy literally took women out of the parlor and into the streets. Parades, outdoor demonstrations, street-corner meetings—these were the marks of modern suffrage agitation. Inasmuch as wage-earning women provided the female army that first breached the walls around the public realm, suffragette militancy was initially "viewed as a specifically working-class initiative." But the challenge to cloistered femininity that it expressed eventually drew passion from women of all classes.[44] Suffragettes were eager to demonstrate their support in public, willing to break the law in service to the "Cause." Some were even determined to die as martyrs for votes for women (they were only successful, it seems, in Britain).

The example of the British suffragettes had tremendous international influence, attributable to the extensive worldwide publicity they received (which they intentionally elicited) and the movement's coincidence with other political radicalisms, socialist and/or nationalist. The International Woman Suffrage Association, established between 1899 and 1902, also spread the example of the suffragettes. Because of organizational factionalism in Britain, the WSPU was prevented by other British suffrage organizations from joining the international association, but the attempt to exclude their example was to no avail. In 1906 the IWSA met in Copenhagen, and delegates brought back the news of the British militants to Hungary, Russia and elsewhere. The IWSA had been designed to meet every five years, but it soon found itself meeting much more frequently, infused despite itself with the spirit of suffragette militancy.[45] In 1909 the IWSA met in London, and delegates were treated to various demonstrations of militant tactics—mass marches, civil disobedience, hunger strikes. Although British suffragettes were not formally invited to the 1913 meetings in Budapest, a radical faction of the Hungarian movement brought Sylvia Pankhurst to talk about her working-class-based version of militancy. She also lectured in Brussels and Vienna, though police prohibited her from holding meetings in Berlin and Dresden.[46]

The IWSA provided a conduit for the militants' influence, much as the Second International did for the socialist suffragism of Zetkin and Kollontai. The relation of the IWSA to the Second International is an interesting one, combining imitation and competition, and signifying the complex interaction between suffragettes and socialists in the international reinvigoration of the movement for political equality. Whereas an earlier international organization of bourgeois women reformers (the International Council of Women, formed in 1888) had avoided the issue of woman suffrage as too radical, the rise of international socialism had emboldened non-socialist suffragists, who formed in the IWSA their own international society. The IWSA also helped bourgeois suffragists to compete with socialists, by providing them with an international resource to counter the influence of socialists in the suffrage politics of their home countries. In turn, women of the Second International, who had helped to inspire the formation of the IWSA by their example, were much influenced by the feminist militancy it spread. Despite their oft-repeated opposition to "collaboration" with "bourgeois suffragists," they could not resist the energy of the suffragette example: Richard Evans believes that the mass demonstrations of International Proletariat Women's Day from 1911 through 1913 were imitations of the "monster parades" organized by British militants.[47]

A new generation of American suffragists—college-educated, middle-class women bored by the "pink parlor teas" of the aging suffrage establishment—were especially quick to pick up the inspiration of the British militants. Many of them were influenced by and sympathetic to socialism, although not party members. In San Francisco, trade-union activist Maud Younger ("the millionaire waitress") organized the Working Women's Suffrage Society. In Manhattan, a group called the "American Suffragettes" began to hold outdoor meetings every night and to tease the press with their love of the outrageous. Harriot Stanton Blatch, herself a veteran of British Fabianism in the 1890s, returned to the United States to organize a working-class-based, tactically militant, independent woman suffrage insurgency; her position as the daughter of Elizabeth Cady Stanton gave her special influence.[48] By 1913, under her leadership, tens of thousands of women were marching in New York City, and the example of suffrage parades was spreading across the country. Despite the dictums of the Second International, American socialist women cooperated closely with these independent suffragettes. In California in 1911, in Wisconsin in 1912, even in New York, it was often difficult to distinguish the two groups or to predict which feminists would show up inside the Socialist Party, and which outside. In 1913 the suffrage revival culminated with a mass suffrage parade in Washington, D.C., and the creation of a national suffragette society.[49]

The suffragette example also shaped the Irish woman suffrage movement, which was only fitting given the role that Irish constitutional nationalists played in holding up a final parliamentary solution to votes for women in Britain. The Catholicism of France and Italy is often cited as an explanation for their outrageously delayed enfranchisement of women, but the influence of Catholicism proved no serious barrier to the flourishing of militant suffragism in Ireland. The leading figure here was Hanna Sheehy-Skeffington, a socialist, friend of Irish labor and militant suffragist. Inspired by the Pankhursts, she organized the Irish Women's Franchise League, which heckled politicians (Churchill at Belfast), held demonstrations and engaged in that signature suffragette activity—breaking windows with stones. Their political focus was on the amendment of the Home Rule Bill to include woman suffrage. In their struggle to influence the shape of the coming Irish nation, the suffragists eventually gained the support of the Irish Labour Party. Irish women got the vote on equal terms with men in 1922 in their new republic, six years before the British.[50]

Nor was it only Europeans and North Americans who responded to the feminist excitement of the British suffragettes. In 1912 in Nanking, China, the Woman Suffrage Alliance, an independent socialist-feminist group, petitioned the provisional parliament to "enact equality of the sexes and recognize women's right to vote." Convinced that the men would not take their demand seriously, they armed themselves with pistols, stormed the parliament building three days in a row and had to be dragged off by guards. In imitation of the WSPU, they broke windows, "drenching their hands in fresh blood." Around the world, suffragette sisters celebrated their dedication. The WSPU itself sent a message of support, and in New York the president of the national suffrage organization paraded under a sign declaring "Catching Up with China."[51]

France provides a useful contrast. Here British militants also inspired independent suffragists, but there was no parallel socialist suffrage movement, little organized suffragism among working-class women, and thus suffragette passions did not flourish in the same way. A militant and socialist-feminist organization, Solidarité des Femmes, was organized as early as 1893 but could find no men's socialist organization willing to work with it. Inspired by the WSPU's first efforts at civil disobedience, Solidarité activists organized a series of public, outdoor demonstrations, culminating in physical attacks on men's ballots (voting urns were upended and their contents destroyed). Despite the heritage of the revolutions of 1789, 1848 and 1871, French women did not respond to Solidarité's challenge for women to take to the streets. Steven Hause and Anne Kenney attribute what they call the French "taboo against activity in the streets" among women to the absence of "the leavening [effect] of working-class experience" on women's sense of the politically possible. In 1914, independent feminists tried once again to organize a militant suffrage movement directed at working-class women, but by then it was too late and war was upon them.[52]

As suffragist activism accelerated among masses of women, the issue of property limits on enfranchisement ceased to be a point of contention between socialist and non-socialist suffragists. In 1911, in response to persistent pressure from a wide range of suffragists, the British ILP dropped its historic objection to any form of enfranchisement that did not include all adults of both sexes and agreed to support a compromise bill, which set the level of female enfranchisement at an intermediate position. When a wartime coalition government finally began to enact parliamentary female suffrage in Britain in 1918, only women householders and wives of male householders over thirty got the vote, a restriction designed to keep women from being the majority of the electorate. After 1918, the suffrage movement was far more concerned about this limitation than Labour and continued to battle for the inclusion of the excluded women. The enfranchisement of women on equal terms with men—for whom householder limitations had been *abolished* in 1918—came relatively late to Britain, in 1928.

In the United States there was no significant tradition of property-based enfranchisement, and this undoubtedly defused class antagonisms among woman suffrage forces and allowed socialists and non-socialists to cooperate to a high degree. The reactionary force in American suffrage politics was rather the question of race, which interfered with the drive for woman suffrage much as the dilemma of householder suffrage did in Britain. While African American women were proportionately more active than white women on behalf of votes for women, the rise of the female suffrage movement coincided with the brunt of the attack on black political power. The leaders of American suffragism included founders of the National Association for the Advancement of Colored People and they included racists, but the forces in American politics favored the latter. In particular, the Democratic Party—the party of labor and of nostalgia for slavery—was the place where female enfranchisement and black disenfranchisement met in confrontation. Despite increasing determination, size and power, the woman suffrage movement was held up in its final drive to amend the federal Constitution by opposition from southern Democrats, unwilling to enfranchise any more black people. As was the case with Labour in Britain, it took time for suffragists to bring the Democratic Party around. In the end, suffragists won enough victories at the state level (notably New York in 1917) to increase their congressional power and break the national political log jam.[53]

Winning the Vote

In the classic account of woman suffrage—the one that assumes its fundamental conservatism—the war is given a great deal of credit for enfranchising women. As Steven Hause and Anne Kenney observe, this is a way of denying the "generations of feminist labor that made enfranchisement possible." Involvement in the war does not correlate particularly well with the enfranchisement of women. Combatant countries—France, Italy and Belgium—did not enfranchise women, while neutral nations—the Netherlands and the Scandinavian countries—were among the first to do so. In some countries, for instance Denmark and Iceland, the war held up the enfranchisement of women, which was already in place by 1914. In France, according to Hause and Kenney, the war was actually "a setback for the woman-suffrage movement"; the world war after which French women were enfranchised was, of course, the second one.[54] Only in Germany and Austria, where defeat and revolution brought in socialist governments which enfranchised women, can a more direct causal role be attributed to the war. In Britain and the United States the war provided time (and a suprapartisan environment) for the political forces necessary to enfranchise women to mature.

Indeed, a case can be made that the fundamental impact the war had on the woman suffrage movement was much more negative: it shattered the socialist-feminist link that underlay suffragism's growth and vigor. The war split the suffrage movement in two, just as it did international socialism. The majority of socialists and suffragists advocated preparedness, war work and service to the state. In Germany, the SPD formally embraced the war, as did the non-socialist woman suffrage movement. In Britain, Christabel and Emmeline Pankhurst became intensely pro-war, renaming the *Suffragette* magazine *Britannia*. Elsewhere, independent militants tended more to the anti-war camp. In the United States the suffragette National Woman's Party resisted pro-war jingoism, running afoul of anti-sedition laws even before the Industrial Workers of the World. In Ireland, Sheehy-Skeffington became a militant pacifist. In Britain, Sylvia Pankhurst became one of the leading anti-war feminists. The international feminist pacifist network that these activists formed became the Women's International League for Peace and Freedom. Among women leaders within organized socialism, Clara Zetkin, who had long since been driven from the SPD's leadership, opposed the war.

The rise of Bolshevism also made the distance between socialism and feminism much greater—stretched the hyphen to breaking point, as it were. As parliamentary socialism was repudiated, woman suffrage ceased to have much relevance. "The subject of political rights . . . is one about which radical women have already stopped thinking," wrote American socialist (and former suffrage activist) Anita Block. "The radical woman is now looking forward to voting as it is done in the Soviet Union [i.e., in soviets], and pure political suffrage has ceased to have interest or value for her."[55] She made this statement in November 1917, days after women had finally won suffrage in her home state of New York and while the October Revolution was still fresh as flowers in her heart. In

France, "Bolshevism enlarged the disagreements between bourgeois feminists and socialist women, driving each group away from conciliation."[56] As Communism developed, it preserved the formal support of women's rights that had characterized the socialist tradition, but refused to tolerate the independent organization of women necessary to give it meaning. In the whole history of the left, the Third International stands out for its failure to generate a corollary feminist movement.[57]

As for the non-Communist remains of the suffrage movement, those who refused to repudiate the left were relentlessly red-baited, themselves treated as subversives. In the United States, Jane Addams was hounded, and in Hungary, Rosika Schwimmer was pursued. The worldwide reaction against Bolshevism drove many feminists to the right. In the United States, the National Woman's Party became devoted to the single issue of the Equal Rights Amendment; that is, it jettisoned all the other social justice concerns that had surrounded suffragist feminism. Under the leadership of Alice Paul, American radical feminism was reformulated as a women's movement which dissociated itself from other progressive movements, a far cry from what it had meant before the war. In France, a small Catholic suffrage movement developed immediately after the war, largely, it seems, because the left had dropped the issue; it was unable to win women the vote. In Italy, the unfilled promises of votes for women were waiting for Mussolini to exploit, and in the 1920s Fascists gave Italian women municipal suffrage, only to gut local governments of any autonomy or power. Only in Argentina did the right successfully seize on and deliver the unmet demand of votes for women.[58] Between the revived hostility on the left to feminism and the rightward turn of suffragist successor organizations, the charge of women's political conservatism was revived. Without socialist-feminists to develop a left politics that spoke to women's needs, or to bring socialism to women once it did, why should this not have been the case?

The history of the movement for woman suffrage goes beyond the 1920s, as do the efforts of some women to hold on to both feminism and the left despite the tensions between them. What little we know of women's movements for political equality in the Third World suggests similar patterns to those in Europe and North America in the early twentieth century. There were left-wing, working-class-based efforts for the enfranchisement of women in Iran, Puerto Rico, Mexico, Uruguay, Argentina, Indonesia and perhaps Turkey.[59] It is possible to argue that, between 1920 and the late 1960s, this is where the left-feminist tradition, the politics which situated women's emancipation in the context of a larger vision of human justice (and which, conversely, insisted that any vision of social transformation must include women as well as men), found its home.

North American and European New Left women of the late 1960s, eager to apply the promise of "liberation" to their own sex, found their initial inspiration less in the history of feminism at home, which seemed pale and reformist, than in the militant women activists of Cuba and Vietnam. Nor was this simply a new left fantasy of Third World revolution, female style, for there had been vigorous dialogues over women's rights that had occurred within and influenced the Third World left.[60] A young American woman anti-war activist recalls that she was first exposed to feminist consciousness at an international conference between Vietnamese revolutionaries and American peace activists in Czechoslovakia in 1967, and she drew on the lessons learned from the Vietnamese women she had met to build a women's liberation movement at home.[61] At about that time, International Women's Day came home.

Indeed, for women in colonial situations, it may be less tempting and/or possible to choose gender over class, or vice versa, than it was for First World feminists. Black and Chicana feminists in the United States are beginning to make a similar argument explicitly with respect to race: their political concerns are simultaneously those of their people and their sex. "The necessity of addressing all oppressions is one of the hallmarks of black feminist thought," writes Deborah K. King.[62] So long as the politics of resistance insists that "one particular domination precipitates all really important oppressions," she argues, black women's "history of resistance to multiple jeopardies is replete with the fierce tensions, untenable ultimatums, and bitter compromises between nationalism, feminism and class politics." But "multiple jeopardy" needn't mean only marginality and exclusion from what King calls "monist" political ideologies. It can also generate "multiple consciousness," a flexible, complex and inclusive perspective on social oppression and human liberation. "'Women of color' have a chance to build an effective unity that does not replicate the imperializing, totalizing revolutionary subjects of previous Marxisms and feminisms," writes Donna Haraway. Such a perspective is crucial to modern politics, to crafting an effective response to what she calls the "disorderly polyphony emerging from decolonization."[63] However difficult it is, we have no choice but to reject false oppositions, to refuse to yield to unnecessary "either-ors" and to hold to the territory of the hyphen.

NOTES

1. During the 1875 debate over whether to include woman suffrage in the founding document (the Gotha Program) of the German Social Democratic Party, opponents cited the allegedly reactionary political tendencies of women, to which Wilhelm Liebknecht responded: "Opponents of female suffrage often maintain that women have no political education. But there are plenty of men in the same position, and by this reasoning they ought not to be allowed to vote either. The 'herd of voters' which has figured at all the elections did not consist of women. A party which has inscribed 'equality' on its banner flies in the face of its own words if it denies political rights to half of the human race." Quoted in Werner Thonnesson, *The Emancipation of Women: The Rise and Decline of the Women's Movement in German Social Democracy 1863–1933*, London 1969, p. 32.

2. Despite sympathetic treatment of the early phases of woman suffragism, Richard Evans maintains this approach to the later period, during which, he argues, suffragism abandoned its egalitarian roots and accepted property restrictions in order to get the vote for privileged women. These claims are drawn primarily from the German example. See his book *The Feminists: Women's Emancipation Movements in Europe, America and Australasia, 1840–1920*, London 1977, p. 217.

3. See Mary Bailey's 1979 characterization of the necessary tension in "Marxism-Feminism," quoted in Rosalind Petchesky, "Dissolving the Hyphen: A Report on Marxist Feminist Groups," in Zillah Eisenstein, ed., *Capitalist Patriarchy and the Case for Socialist Feminism*, New York 1979, p. 375: "As Marxist-Feminists we straddle an uneasy horse. We have not worked out what this means, this hyphen. . . . All too often, all this has meant is that we are Marxists to our feminist sisters and feminists to our Marxist brothers. The gravest danger facing us right now is that we will settle for this hyphen . . . as a self-explanation

. . . a counter, a cipher, instead of a project. . . . What intervenes in this relationship of two terms is desire, on every level. Hyphen as wish. We have heard its whisperings."

4. See, for instance, Karen V. Hansen and Ilene J. Philipson, eds., *Women, Class and the Feminist Imagination: A Socialist Feminist Reader,* New York 1990.

5. The meaning of "feminism" is highly contested, by both scholars and activists. See Karen Offen, "Defining Feminism: A Comparative Historical Approach"; and Nancy Cott and Ellen Carol DuBois, "Responses," *Signs,* vol. 14, no. 1, 1989, and vol. 15, no. 1, 1990. In *The Grounding of Modern Feminism,* New Haven 1988, Nancy Cott argues that the term, which first appeared about 1900, should be reserved for the more modern ideological strains with which it was originally associated. Because I am trying to establish links between the present and the past, I have chosen to use the term "feminism" in a broad sense, to mean a very large, long and complex tradition calling for the "equality," "elevation," or "emancipation" of women, but often disagreeing within itself as to how to achieve that. In particular, I am using the term "feminism" to describe a historical movement larger and more general than the demand for woman suffrage. Here and elsewhere, my work has concentrated on illuminating intellectually and advancing politically the "left feminist" wing of that tradition. It has frequently been observed that the terms "left" and "right" translate to feminism with real difficulty. Nonetheless, I find the term "left feminism" helpful, and therefore use it, albeit with imprecision. Steven C. Hause and Anne R. Kenney *(Women's Suffrage and Social Politics in the French Third Republic,* Princeton 1984) use the term to describe a wing of the late-nineteenth-century French movement. In this connection, I have found Richard Flacks's *Making History: The Radical Tradition in American Life,* New York 1986, very useful; he defines "left" to mean democratic movements for social change, a tradition which includes but is not limited to socialism.

6. See Meredith Tax, *The Rising of the Women: Feminist Solidarity and Class Conflict, 1880–1917,* New York 1980, a study of the American movement for working women's emancipation that coincided with the 1890–1920 suffrage movement. Tax traces a similar political dialectic, which she calls "the united front of women": "Gradually a shape—a theme—emerged from the clay. . . . I have called it the 'united front of women', by which I mean the alliance, recurring through time in various forms, of women in the socialist movement, the labor movement, the national liberation movements, and the feminist movement. I am using the term 'united front' not in the catch-all sense of the 1930s, but as it is used currently, particularly in the Third World, to describe the coming together . . . for a goal of some magnitude that takes a considerable length

of time to achieve" (pp. 13–14). While I do not use the same term as Tax, because I see more tension and conflict than the term "united front" suggests, I agree with Tax's sense of the complex dialectic at work and its importance to the long history of feminist politics.

7. Barbara Taylor, *Eve and the New Jerusalem: Socialism and Feminism in the Nineteenth Century,* New York 1983.

8. Elizabeth Cady Stanton, Susan B. Anthony, Matilda Joslyn Gage, eds., *History of Woman Suffrage,* Volume 1, New York 1883, pp. 234–36; Ellen Carol DuBois, ed., *Elizabeth Cady Stanton. Susan B. Anthony: Correspondence, Writings, Speeches,* New York 1981; Claire Moses, *French Feminism in the Nineteenth Century,* New York 1984.

9. Moses. See also Ruth-Ellen Joeres and Mary Jo Maynes, eds., *German Women in the Eighteenth and Nineteenth Centuries,* Indiana 1986.

10. Ono Kazuko, *Chinese Women in a Century of Revolution, 1850–1950,* California 1989. Cynthia Jeffress Little, "Education, Philanthropy and Feminism: Components of Argentine Womanhood, 1869–1926," in Asuncion Lavrin, ed., *Latin American Women: Historical Perspectives,* Greenwood, Conn. 1978. A lone but intriguing counter-example can be found in England, where the prohibition against paid partisan organizing (i.e., among men) in 1883 opened the doors of political support work to women.

11. Moses, p. 152.

12. Thönnesson, pp. 31–2.

13. It is interesting that in both the U.S. and British cases, these early efforts were not aimed at enfranchising women as a particular group, but rather at *removing* the linguistic qualifier "male" to enable the inclusion of women in non-gendered categories such as "person," "citizen" or "voter."

14. Ross Evans Paulson, *Women's Suffrage and Prohibition: A Comprehensive Study of Equality and Social Control,* Illinois 1973, p. 100.

15. In 1879 Auclert petitioned socialists to support woman suffrage and forge "a pact of alliance against our common oppressors." Hause and Kenney, p. 9. After years of alliance with liberals, Mozzoni "began calling herself a 'socialist'" and saw new possibilities for a woman suffrage movement in "the young female factory workers of the Italian textile industry." Donald Meyer, *Sex and Power: The Rise of Women in America, Russia, Sweden and Italy,* Middletown, Conn. 1987, pp. 124–5.

16. Thus Elizabeth Stanton, in her closing address to the International Council of Women in 1888, predicted that unless women's demands for freedom were speedily met, "it requires no prophet to foretell the revolution ahead when women strike hands with Nihilists, Socialists, Communists, and Anar-

chists, in defense of the most enlarged liberties of the people." DuBois, ed., *Elizabeth Cady Stanton, Susan B. Anthony*, p. 177.

17. Thönnesson, p. 31.

18. In contrast to property-bound traditions of votes for women, these movements were more likely to restrict their demands to married rather than to unmarried women.

19. Mari Jo Buhle, *Women and American Socialism, 1870–1920*, Illinois 1981. Ella Reeve Bloor, legendary founder of the CPUSA, made her political start in the WCTU.

20. Bonnie Smith, *Changing Lives: Women in European History since 1700*, Lexington, Mass. 1989, p. 313.

21. Marilyn Boxer and Jean Quataert, eds., *Socialist Women: European Socialist Feminism in the Nineteenth and Early Twentieth Centuries*, New York 1978; Richard Evans, *The Feminists*, New York 1977; and *Comrades and Sisters: Feminism, Socialism and Pacificism in Europe, 1870–1945*, New York 1987; Charles Sowerwine, "The Socialist Women's Movement from 1850 to 1940," in Renate Bridenthal, Claudia Koontz, and Susan Stuard, eds., *Becoming Visible: Women in European History*, Boston 1987; Jane Slaughter and Robert Kern, eds., *European Women on the Left: Socialism, Feminism and the Problems Faced by Political Women, 1880–Present*, Westport, Conn. 1981.

22. Cynthia Little has found evidence of a socialist women's organization in Argentina, the Feminist Center, working from 1906 through 1912 with socialist deputy Alfredo Palacios, advocating the Second International feminist platform, including woman suffrage and special labor legislation for women. "Education, Philanthropy, and Feminism: Components of Argentine Womanhood, 1860–1926" in Lavrin, ed., *Latin American Women: Historical Perspectives*. On Second International feminism in South Africa, see Cheryll Walker, *The Women's Suffrage Movement in South Africa*, Cape Town 1979; this was, of course, an all-white movement. On Galicia, see Martha Boyachevsky-Chomiak, "Socialism and Feminism: The First Stages of Women's Organizations in the Eastern Part of the Austrian Empire," in Tova Yedlin, ed., *Women in Eastern Europe and the Soviet Union*, Ottawa 1975.

23. Socialist Women's Day seems to have begun in the United States in 1909, as part of the International-authorized socialist campaign for woman suffrage (Tax, *Rising of the Women*, p. 188). Zetkin picked it up within the International in 1910. The holiday was adopted by the Comintern and became a solely Communist observance, until the American women's liberation movement, itself inspired by Communist women activists in the 1960s, reimported the celebration to the United States. By the late 1970s, liberal De-

mocrats took the holiday through one more political transformation, and it became the federally mandated Women's History Month. See Temma Kaplan, "On the Socialist Origins of International Women's Day," *Feminist Studies*, 11, 1, 1985, pp. 163–71 for the history of this event, a rich example of the complex relation between the present and the past in the creation of a historical tradition.

24. Buhle's first account of American socialist women emphasized left sexism: "Women and the Socialist Party, 1901–1914," *Radical America*, vol. 4, no. 2, 1970; the collection edited by Boxer and Quataert, *Socialist Women*, stresses the antagonism to bourgeois feminists.

25. Sowerwine, p. 409.

26. Jean Quataert, *Reluctant Feminists in German Social Democracy, 1885–1917*, Princeton 1979, p. 94.

27. "The socialist parties of all countries have a duty to struggle energetically for the introduction of universal suffrage for women." Sowerwine, p. 416.

28. Evans, *The Feminists*, pp. 109–12.

29. Charlotte Perkins Gilman, whose historical account of women's evolution toward emancipation is indistinguishable from that of Engels, was a major force in popularizing the socialist approach to women's equality throughout the non-socialist women's movement in America. Buhle, *Women in American Socialism*, chap. 2.

30. Susan Groag Bell and Karen M. Offen, eds., *Women, the Family and Freedom: The Debate in Documents*, vol. 2, Stanford 1983, p. 87.

31. Thönnesson, p. 63.

32. Linda Edmondson, *Feminism in Russia, 1900–1917*, London 1984.

33. In her survey of the history of women workers, Alice Kessler-Harris concludes that this is the way that special labor legislation for women ultimately functioned. *Out to Work: A History of Wage-Earning Women in the United States*, Oxford 1982, chap. 7. In her later work, she has backed away from this assessment to some degree; see *A Woman's Wage: Historical Meanings and Social Consequences*, Lexington, Kentucky 1989.

34. In England, the conflict between these two positions occurred early in the history of the Fabian Society, over the 1896 Factory Act. Socialist-feminists, among them Stanton's daughter, Harriot Stanton Blatch, criticized the limitation of hours only among women workers, while Beatrice Webb, representing the classic trade-union position and the leading faction within the Fabians, argued (successfully) for laws only against the exploitation of women workers. Polly Beals, "Fabian Feminism: Gender, Politics and Culture in London, 1880–1930," Ph.D. thesis, Rutgers University, 1989.

35. On Germany, see Ute Frevert, *Women in German History: From Bourgeois Emancipation to Sexual Liberation*, New York 1989.

36. B. Clements, *Bolshevik Feminist: The Life of Aleksandria Kollontai*, London 1979, p. 59. Similarly, Linda Edmondson, in *Feminism in Russia, 1900–1917*, argues that "such was the abhorrence felt by Orthodox Marxists toward the idea of separate women's organizations that the potential value of the female proletariat went almost unnoticed" until the non-bourgeois women's movement forced it upon socialists' attention (p. 171).

37. John D. Buenker, "The Politics of Mutual Frustration: Socialists and Suffragists in New York and Wisconsin," in Sally Miller, ed., *Flawed Liberation: Socialism and Feminism*, Westport, Conn. 1981.

38. In the United States, socialist women had their own organization, the Socialist Women's National Union, even before Debs formed the American party in 1902; in 1908 it metamorphosed into the Women's National Committee of the Socialist Party.

39. Kollontai's biographer says that when Kollontai discovered that the separate organizing of socialist women, to which she was passionately committed in Russia, was the child of German necessity, she was astonished. Clements, p. 64.

40. Sandra Holton, *Feminism and Democracy: Women's Suffrage and Reform Politics in Britain, 1900–1918*, New York 1986; Jill Liddington and Jill Norris, *One Hand Tied behind Us: The Rise of the Women's Suffrage Movement*, London 1978; Lisa Tickner, *The Spectacle of Women: Imagery of the Suffrage Campaign, 1907–1914*, London 1988. In addition, there is another group of contemporary feminist historians of British suffragism who have emphasized instead the degree to which the sexual politics of Christabel Pankhurst anticipate modern anti-pornography feminism. See Susan Kingsley Kent, *Sex and Suffrage in Britain 1860–1914*, Princeton 1987: and Sheila Jeffreys, *The Spinster and Her Enemies: Feminism and Sexuality, 1880–1930*, London 1985.

41. Holton, p. 33.

42. Sylvia Pankhurst, *The Suffragette Movement: An Intimate Account of Persons and Ideals*, London 1977, p. 195.

43. Rosemary Cullen Owens, *Smashing Times: A History of the Irish Woman Suffrage Movement 1889–1922*, Dublin 1984, p. 40. Christabel Pankhurst, referring in 1908 to the "Fenian outrages in Manchester and the blowing up of Clerkenwell Gaol," wondered "how anybody after that can say that militant methods are not effectual." Jane Marcus, ed., *Suffrage and the Pankhursts*, London 1987, p. 48.

44. Holton, p. 35; Ellen Carol DuBois, "Working Women, Class Relations

and Suffrage Militance: Harriot Stanton Blatch and the New York Woman Suffrage Movement, 1894–1907," *Journal of American History*, vol. 74, no. 1, 1987.

45. International Council of Women, *Women in a Changing World: The Dynamic Story of the ICW since 1888*, London 1966.

46. Pankhurst, p. 535.

47. Evans, *Comrades and Sisters*, pp. 68–75. Richard Evans, "Appendix: International Feminists Movements," in *The Feminists*; Edith F. Hurwitz, "The International Sisterhood," in *Becoming Visible*, ed. Bridenthal, Koontz, and Stuard; Mineke Bosch and Annemarie Kloosterman, eds., *Politics and Friendship: Letters from the International Woman Suffrage Alliance, 1902–1942*, Columbus, Ohio 1990.

48. Susan L. Englander, "The San Francisco Wage Earners' Suffrage League: Class Conflict and Class Coalition in the California Woman Suffrage Movement, 1907–1912," M.A. thesis, San Francisco State University, 1989; DuBois, "Working Women." After American women won the vote, Blatch became an active member of the Socialist Party and ran for office on its ticket.

49. M. J. Buhle, M. Tax, J. Buenker and C. Lunardini, *From Equal Suffrage to Equal Rights: Alice Paul and the National Woman s Party, 1910–1928*, New York 1986.

50. Leah Levenson and Jerry H. Natterstad, *Hanna Sheehy-Skeffington: Irish Feminist*, Syracuse 1986, p. 37.

51. Kazuko, pp. 80–92. Argentinian suffragists, exasperated with a ridiculously limited municipal suffrage, organized the Partido Feminista Nacional, in imitation of the British WSPU. Argentine municipal woman suffrage was available only to women "of majority age who were free to administer their own estates or who had university degrees that allowed them to work in professions." Ann Poscaletto, *Power and Pawn: The Female in Iberian Families, Societies and Cultures*, Westport, Conn. 1976, p. 191.

52. Hause and Kenney, p. 118.

53. Paula Giddings, *When and Where I Enter: The Impact of Black Women on Race and Sex in America*, New York 1984. A distinctive feature of American suffrage politics is dual sovereignty over the franchise. States can grant full voting rights (including the vote in federal elections) by amending their constitutions. From the viewpoint of a popular suffrage movement, this meant that activists could pursue their goal at either the state or the federal level, so that when one route was blocked they could turn to another. Women in many states thus voted, including for federal offices, before the federal Constitution was amended in 1920. Thus, office holders dependent on women's votes played a

role in the final stages of female enfranchisement; in other words, women's votes helped to win women's votes.

54. Hause and Kenney, p. 202; Evans, *The Feminists*, p. 223.

55. Buenker, p. 126.

56. Hause and Kenney observe that among the fourteen reasons given by a government commission against woman suffrage in 1919 were the contradictory assertions that women were too backward to vote ("their uninformed participation would pose a grave threat to the republic") and that feminists posed a violent threat to social order "like the Bolsheviks" (p. 238).

57. From 1920 to 1925, Zetkin led a Communist women's international, and there are some national exceptions to this generalization.

58. Marifran Carlson, *Feminismo: The Woman's Movement in Argentina from Its Beginnings to Eva Peron*, Chicago 1988.

59. The English-language scholarship on post-1920 suffrage movements is just beginning to accumulate. Kumari Jayawardena, *Feminism and Nationalism in the Third World*, London 1986, is particularly worthy of note. Also see Jane Macias, *Against all Odds: The Feminist Movement in Mexico to 1940*, Westport, Conn. 1982; Deniz Kandiyoti, "From Empire to Nation State: Transformations of the Woman Question in Turkey," and Sylvia Villamil and Graciela Spariza, "Feminism and Politics: Women and the Vote in Uruguay," in S. Jay Kleinberg, ed., *Reviewing Women's History*, Oxford 1988.

60. See, for instance, David Marr, "The 1920s Women's Rights Debates in Vietnam," *Journal of Asian Studies*, vol. 35, no. 1, 1976.

61. The first contact between Vietnamese revolutionaries and American peace activists was made through the Women's International League for Peace and Freedom in Jakarta a year or two before (personal communication by Vivian Rothstein to the author, 1990). Nor was this merely token female equality, Soviet style: Madame Binh was a leader of the NLF, when such women leaders were a rarity in international politics.

62. Deborah K. King, "Multiple Jeopardy, Multiple Consciousness: The Context of a Black Feminist Ideology," *Signs*, vol. 14, 1988, p. 43.

63. Donna Haraway, "A Manifesto for Cyborgs: Science, Technology and Socialist Feminism in the Last Quarter," in Hansen and Philipson, p. 587.

14

A Vindication of Women's Rights

Of all the terms associated with what we now call feminism, the one that has been used for the longest time is *women's rights*. It dates back to the late eighteenth and early nineteenth centuries, when it signified a revolutionary approach to women's nature and prospects, advocated by a tiny group of Anglo-American radicals and tainted by its association first with the French Revolution and then with socialism. Two hundred years later, the term women's rights is used much more widely than in earlier centuries and its contemporary associations are far less terrifying. The current meaning of women's rights leans to the more conventional and legalistic aspects of modern women's struggle for freedom and equality and is sometimes invoked, in contrast to *feminism*, as a temperate call to change.[1]

I suggest a more precise meaning for women's rights, which retains some of its original pointedness and militancy, yet reflects two hundred years of changing contexts, meanings, and goals for women's advancement. When the term women's rights first began to be used, especially in the United States, it had a very specific content: it was understood to be a critique of women's dependence within marriage and a call for full individuality (or personality or autonomy) for women, regardless of marital status. The initial target of women's rights protest was the legal doctrine of "coverture," which determined that marriage removed from women the right to own and contract for property, transforming them instead into property. A classically liberal ideal that focused on the emancipation of the individual more than on the reorganization of society, the women's rights perspective nonetheless opened up dramatic new aspects for human freedom, especially with respect to sexuality and reproduction, precisely because the individuals it sought to liberate were women and the oppressive structures it targeted were so literally close to home.

Traditionally, it has been assumed that coverture was a remnant of feudalism and was dismantled in the nineteenth century, but feminist legal scholars are beginning to rewrite this story. They have traced what Reva Siegel calls the modernization of coverture into the twentieth century and explored the continuing power of marital subordination to function as a framework for modern family life and the fundamental inequality of gender relations.[2] I am interested in a similar project, although from a less singularly legal perspective and with more of a focus on women's organized protests against their subordination. I treat marriage here not solely as a legal category but also not merely as a personal relationship, varying widely in character and satisfaction for its many participants; rather, I address marriage as an institution and a social structure, created and enforced not only by law but by economic forces, culture and other means as well and responsible for the creation and re-creation of the relations between the sexes that we call *gender*.[3]

Within the history of feminism, then, the battle against coverture was also modernized and can be traced into the twentieth century and through to our own contemporary concerns. I suggest that protests against women's subordination in and through marriage, first raised in the nineteenth century by those who gathered under the mantle of women's rights to attack the laws and social conventions of coverture, can be linked to such twentieth-century feminist concerns as equality for women in the labor force, regardless of marital status, and sexual and reproductive freedom. Since the 1970s, the term women's rights has become so identified with the campaign for the Equal Rights Amendment that it has lost its distinctive and still disruptive emphasis on the conflict between the institution of marriage and women's personhood. I here trace the continuing radical possibilities to be found in protesting the institution of marriage as the root of women's subordination and seek to reidentify these with the term women's rights.

Mary Wollstonecraft is generally recognized as the first major figure in the women's rights tradition. Previous female polemicists had argued for the necessity of transforming and elevating women's status, but Wollstonecraft was the first to frame her arguments in terms of women's rights, a term that reflected her identification with the French Revolution. Her program, a liberal education for women, was rather modest; but her most intense rage was reserved for women's reduction to men's trivial playthings, a loss of individuality so great that women no longer even aspired to selfhood. Not only in her writings but in her life, Wollstonecraft struggled against the subordination of women in marriage—refusing to marry her lovers and the fathers of her children until the very end of her life and then dying in childbirth.

After Mary Wollstonecraft, the argument for women's rights passed into the hands of the utopian socialist followers of Robert Owen. The Owenites took Wollstonecraft's critique of the negative impact on women of a narrow and antidemocratic domestic life and linked it to their own hostility toward the private, bourgeois family. In their hands, the women's rights tradition developed into an even more precise perspective on women's emancipation, focusing on the position of women within marriage and calling for their liberation from their (non)status as the property of their husbands. The Owenites understood the doctrine that women "disappeared," upon marriage, into the persons of their husbands not merely as a legal fiction but as an organizing premise for the unequal relations of the sexes, the male-dominated structure of the family, and the rigid sexual division of labor. As utopians, they imagined and tried to establish an alternative social order not organized around the bourgeois family, with its private, isolated economic basis and its strict sexual hierarchy.[4]

The women's rights tradition was brought from England to the United States in the 1820s by the Scotswoman Frances Wright and by Robert Dale Owen, Robert Owen's son. Robert Dale Owen made his mark on U.S. history by advocating two radical reforms that were derived directly from the utopian socialist critique of women's loss of autonomy in marriage: First, he pioneered in spreading contraceptive information, especially to women and, second, he supported liberal divorce laws, to permit an escape from intolerable unions. His political companion Frances Wright literally embodied female autonomy, especially with respect to sexual self-determination, until, as with Woll-stonecraft, pregnancy drove her into marriage and retreat. For decades, her name was virtually an epithet for monstrous female independence.

Owen's and Wright's protégé Ernestine Rose, the heroic Polish-born freethinker, forms the link between these transplanted British socialists and the establishment of a full-fledged women's rights movement in America. From 1840 through 1848, Rose agitated for reform of the laws governing married women's economic status in her adopted state of New York. This was the campaign in which Elizabeth Cady Stanton served her political apprenticeship.[5]

In 1848, the year in which the New York legislature finally began to reform wives' economic status, Elizabeth Cady Stanton called a public meeting to begin to organize a more sustained agitation around women's rights. "We are assembled to protest against a form of government, existing without the consent of the governed," she declared at Seneca Falls in 1848. By government she meant not only the public but the private rule under which women lived, that is, marriage. The Seneca Falls Declaration specified the poisonous fruits of coverture: "such disgraceful laws as give man the power to chastise and imprison his wife, to take the wages which she earns, the property which she inherits and, in case of separation, the children of her love; laws which make her the mere dependent on his bounty."[6]

Other perspectives that called for the improvement and elevation of women's status circulated in Jacksonian America—for instance, the evangelical notion of enhancing women's social role on the basis of their moral superiority, as well as the romantic goal of women's developing their "true nature," which Margaret Fuller elaborated so well. But these alternative discourses were not the same as women's rights and sometimes even emerged to refute and replace it. Catharine Beecher offered her domestic science and social maternity program in the 1850s as a conservative antidote, literally a reaction, to the much more radical claims of women's rights spokeswomen, whom she characterized as "bewailing themselves over the fancied wrongs and injuries of women in this Nation."[7]

In the 1850s, the American women's rights movement focused very clearly on women's loss of rights and personhood in marriage. The primarily legal goal was the establishment of basic property rights for women once they were married, which went to the core of the deprivations of coverture. Lucy Stone's distinctive contribution to the women's rights campaign was her 1855 protest against the convention by which the wife took the husband's name, which was the classic sign of women's marital subordination.[8] Finally, in 1860, activists in New York achieved the passage of the most comprehensive married women's property law in the United States. Other states had revised their laws before—a half dozen Southern states had moved to insulate wives' separate property (especially slaves) from husbands' indebtedness. But the New York reforms of 1860 were the first to give rights to women themselves (as opposed to their fathers' property as invested in them). Wives in New York won the right to buy and sell property, to retain custody of their children on divorce, and to make legal contracts. As historians have pointed out, judges limited the impact of wives' new rights by conservative interpretations, but the mark of the women's rights movement lies nonetheless clearly on these legal reforms, which were intended to allow women to continue to be individual economic actors after they had married.[9]

The 1860 legislation in New York was also the first to include wives' right to earn and control wages, along with the right to own and contract real property, in the framework of married women's economic rights. This redefinition of the meaning of property rights from land to wages was fundamental in making the women's rights tradition meaningful to the growing masses of working people in industrializing America who owned only their own labor power. Women's rights claims, which had come into being to protest restrictions on wives' real-property owning, gained greater relevance by including wives' rights to their property in their own labor.[10] By the twentieth century, wives' labor-force equality would be at the forefront of the battle for women's emancipation.

But the mid-nineteenth-century women's rights movement went even further. It not only demanded women's equal rights to hold property and make contracts but named as an issue men's claims to property in women and demanded instead women's rights to claim property in themselves. This included women's right to dispose of their own labor, but it involved more. If anything, women's rights arguments centered on uses of the body other than productive labor, especially on the question of who controlled women's sexuality and reproductive capacities, their husbands or themselves. Women used these premises to level an attack on that aspect of the tradition of coverture which withdrew sexual and reproductive as well as economic individuality from women on marriage. Under the banner of women's rights, the political meanings associated with the individual thus became more than a contractual fiction and began to move in the direction of the person as an embodied reality, whose physical integrity and self-determination were at the core of her being.

This interpretation of the women's rights movement, that it aimed to emancipate wives from being—to borrow Patricia Williams's phrase—themselves "the object of property," brings us to the abolitionist movement and women's rights' debt to it.[11] In large part, the historical coincidence of women's rights with abolitionism made it possible to articulate why and how it was immoral for a "nominally free woman" (Angelina Grimké's phrase) to be considered the property of another human being (her husband). Women's rights leaders regularly conceptualized marriage's injustices by analogy to slavery. Stanton was particularly strong on this point: Wives took on their husbands' names, as slaves did their masters'; neither could testify against their masters in court; the wife who escaped an abusive husband was like a fugitive slave, except that she lacked a Canada to which she could flee. Through participation in abolitionism, women's rights activists developed an analogy between slavery and marriage that was not simply rhetorical but analytical as well. In 1871, Victoria Woodhull argued that women were already enfranchised by the Constitution as amended, relying not only on the Fourteenth Amendment for its expansive definition of national citizenship but on the Thirteenth Amendment as well; by banning slavery and all its badges, she argued, constitutional abolition had emancipated wives as well, inasmuch as marriage was a form of slavery.

The Civil War had another effect on the women's rights movement. Following the path laid out by the constitutional enactment of suffrage for freedmen, women's rights activists shifted their attention from married women's economic rights to the achievement of equal political rights for women, regardless of marital status. The women's rights focus

on the oppressions of marriage was not lost entirely; economic independence (which marriage denied to women) was the *sine qua non* of enfranchisement. Thus, demanding the vote for women regardless of marital status called into question wives' categorical inability to hold property.[12] In addition, women needed political power to dismantle the legal
apparatus that kept them subordinate within marriage.

And yet, woman suffrage soon developed into a program that appealed to a much wider audience than just women's rights enthusiasts.
The republican motherhood and female moral superiority approaches to
women's advancement saw in votes for women a way to bring women's
special, maternal-based vision to bear on the larger society. This was
quite different from the initial advocates' demand for political equality
as a confirmation of and weapon for women's individualization. Indeed,
the great value of the woman suffrage claim was precisely that it appealed
to so many of the forms that women's discontent had taken, not just to
the women's rights variant. As innumerable historians have observed, the
focus on suffrage made possible one of the widest coalitions in the history of organized women's reform.

Charlotte Perkins Gilman provides a fine guide for following the
women's rights tradition through the late suffrage period and into the
early twentieth century. Gilman was the first thinker since Elizabeth
Cady Stanton to explore the core of women's marital subordination in
a way that still remains compelling to us a century later. Her subject
was precisely women's loss of personhood within marriage. She wanted
to separate marriage out—to perfect it, as it were—from what she
called "the family," all the other public functions that did not belong
in and interfered with personal life. Gilman's perspective on marriage
was complex and, at times, openly contradictory. She vigorously condemned what she called the "sexuo-economic" nature of the marriage
relationship, but ultimately her goal was to free the personal relationship from the corruptions of the institution. Gilman became the guru
of the "new woman" of the Progressive Era precisely because she spoke
for women's rights to personal autonomy and economic independence
within as well as outside marriage. Notably, her own marital history included both suffering of the sort that felled earlier feminists and satis-

faction (in her second marriage) of the sort to which modern women now aspired.

Among these twentieth-century radicals, the first to assume the neologism *feminist*, the women's rights tradition was revived. The nineteenth-century women's rights movement had sought economic alternatives to marriage, so that women would not be forced to demean themselves by marrying for support rather than for love. Twentieth-century feminists pushed the women's rights approach further by insisting on personal freedom and economic independence within as well as instead of marriage. They protested laws that banned married women from working, and they revived Lucy Stone's campaign against the convention of wives taking their husbands' names on marriage. They responded to the wage-earning mothers, whose numbers were so dramatically increasing in this period, by reformulating the ethic of female self-support as a standard within marriage and not just as an alternative to it. To address the dilemmas of wage-earning mothers, some called for a government policy of providing "motherhood pensions" rather than of reinforcing male breadwinning and the family wage. Their perspective was distinctive even among women reformers of the period, many of whom sought to maintain the separation between motherhood and wage labor for women.[13]

This same pioneering generation of feminists also became the initial shock troops of Margaret Sanger's birth control movement, which began in the 1910s as the suffrage movement was nearing victory. The birth control movement, which sought to disentangle sexuality from reproduction for women, tremendously advanced the women's rights campaign against that other great pillar of modern women's conjugal subordination: the confining of women's sexuality and reproduction within marriage.[14] Feminists' enthusiasm for birth control in combination with their commitment to economic independence for women within marriage led them to envision a future of heterosexual freedom and independence for women; in essence, they imagined a revolution within marriage. Of course, their hopes were in no way matched by their accomplishments, their personal efforts at egalitarian marriages failed, and they can easily be criticized for their naïveté with respect to men's ability to reassert and maintain their sexual privilege in the modern era. For the most part, their capacity to imagine unlimited sexual freedom for women stopped at the boundaries of what later generations would call "compulsory heterosexuality." But it is also true that they dramatically updated a perspective that had ceased to inspire women's passions for emancipation, invented a new vision of women's freedom, expanded the horizons of the women's rights promise of autonomy and personhood beyond that of the nineteenth-century perspective, and began to make the promise of liberation newly compelling to modern women, ourselves included.[15]

The final victory of the woman suffrage movement reopened questions, long put aside, about a larger vision of women's emancipation. To pursue a postsuffrage program, the National Woman's Party was founded. After much debate—including arguments by those who sought to concentrate on birth control, peace, suffrage enforcement for black women, and many other demands—the National Woman's Party agreed on a single plank: the Equal Rights Amendment. This is a crucial moment in the history of the women's rights tradition. While it might appear that the battle for the Equal Rights Amendment constituted a principled return to the women's rights tradition, the moment can be interpreted quite differently, as a turn away from the focus on marriage that had historically distinguished women's rights. Instead of seeking the causes of women's subordination in the lived relations between men and women, the campaign for the Equal Rights Amendment defined women's freedom on the basis of a formalistic legal fiction of their indistinguishability from men.

Most accounts of the three-year process by which the National Woman's Party settled on the language of the Equal Rights Amendment concentrate on Alice Paul's efforts to preserve the principle of equal rights before the law and at the same time shield sex-based labor legislation from any attack on the basis of that principle, an effort that she eventually abandoned. (Ironically, it can be argued that sex-based labor legislation was one of the most important sites within the law in which the tradition of coverture was relocated.)[16] However, another transition lies in the evolution of the proposed amendment's language: The wording of early versions of the amendment prohibited discrimination not only on the basis "of sex" but also "of marriage." Historian Joan Zimmerman thinks Paul's experiments with this approach reflected her concern with the legal remnants of coverture, which were the discriminatory legal practices in which she first took interest. In the end, however, the reference to discrimination in and through marital status was dropped, and the Equal Rights Amendment prohibited only discrimination by something it called "sex."[17] This is the constitutional principle that generations of feminists, ourselves included, have been honor bound to defend; but by dropping any criticism of the marriage institution, Paul turned away from the women's rights tradition and its historically based and sociologically engaged understanding of subordination as women lived it.

With the ascendance of the Equal Rights Amendment as the measure of feminist loyalty, the cutting edge of the women's rights tradition was seriously dulled for many decades. The Equal Rights Amendment was little help in the achievement of a sexually egalitarian future, precisely because its implications for marriage were so unclear. As Harriot Stanton Blatch observed when the measure was first introduced and she declared her objections to it, no consensus existed on what constituted equality within marriage, and the Equal Rights Amendment was not going to provide one. Blatch's convictions about marital equality led her to believe "that the wife should stand on her own economic feet," but she understood that supporters of the Equal Rights Amendment also included what she characterized as "an extreme right . . . [which] would like to see the husband forced to pay the piper while the wife called the tune." The abstractions and formalism of the Equal Rights Amendment, she argued, avoided this fundamental conflict about the meaning of equality between the sexes rather than resolved it.[18]

The decision to pin feminism's future on the single goal of the Equal Rights Amendment precipitated a disastrous split within organized women's reform that lasted many decades. As Nancy Cott has argued, the National Woman's Party took equality as its watchword and generated an opposition that gathered under the banner of economic justice.[19] Into the gap created by this false opposition fell the dilemma of the working wife and mother, to whom neither side attended. Neither wing was able to criticize the reimposition of the norm that adult women were properly their husbands' economic dependents, and the ancient tradition of coverture began to flourish in new, more modern forms. These sectarian antagonisms receded slightly during the 1930s, in response to intensifying job discrimination against wives. Both sides protested the introduction of "the marriage bar" into New Deal legislation, especially Section 213 of the National Economy Act, which federalized state laws against hiring wives as government employees. However, the disrepair into which women's rights arguments had fallen, combined with the economic pressures of the Great Depression, kept either side from protesting such laws in terms of married women's right to work. Even supporters of the Equal Rights Amendment fell back on the argument that married women worked because of family need, presumably only under exceptional conditions. This left the norm of the nonworking economically dependent wife unchallenged when economic conditions improved, during and after the war.

In 1966 a new feminist organization, the National Organization for Women, revived the campaign for the Equal Rights Amendment under very different conditions. The organization's founder, Betty Friedan, had rocketed to prominence as the author of *The Feminine Mystique*, the 1963 indictment of women's loss of personhood in marriage.[20] So weak had the women's rights tradition become that Friedan characterized women's loss of identity and purpose in marriage, which activists had been attacking for over a century and a half, as "the problem which has no name." Like Wollstonecraft 160 years before, Friedan offered a very modest solution to an enormous problem. She called for a change in lifestyle rather than social policy, and her vision of women's independence within marriage centered on women with money enough to employ other women as domestic servants. Still, it would be a mistake to underestimate the power that her indictment of women's subordination in marriage had on a whole generation of women.[21]

Even more than the National Organization for Women, however, it was the radical wing of 1960s and 1970s feminism, the young militants who initially gathered under the call for "women's liberation," who may best be seen as the legatees of the women's rights antimarriage tradition. No doubt this seems a strange claim, inasmuch as women's liberation, like the New Left from which it grew, was wildly contemptuous of liberalism and all its rights-oriented claims. Nonetheless, young women's liberationists learned from the civil rights movement an aggressive notion of human rights, which provided a language for asserting women's suppressed personhood. They were also deeply affected by the counterculture, with its utopian repudiation of the nuclear family. This multifaceted and youthful disdain for every aspect of conventional personal life from the single family household to monogamy itself fueled renewed criticism among women—especially those just at the age at which they would normally marry—of the institution of marriage. One has only to think of Shulamith Firestone's indictment of "the nuclear family" in all its aspects, from romantic love to nontechnological reproduction.[22] Together these two influences—modern civil rights and the counterculture—created women's liberation and gave the women's rights critique of marriage a new focus: sexual and reproductive autonomy for women.

The core of the movement for women's sexual and reproductive self-determination, which I am arguing is the latest phase of the long women's rights tradition, has been the abortion rights movement. The movement for abortion rights, far more than the Equal Rights Amendment, has provided the dynamic and passionate core of a vision for women's emancipation over the last quarter century. This can be explained only when abortion is understood not as a particular birth control practice, one of the many discrete acts that together constitute women's reproductive repertoire, but as a potent symbol for women's sexual and reproductive self-determination, the latest stage in women's revolt against marital dependence and female subordination. What began two centuries ago as a protest against women's formal, legal loss of individuality within marriage has become, in our own time, an insistence that marriage need not be the sole legitimate arena within which women can expect to be mothers and sexual persons.

In her definitive exploration of abortion from a modern women's rights perspective, political theorist Rosalind Pollack Petchesky has argued that the tremendous passion that the abortion issue generates, among both adherents and opponents, has to do with its close association "with the increasing visibility of women's sexuality outside the patriarchal family." "We sense that larger issues about women's sexuality

. . . are being distilled into the conflict over abortion." Concretely, the availability of legal abortion has made it possible for more and more women to delay or avoid marriage, without forfeiting their rights to sexual expression. From this anticonjugal perspective, Petchesky has argued that young unmarried women's recourse to abortion and their willingness to carry their pregnancies to term and become single mothers are developments that point in the same rather than in opposite directions. They both signal "the rejection of early marriage as the definite objective in women's lives and at least an expectation of economic independence." "Without minimizing . . . the hardships of single motherhood," she writes, "it is possible to recognize the decline of compulsory marriage as a progressive development" in both these changes.[23]

Given the particular emphases that, I have argued, link these many battles for women's emancipation together into a women's rights tradition that spans the centuries, what might the new frontiers of feminist battles for women's autonomy and personhood be? Two issues flow directly from the terms on which the abortion rights campaign has sought to disentangle sexuality and reproduction from marriage. They have already moved into contemporary political prominence and call for a clear and radical women's rights position.

First, in response to right-wing efforts to "reform" the welfare system by dismantling it, modern feminists need to make clear the real intent of the unilateral elimination of what pitiful support the state has been providing impoverished single mothers and their children: the reassertion of male headship, by insisting that all mothers properly owe economic dependence on men. We need to insist what our own political tradition teaches us: that the proper response to this situation is to fight for decent jobs and better pay for women and for the legitimacy and dignity of the female-headed household.[24]

Second, feminists need to defend and expand the personal rights of lesbians to be sexual people and to be mothers without recourse to men even outside of marriage. "By permitting the separation of sexuality and reproduction," writes Rhonda Copelon, a radical feminist litigator for abortion rights, "the right to abortion indirectly protects the rights of lesbians to be sexually self determining."[25] Rosalind Petchesky has argued that a campaign for women's "sexual rights," especially freedom of sexual preference, is most clearly occurring in the international political arena. In human rights campaigns and at United Nations-sponsored venues, a global women's rights movement has begun to outline a doctrine of what she calls "affirmative sexual rights," not simply against violence and abuse but in favor of self-definition, self-determination, and self-expression.[26]

To these already politicized dimensions of the continuing battle for women's autonomy from the institutionalized constraints of marriage I would add a plea for a third horizon, this one even more utopian: the aspiration, no longer embraced as enthusiastically as it has been at other times in the women's rights tradition, to rethink and reorganize the intimate relations of women and men so as to be totally compatible with full freedom for women. I trust I will not be misunderstood as standing in opposition to a program of ever greater lesbian rights. On the contrary, to the degree that heterosexuality is seen as fundamentally incompatible with women's liberation, as irredeemably productive of male domination and women's subordination, an emancipatory lesbianism must also remain an unfinished project, undermined in practice by silences and idealization.[27]

The revolution that feminism began in heterosexuality needs to be completed. Women's expectations of their relations with men, which the revival of feminism in the 1970s did so much to expand, have now risen far beyond the capacity of current conjugal practices to meet. And yet, it often seems as if only the forces of traditional patriarchy—organized religion, the political Right, nationalist movements—are there to respond, to speak to women's frustrations and men's dissatisfactions, and to offer any hope for change. By contrast, in the face of this crisis of marriage and heterosexuality, the only remedies still associated with feminism are therapeutic ones, advice delivered and consumed at the individual level, to adjust one's expectations and make one's compromises with men and with marriage. Surely, this is a serious failure of political initiative. Feminism must not abandon its role in leading the way to women's *collective* achievement of better lives and greater satisfactions. To do so would be to abdicate the historical tradition of women's rights, which has never been a matter merely of changing laws but rather of winning the battle for women's hearts and minds, and deserving to do so.

NOTES

1. See, for instance, Gerda Lerner's approach in "Women's Rights and American Feminism," in *The Majority Finds Its Past* (New York: Oxford University Press, 1979), pp. 48–62.

2. Reva B. Siegel, "The Modernization of Marital Status Law: Adjudicating Wives' Rights to Earnings, 1860–1930," *Georgetown Law Review* 82, 7 (1994): 2127–2211.

3. The two American historians who are working most pointedly in this area are Peggy Pascoe ("Race, Gender and Intercultural Relations: The Case of Interracial Marriage," *Frontiers* 12, 1 [1991]: 5–18) and Nancy Cott ("Giving Character to Our Whole Civil Polity: Marriage and the Public Order in the Late Nineteenth Century," in *U.S. History as Women's History*, ed. Linda Kerber, Alice Kessler Harris, and Kathryn Kish Sklar [Urbana: University of Illinois Press, 1995], pp. 107–21). Pascoe focuses primarily on the mutual constructions of race and gender, and Cott on the role of the state in creating and monitoring "private life." My interest, related but different, is on the way in which feminist activists have understood, protested, and altered the role of marriage in women's subordination.

4. Barbara Taylor, *Eve and the New Jerusalem* (New York, Pantheon, 1983).

5. Norma Basch, *In the Eyes of the Law: Women, Marriage and Property in Nineteenth-Century New York* (Ithaca: Cornell University Press, 1982).

6. Elizabeth Cady Stanton, "Address Delivered at Seneca Falls," in *Elizabeth Cady Stanton, Susan B. Anthony: A Reader*, ed. Ellen DuBois (Boston: Northeastern University Press, 1993) p. 31.

7. Catharine Beecher, *A Treatise on Domestic Economy*, (1841; New York: Schocken Books, 1977), p. 9.

8. See Una Stannard, *Mrs. Man* (San Francisco: Germainbooks, 1977), for a very original history of feminism that centers on the coverture-based naming convention for wives in marriage.

9. See Basch, *In the Eyes of the Law*, pp. 200–223; and Siegel, "Modernization of Marital Status Law," pp. 2137, 2148.

10. Amy Dru Stanley, "Conjugal Bonds and Wage Labor: Rights of Contract in the Age of Emancipation," *Journal of American History* 75, 2 (1988): 471–500.

11. Patricia Williams, *Alchemy of Race and Rights: Diary of a Law Professor* (Cambridge: Harvard University Press, 1991).

12. Contrast this with the British suffrage movement's insistence, until the 1880s, that suffrage claims must take into account women's marital status.

13. Ellen Carol DuBois, *Harriot Stanton Blatch and the Winning of Woman Suffrage* (New Haven: Yale University Press, 1997), chap. 8.

14. The definitive feminist account of Sanger's birth control leadership remains Linda Gordon, *Woman's Body, Woman's Right: A Social History of Birth Control in America*, rev. ed. (New York: Penguin Books, 1990).

15. On the limits and naïveté of feminists' hope for revolutionizing heterosexual marriage, see Ellen Kay Trimberger, *Intimate Warriors: Portrait of a Modern Marriage, 1899–1944* (New York, Feminist Press, 1991).

16. This is how Harriot Blatch saw it; see DuBois, *Harriot Stanton Blatch*, pp. 214–24.

17. Joan G. Zimmerman, "The Jurisprudence of Equality: The Women's Minimum Wage, the First Equal Rights Amendment, and *Adkins v. Children's Hospital*, 1905–1923," *Journal of American History* 78, 1 (1991): 211.

18. "Can Equality Be Legislated?" *The Independent*, December 22, 1923, p. 301.

19. Nancy Cott, *The Grounding of Modern Feminism* (New Haven: Yale University Press, 1987), p. 142.

20. Betty Friedan, *The Feminine Mystique* (New York: W. W. Norton, 1963).

21. Gloria Hull, at the time a young, Southern black woman struggling unsuccessfully to combine graduate school and a conventional marriage, made this point in her remarks at the conference "What Ever Happened to Women's Liberation?" University of California, Los Angeles, May 1991.

22. Shulamith Firestone, *The Dialectic of Sex: The Case for Feminist Revolution* (New York: William Morrow, 1970).

23. Rosalind Pollack Petchesky, *Abortion: A Woman's Choice* (Boston: Northeastern University Press, 1985), pp. 143–45.

24. See *Women, the State, and Welfare*, ed. Linda Gordon (Madison: University of Wisconsin Press, 1990).

25. Rhonda Copelon, "From Privacy to Autonomy: The Conditions for Sexual and Reproductive Freedom," in *From Abortion to Reproductive Freedom: Transforming a Movement*, ed. Marlene Gerber Fried (Boston: South End Press, 1990), pp. 27–44.

26. Rosalind Pollack Petchesky, "Sexual Rights: Inventing a Concept, Mapping an International Practice" (unpublished paper, 1997).

27. I am grateful for conversations with Alice Echols on this point. It is distressing to note the degree to which the arguments for expanding marriage to include gay and lesbian couples mirror some of the right-wing calls for shoring up the institution: that it is the only antidote to the rampant individualization of our culture; that it is a way to discipline and control promiscuous sexuality; that participants in the institution deserve economic and other benefits that those outside it do not warrant; and even that it is a benign institution, with no role in the establishment of gender inequality. See, for instance, William H. Hohengarten, "Same-Sex Marriage and the Right of Privacy," *Yale Law Journal* 103, 6 (1994): 1495–1531.

Index

About the Author

Ellen Carol DuBois has been active in the development of the field of U.S. women's history since the 1970s. The focus of much her work has been the history of the movement for political equality for women. Her major books on this subject include: *Feminism and Suffrage: The Emergence of an Independent Women's Movement in America 1848–1869* (Cornell University Press, 1978); *Elizabeth Cady Stanton, Susan B. Anthony: A Reader,* second edition (Northeastern University Press, 1990); and *Harriot Stanton Blatch and the Winning of Woman Suffrage* (Yale University Press, 1997).

She is also the editor, with Vicki L. Ruiz, of *Unequal Sisters: A Multicultural Reader in U.S. Women's History* (Routledge, 1991, 1994). She is currently Professor of History at University of California at Los Angeles.

CPSIA information can be obtained at www.ICGtesting.com
Printed in the USA
BVOW06s2315041013

332853BV00001B/15/P